Neal Kinsey's
Hands-On
Agronomy

Before we start, please understand this material is not intended to be "the last word on soil fertility." It is only what I understand and use, explained to the best of my ability so others can understand and use it to the best of their ability. I have no secrets. I do not try to keep certain "keys" for myself. My biggest job is to put everything I understand into terms which others can use.

The better a client understands this program, the better his or her results. My best clients are those who strive the hardest to learn and apply what the soil tests show to be needed.

—*Neal Kinsey*

NEAL KINSEY'S
HANDS-ON
AGRONOMY

by Neal Kinsey
and Charles Walters

Acres U.S.A.
Metairie, Louisiana

NEAL KINSEY'S
HANDS-ON AGRONOMY

Acres U.S.A.
P.O. Box 8800
Metairie, Louisiana 70011

ISBN: 0-911311-39-4
Library of Congress: 92-076121

DEDICATION

This book is dedicated to individuals who helped provide the support and experience that made it possible. First and foremost, to my wife, Linda, whose support made all this possible; to my good friend, Dale Schurter, an excellent teacher, and the best boss I ever worked for; to the late William A. Albrecht, who provided a solid foundation on which to build; and especially to all the clients who have stayed with me over the years.

ABOUT CONSULTANT NEAL KINSEY

Neal Kinsey has been called a "consultant's consultant." He specializes in only one thing—building and maintaining soil for quality crop production. In addition to consulting on standard crops such as corn, cotton, soybeans, rice, wheat and grain sorghum, and specialties such as alfalfa, pastures, clovers, oats, melons, almonds, avocadoes, citrus, grapes and peaches, Kinsey has helped growers with turf and lawn care.

His biography is contained as a broad outline in this book. In discussing sound agronomy practices, he tells much, but not all. For instance, it was once standard practice to provide free lawn or garden sampling to any farmer who employed Neal on his total farmable land of 200 acres or more. Though this was begun as a token of appreciation, it turned out to be a valuable source of knowledge when the opportunity arrived to begin working on commercial vegetable production, and with large-scale lawn, landscape and nursery stock production, and when golf courses were also added to his list of clients.

In time, various companies and private consultants began to call for possible help in growing crops such as potatoes, sugar cane, tobacco and tomatoes. To cope with the demand for information, training sessions for clients were begun. These have now expanded to two- and three-day seminars several times a year.

Foreign work followed, and so coffee and banana production were added to crop experiences. Popcorn, timber and turf grass production came along in the early 1980s, followed closely by rapeseed and ornamentals. Peanut and commercial herb growers were signed up. All of these crops helped to demonstrate that supplying the correct fertility to achieve a proper balance worked in all types of agriculture.

The mails and UPS bring soil samples routinely to Neal Kinsey's service. Thus Canada and the United States have added sunflowers, flax and mustard seed to the consultation service agenda. Various new crops from Asia, including mangoes, spices and medicinal plants for the commercial market also added to acreages and experience. Although work with walnuts and pecans paced the opening of new frontiers, eco-agriculture didn't become significant until the late 1980s.

Neal grew up in southeast Missouri and worked on the farm for his father until he graduated from high school. To pay his way through college, he worked part-time and summers as a crop reporter for the USDA's ASCS in Missouri and Illinois. He obtained his B.S. degree in marketing from Southern Illinois University at Carbondale. In the fall of 1966, Neal enrolled in a master's degree program in Food Industry Logistics in Agricultural Economics at University of Missouri, Columbia. Here is where he first met Dr. William A. Albrecht, who later provided the technical training in soil fertility required by his present profession.

In 1968, Neal and his wife, Linda, moved to Texas. He took a job with a large environmental research project conducted by Ambassador College at Big Sandy. He eventually became assistant to the director. Later, he became business manager, and eventually agricultural operations manager for the Ambassador College Agriculture Department. While serving in this capacity, he became a certified consultant for Brookside Farms Laboratory of New Knoxville, Ohio. In 1977, Neal established Kinsey's Agricultural Services.

TABLE OF CONTENTS

Long before man could make a plow or a test tube, nature was creating life, including man, and providing an environment in which all life could live. She used the resources of air, water, sunshine and soil plant food minerals to make life. If she had created only life, these resources would soon have been tied up in all living things. So she created death. This way resources could be recycled and used again and again. There is a basic law which says, *All life forms must return at death what they took from the resources of the earth during their lifetime.*

—*Eugene M. Poirot*
Our Margin of Life, 1978

WORD FROM THE PUBLISHER

MORE THAN TWO DECADES AGO, *Acres U.S.A.* went about the heady business of defining the foundation for modern agriculture. The publication was not even a year old at the time, and making sense to both the organic camp and the conventional "scientific" crowd seemed impossible. They were at each other's throats, and in the eyes of the true believers on both sides, there was no room for compromise. Nevertheless, "we" sallied forth—the second half of the "we" being the late C.J. Fenzau.

Then, as now, scientific commentary based on the chronological record of thought and theory seemed to explode the organic myth, and we figured we'd make a pass at exploding the chemical myth. The experts who perpetuated the so-called scientific theory of chemical fertilizers were seldom required to answer some very honest and sincere questions. The reason seemed obvious as *Acres U.S.A.* got underway.

Unfortunately, some very basic lessons had to intervene, otherwise farmers would not understand the far-ranging implications of what Neal Kinsey has to say in the present volume. One of those lessons has been styled, *An Acres U.S.A. Primer. The Albrecht Papers*—four volumes—have also helped answer questions and explain answers. But for our present purpose, a two decade-old entry in *Acres U.S.A.* provides a perfect overview for Neal Kinsey's insightful presentation.

There are few, if any, trained soil nutritionists who are able to understand and present any comprehensive judgment, other than mere lip service, to the standard viewpoints that are important to soil bacteria, earthworms, soil drainage, tilth, structure, and particularly the true function of organic materials in the soil system. After all, organic matter converts, regulates and releases nutrients to soil life which, in turn, makes available biological forms of nutrients to the biological system of the soil from which man has originally evolved. His creation and permission to life are profoundly linked to this biotic beginning.

Nature's way is biological. It is a combination both chemical and organic.

A study of histories of civilizations gives mute evidence that life cannot endure unless nature is allowed to produce nutrients for the *biological systems in the soil* for the plants that nourish therefrom and are then consumed by animals and eventually "man." This is possible only if man, in his ignorance, does not tamper either with "organic" or "chemical" systems.

The chemical industry has accumulated a body of *knowledge* and *financial capacity* to sustain the chemical system. On the other hand, the amateurs of "organic" systems have accumulated amateur knowledge to teach others to be good amateurs. We have few professional producers of food and fiber because, in the absence of adequate compensation and/or profit, they have not been able to *support* or *develop* a responsible body of knowledge that could define the ultimate "biological system of life."

Both chemical and organic systems are essential. Both chemicals and organic materials have an important role in nourishing plant life. Neither is capable of doing a proper, sustained job without an ecologically balanced soil system. It is for this reason, that we become infuriated when our authorities and agricultural leaders expound the merits of one system or another. Neither group is willing to comprehend the full meaning of nature's way of providing biological products for the biological sustenance of all forms of life. This concept was detoured by von Liebig's "Law of the Minimum" in 1848, and has been fully perpetuated by "science," by institutions, by laws, and by commercialization, none of which have to account to nature or give credentials to "life."

When "living life" emerges into an ultimate objective of our nation, only then can we begin to construct the understanding of the ecology of the soil and be able to benefit from its minuteness and wondrous patience. Nature has no limit on time. She is patient and forgiving. She is able to repair herself from the ignoble treatment of man in spite of his tremendous physical capacity for destruction. As we continue to replace nature, we assuredly prevent the development of our mental capacity to learn and fully compliment nature—a requirement expected from us—*in permission for life.* Apparently the growing interest of many farmers in searching for answers reflects the beginning of an intellectual attitude in conflict with both agronomic science and industry. This virgin knowledge is finally emerging as a test and challenge to the introverted and integrated industrial exploiters and absconders of our most precious resource.

It is time to stop the folly of both "chemical" and "organic" competition, and buckle down to the great necessity of compatibility. We must let the cocoon burst into a life cycle that may permit eggs of thought to be created. Nature needs our physical help to save her the time because we, as man, cannot endure such time. If we continue in our ignorance, we have little time left to assure much time in which to do our part.

A soil system for nutrient and energy production is a living system in which bacteria and the many soil organisms must receive nutrition and energy from proteins, carbohydrates and cellulose and lignin—all organic materials in a soil that has a managed supply of both air and water within a balanced chemical environment. This chemical balance involves more than just N, P and K. It requires an equilibrium of pH, calcium, magnesium, sodium, potash, humus and a nutritional balance of sulfur to nitrogen, nitrogen to calcium, calcium to magnesium, magnesium to potash and sodium. Without this balanced equilibrium, neither the organic system nor the N, P and K system has any enduring potential for soil building or plant nutrition. This total equilibrium is even more essential for the vital nourishment of man.

On the other hand, hydroponics is not a living system of plant nutrition. It is a synthesized method of supplying elements for plants growing in an environment protected artificially from the hazards and basic elements of life itself. The time clock and configurations of life are continually influenced by hormone-enzyme systems, by light, temperature, carbon dioxide, photosynthesis, antibiotics and a balanced viable plant sap (globulin-blood) system which requires basic hormones and a specific pH equilibrium in order to biologically produce a healthy plant. This plant must grow nutritionally, ripen and dry. The nutritionally ripe plant is essential for complete animal or human nutrition. Neither the chemical nor the organic systems can assure fully matured or "biologically ripe" food production. By co-incidental accident, our agricultural system can produce the desired food quality without the hazards of weather, insects, disease or geographical limitations—and hydroponically, we could be a nation stuffed with partially matured carbon-based compounds that look and feel like food. In reality this so-called food results in partial or complete malnourishment—the predecessor to poor health and eventual metabolic and physiological deterioration.

Perhaps it is unfortunate, but nevertheless essential, that we *must farm soil*. It is only folly that we invite the hazards of hydroponics to sustain a synthetic system of life. Since we must cultivate soil for production of both nutrients and energy as well as fiber, we must begin to feed the soil, not the plant. This is the basic and fundamental change required for progress to begin.

In the past 50 years, many scientists and educators have brought attention to this principle. Industry astutely avoided this philosophy, and farmers honestly accepted the counterview. The farmers now are beginning to express their own experiences, and this is irritating to the authorities. To illustrate, we must regard nitrogen as a source of nutrition and energy for the actinomycetes fungi to digest and break down the complex carbons contained in lignated organic matter. Some mild and gentle form of nitrogen must be used until our soils can sustain a regular supply of nitrogen. This will furnish a renewable source of carbon dioxide, the by-product mild-gentle organic acids needed to release the mineralized nutrients in the soil complex into a form available to plants. The remains of this decay process is humus, which is also essential to the soil and its capacity for total function and performance. It is not practical to handle the tons of organic materials already in position on every farmed acre. Let us learn how to manage both the soil and this organic material and let nature function for us.

Whenever we use N, P and K as a computerized supply of nutrients, or plant food, we may eventually violate the natural equilibrium in the soil system. This accounts for the many disappointing production results from one soil type to the next within a field and the unexpected variations from one year to the next. To supply exact pounds of N, P and K per unit of crop production is sheer nonsense.

Farmers, without their own body of knowledge, have been innocently led by this theory, and coached along into propagandized obedience. Just ask any fertilizer expert to guarantee results and you will begin to flush out the truth.

Life in the soil sits at the table first, and compost, manures, green manure crops and crop rotations are subject to the same antagonisms. Historically, neither chemicals nor organic systems have produced consistent results unless the equilibrium factors were natural or properly managed.

It is possible to compete one system against the other in a given soil environment, to show favorable and significant results either in productivity or quality. On the other hand, in a measured quality soil system, a thoroughly managed chemical and organic system will produce consistent results. By chemicals, it is meant, in addition to nitrogen, the proper amounts of calcium, magnesium, potash and sodium along with ripe humus. These must be biologically positioned to create a living soil system.

This living soil will release the phosphorus and trace elements at a compatible level for plants to utilize the sunlight energy, water, air and carbon dioxide supply available. The growing period, yield and character will be in direct proportion to the elements and timing of weather from one year to the next.

In seasons of poor crop performance, we always blame the weather. This is cowardly. In good years, we never give adequate credit to the weather. Since weather can be easily criticized, our ignorance continues to endure, and human pride can be maintained in spite of its error. In reality, however, we simply rely on the "crutch" to explain away our ignorance. After all, next year we can try again with the hope that things will be better. There is much we can do through feeding the soil to eliminate the hazards of weather, or at least diminish the effects it might have on crop performance.

We need quality food. More people can be fed with less quantity. The general public, as well as commercial leaders, do not have sufficient background information to make judgments concerning either the effects of various kinds of fertilizer, or the values of organic matter on the living systems with a given soil. A living soil will not require any of the existing soil conservation or crop production practices thought necessary to assure a quantity food supply. Instead, quality foods can be produced, of which less is required for optimum nutrition, not only of man, but in animals and plants as well.

Yes, the general public can be swayed by health food promoters, just as they can be "quacked" by the chemical promoter, however respectable their financial and political credentials. Let's not forget that in the beginning farmers were once "promoted" to be aware of the "quacks" selling nitrogen for crop production in states now boasting to be number one. At one time it was disgraceful. By what promotional means did it become respectful?

Our population cannot survive on pre-1930s organics alone, but neither is it healthfully surviving through chemicals. Witness the millions of livestock that are carcassed to rendering factories across our land. Then witness the overflowing hospitals treating the symptoms and diseases which could be averted by wholesome and nutritionally ripe foods. Witness the billions spent on fuels and dryers to take water from physiologically immature grain crops, the nutrients of which were not able to fully mature into nature's intended ripeness. Animals and people cannot experience health and ripeness in life from this type of food. Through chemistry, we can too "hopefully" keep trying, but it is futile.

Witness the cost of keeping sick plants alive in the sick, sick soils of our nation, and yet we have the audacity to simply treat this problem with N, P and K aspirin tablets while we close our eyes to the actual causes of these diseases and problems. No, the aspirin treatment is not the answer either, because with ineffective life in these sick soils, nature is not able to supply adequate calcium, humus or water to all regions. Neither can the proper decay of organic materials be accomplished. Organic composting illustrates this weakness of nature also—and out of sheer economic impracticality, we cannot compost all of our land either. We must learn how to make every acre a compost acre—and this is not done by chemicals or by organics. We must create a unity of both to permit the biological system to work. Herein must lie our fundamental objective.

It may seem odd that "we"—Neal Kinsey and I—chose not to comply with scientific conduct and forgo the use of the personal pronoun "I." For now it is enough to point out that to write in the first person does not offend science. As Phil Callahan put it, this stilted anti-"I" conceit is "inappropriate because it gives to the literature of science a facade behind which its authors appear to be infallible and is the reason why science—which is, or should be, the study of nature, and thus altogether fascinating—is presented to mankind in such a dull guise."

The "I" in *Hands-On Agronomy* is Neal Kinsey, and not this writer and publisher. Kinsey speaks through the experiences he has held in escrow for over two decades, and the other I—Charles Walters, the scribe—handles the mechanical chore of wordsmithing, no more, no less.

How well Neal Kinsey complies with that early *Acres U.S.A.* vision will become apparent as readers proceed with Chapter 1, and the other chapters that follow. For now it is enough to call for open minds in every camp. Indeed, our "permission for life" demands it.

—*Charles Walters*
founder, *Acres U.S.A.*

Hu-mus / 'hyü-mes, 'yü- / *n* [NL, fr. L., earth] **1** a brown or black complex variable material resulting from decomposition of plant or animal matter under proper environmental and biological conditions **2** composed chiefly of hydrogen and carbon-hydrogen and oxygen with varying percents of nitrogen attached **3** a long chain-like affair with the capacity to bind plant nutrients—phosphate, nitrate, for instance—to itself **4** it can coat itself with some amino acids, certain sugars and many trace minerals **5** a veritable sponge for nutrients **6** it cannot have more than 6% nitrogen on a dry matter basis, 20 to 50% of which is in the amino acid form, and 1 to 10% in the form of amino sugar nitrogen **7** a buffer and a source of nutrients **8** manufactured by microorganisms, including the actinomycetes, yeasts, molds, and clostridium types

1

The Farming Dilemma

NO ONE USED THE TERM *killer agriculture* or *knowledgeable mining* when I was a youngster growing up on a farm in southeast Missouri. We raised corn, wheat, cotton, soybeans and a little hay. We also finished a few cattle. Now, a mature sense of values brings the reality of our farming operation into focus. Sir Albert Howard identified the horns of the modern farming dilemma: partial and imbalanced fertilization, and toxic rescue chemistry.

Neither I nor my father heard or understood that dictum then, *then* being the 1950s and 1960s. All we knew was that the crops faltered—not occasionally, but year after year. My father had five sons and he concluded, "I hope you won't even think about going into agriculture because it costs too much and I am not going to be able to help you get started. I hope you will go into business and be an accountant or something like that." Accordingly, I went to college with the intention of becoming an accountant. There was a problem with this. I couldn't stand being inside four walls all the time. So I changed my direction while I was at the University of Missouri. I met William A. Albrecht, the legendary professor who contributed so much to what *Acres U.S.A.* calls eco-agriculture. Albrecht gave the Department of Soils its well-deserved reputation, but by the time I arrived, he had been retired—forcibly, I am told—in the wake of a great grant from a fossil fuel company. In any case, his classroom days were over, for which reason I was able to get more of his ear than might have been possible as classroom fare. He taught a private study course for Brookside Farms, and I decided to avail myself of this extra-curricular opportunity. He changed my entire way of thinking.

My family farmed a nice sandy loam farm at first, and then my dad had an opportunity to get a larger farm with some heavy clay soils. We had no irrigation. In fact there was none in the area at the time. This is one of the reasons we finally moved close to the Mississippi River, to what we call heavy clay gumbo soil. We had some sandy ridges, but most of the soil was heavy clay and gumbo. Farming that territory presented a host of new problems. Our soybeans grew only half-size before foxtail took over. Cotton sometimes grew knee high. When you talked to the old-timers they would recall cotton up to waist high and soybeans that buried a man's shoulders. Yields in either case were great. But when we started to farm the clay soils, foxtail took over, not just our acres, but the general landscape. No one had an answer. I remember a next-door neighbor talking to my dad. "If we could find a way to market this foxtail seed, we could make some money," he said; "a lot more than we could from beans, because I think we grow more bushels of foxtail seeds than we do beans." I believe this was true in some years. Beans that used to make 40 bushels were making 15 bushels because the foxtail was taking over.

Nobody had clean beans and then Randox came along from Monsanto, and we thought that was the best thing in the world. It at least kept the foxtail out of the row. If you took a standard soil sample, the readout said nothing was needed. It usually came back with a notation that no lime was required, and that fertilizers were superfluous, other than nitrogen and a little starter on cotton. These reports even said phosphate and potash were not needed to grow soybeans. For corn, only a maintenance level became the general recommendation. Some farmers who became clients when I started in the consulting business had grown nothing but soybeans for 20 or 25 years, always on the same soil. On the average, they made 30 to 40 bushels per acre, year after year, always without fertilizers, lime or other inputs. Most of the money was spent on herbicides when killer technology came along.

I wondered aloud, "Why did this happen?" So when a friend at the University of Missouri told me about William A. Albrecht, Ph.D., a connection was made. On the first visit to his office I explained where I lived. At some point during the visit the opportunity came to ask, "Why are our soybeans so short and why is our cotton stunted, because it hasn't always been that way." I related how when farmers cleared out timber in our area and planted soybeans, the first year delivered a yield of about 50 bushels of beans. The next year the yield would go down in the 40s and the next year it would be 30 bushels or so per acre, which is where it would generally stay. When analyzed for pH, P and K in the soil, the audits showed nothing wrong. Dr. Albrecht knew soils. He knew what the basic soils were in the entire Midwest. And he provided sensible, practical answers to my questions. "Well, now wait a minute. You live over by the Mississippi and you are in that heavy gumbo soil? That is why your beans didn't get very tall. They got tall in the first place because you had free calcium. Now, when you take a regular soil test and send it in, and if you just check pH, phosphate and potash, you will never find the problems. Actually pH is influenced by a lot more than calcium. Heavy clay soils are high in magnesium, and that is what is keeping your pH high. If you had known to check the various nutrients in the soil and put on the limestone needed to get your calcium up, then your beans would have gotten back to the size they were in the first place. You are losing out because the calcium is what puts all the other nutrients in the plant."

One of my first clients was our next-door neighbor during my high school years. He had grown soybeans on 750 acres every year for 20 years, plus! He told me he had never made a 40-bushel bean crop. He said he had always averaged 30 to 32 bushels per acre. He did what Albrecht taught should be done.

The first year we followed through on the program, this farmer averaged 45 bushels of beans per acre on the entire 750 acres. The second year, the average was 48 bushels of beans. We merely analyzed the soil in detail and found out what was missing, and supplied what was needed in the proper amounts. But herein lies a problem. Most farmers do not trust a soil test. If a soil test is to be trusted, which one and why? This book will endeavor to provide those answers.

Today I have clients in 42 states and 22 countries. The fact is, it doesn't make much difference where you live. What makes the difference is whether or not you follow through on the things that don't change. The things that do not change are the laws of science—physics, chemistry and biology. These laws show that you may be able to produce crops without fertilizers, but you can't produce crops without fertility. That is why I look at fertility, evaluate fertility, and then use fertilizers where necessary to achieve it. The more information a farmer gives as to what he expects to accomplish, the better the job I can do for him.

Remember That You are Dust

We should frequently meditate on the words of Ash Wednesday: "Man, remember that you are dust and that you will return to dust." This is not merely a religious and philosophical doctrine but a great scientific truth which should be engraved above the entrance to every Faculty of Medicine throughout the world. We might then better remember that our cells are made up of mineral elements which are to be found at any given moment in the soil of Normandy, Yorkshire or Australia; and if these "dusts" have been wrongly assembled in plant, animal or human cells the results will be the imperfect functioning of the latter. . . .

In 1897, for the first time, Gabriel Bertrand of the *Academie d'Agriculture* [in France], succeeded in showing that a "dust" of the soil, that is to say a mineral element in trace form, was essential to the functioning of living cells. All observations have since confirmed this discovery. An attempt will be made . . . to show how "dusts" of the soil are "assembled, bolted and screwed" to form the cells of our body and allow them to function. The special aim will be to demonstrate how illness can be due to an upset in the balance of this "assembly."

—*Andre Voisin*
Soil, Grass & Cancer, 1959

Fertilizers, limestone and other materials can add to the soil's fertility levels. In certain instances, these same materials can actually damage the soil's level of fertility. You can overdo anything. For the last 20 years at least, farmers have stopped looking at what we call the *law of the maximum*. They are not looking at the basic laws which say that if you overdo one thing, something else has to give. Needed is a program for fertility that works in all types of situations— on clay or sand, in weather both hot and cold, in a tropical environment. We can work out each situation, as long as we use physics, chemistry and biology.

Therefore, the first principle of soil fertility is *feed the soil* by providing the necessary nutrients in the proper amount. I am not talking about feeding the plant. I am talking about feeding the soil and letting the soil feed the plant. This means broadcast applications. If we want to build up the soil, we must use fertilizers that last. In such a situation, any long-term fertilizer should be broadcast. Because if there really is such a thing as the Law of the Maximum, then you are actually creating some possible problems for yourself if you band. Some fertilizers are soil feeders. They build levels of fertility in the soil. These should be broadcast. Some fertilizers are plant feeders. This means there will be no soil build-up. Response is immediate, after which the fertilizer no longer shows up. It is almost impossible to pick up plant feeders later on in the soil. An extra load will not materially change the nutrient profile. These materials are merely an insurance policy for continued expense, year after year. Side-dress fertilization feeds the plant, not the soil. This is the reason I try to get away from a situation that requires side dressing. My objective always is to get to the point where fertilizers can be broadcast, with materials being effective at feeding the crop. The bottom line: side dressing or plant feeding is not best in the long run.

To feed the plant, fast-acting, quick-impact, short-range fertility is required. In terms of such a program, the usual procedure is to supply the biggies—nitrogen, phosphate and potash. A consequence of this procedure is to tie up certain of the trace nutrients via the glut.

When trace elements are borderline, a deficiency situation will be the observed result. Yet farmers dance to the tune of N, P and K every day. They create their own yield limiting situations. Still, it must be observed that fast action is often required. But such nutrients should not be introduced into the soil as side dressing. A better system is to feed plants through the leaves using a foliar.

A lot of farmers do not believe foliars will work, and certain other professionals have still to tune in on this eco-technology.

In fact, valid technologies have been used to make foliar feeds and liquid fertilizers since 1951. According to *An Acres U.S.A. Primer*, "These developments went on virtually without the agricultural community knowing anything about them." Sylvan H. Wittwer, under whose leadership Michigan State University conducted investigations on foliar fertilization of plants, correctly summarized: "There is probably no area of agricultural crop production of more current interest, and more contradictory data, claims and opinions, or where the farmer in practice has moved so far ahead of scientific research." Even today, the average land grant college often does not have a single scientist who has the working knowledge necessary for using liquid fertilizers in crop production. There will be those who object to this statement, citing Hanway's Iowa State University research, which came some 12 years after Wittwer's, but this hardly qualified because it failed as a result of using the wrong type of ingredients.

Credentialed and uncredentialed outsiders standing in the wings knew that Hanway's foliar N, P and K efforts would fail because the compound being used did not answer plant requirements, would burn crops, and because it would cost too much. It involved the application of gross amounts of nitrogen, phosphorus and potassium to soybeans in three applications, using amounts required by the holy writ of soil fertilization.

Working with nursery crops, flowers for market, strawberries, apples, pears, and cherries, agronomists started answering growth cycle requirements with seaweed extracts many years ago, all with successes that were spectacular, erratic, and rejected. There were things that could be done with the leaf that proved next to impossible when working with complex soils.

In the early 1950s, Wittwer was working under arrangements with the Division of Biology and Medicine, Atomic Energy Commission. Experiments entailed the use of radioactive isotopes in assessing the efficiency of foliar applied nutrients compared to soil applications of those same nutrients. It was found that the efficiency of the foliar fertilizers was from 100 to 900% greater than the dry-applied fertilizer materials.

Trees, grasses and field crops all respond to the foliar assist. Even so, foliar nutrition is the second part of fertility management.

The first principle is feed the soil and let the soil feed the plant. If, in the meantime, there is something missing, it must be supplied in the most economical way. Many nutrients obey the "law of the little bit." The plant will take most of what it needs from the soil in any case. It is the last bit that puts support over the top when there is a deficiency. The second principle is concerned with the nutrient balance we are required to achieve. In other words, the fertility level we are working to achieve for each soil is the foundation required for plant growth. Our objective is the right amount of everything. Once we achieve the proper nutrient load, then we have the foundation to begin achieving proper fertility support for plant growth. Whatever the crop in the production sequence—corn, soybeans, rice or wheat—these generally can be grown in the same soils without too much trouble. Rice production can work with a little less calcium. Soybeans, on the other hand, can use a little more calcium. Clover, alfalfa, sugar beets, sugar cane, vegetables, citrus groves, pasture grasses, trees, and flowers or turf grass, all will grow best in the very same soil. That soil is the one which contains all of the necessary nutrients we know to test for in the proper relationship to every one of the other nutrients. A soil that grows the very best corn will also grow the very best alfalfa. Should we analyze a soil and discover a nutrient content proper to production of the above named crops, and the crop is timber, it will be top quality timber. If the crop is barley, it will be top quality barley.

There are some elements that barley can endure, which other crops can't, one being extra high sodium. Barley does not have to have high sodium, but it can live with it. A pine tree can live in an extremely acid soil. But the pine tree that lives in extremely acid soil doesn't produce the best wood. That record is reserved for the pine tree grown in the same soil that will produce the most excellent stand of corn or alfalfa. Much the same is true of barley. Top quality barley relies on the common denominators that underwrite quality corn.

I have never seen a soil, not one, that didn't confirm and conform to the design unlocked by analysis. I have never seen a soil that required me to say, "I honestly can't tell you anything that you can do to improve your crop."

Most soils tell us about many things that can be done. But the general principle holds: top quality blueberries grow on the same soil as the very best corn. Yet once you get even one of the nutrients out of balance, a whole new set of factors becomes inserted into the equation.

Some basic proofs have been provided by the man I mentioned in the opening paragraphs of this book, Dr. William A. Albrecht. Dr. Albrecht retired in 1955. I received a certificate as an agronomist from him in 1973. He passed away a year later. Albrecht received his doctorate from the University of Illinois. He originally intended to be a medical doctor, but his studies convinced him he could do more to help people's health by concentrating on the soils that feed them. While studying plant pathology, plant physiology and soils, he concluded that soils are more a cause, whereas doctors treat effects. He taught soils at the University of Missouri. He also helped the Midwest develop inoculates for legumes. In the process he started looking for answers to why crops didn't respond properly. A lot of the information that he used came from Germany and Holland. In particular, there was a Dr. Oscar Loew in Germany who put forth the idea that excess magnesium was a poison to the calcium in the nucleus of the plant cell. Equally important was the Albrecht revelation that a nutrient balance was the foundation for achieving proper fertility.

If I consult with a farmer within a 100-mile radius of where I live, I will not accept soil samples sent in by him. I insist on total supervision of the sampling process. There is a reason for this. Most farmers skimp when it comes to pulling soil samples. What I do is contract with a farmer on an acreage basis, then go in and map the farm and pull the samples. It costs him the same amount of money whether there are many or just a few samples. Generally, I will pull twice as many soil samples and will probably pull ten times more probes of soil than the farmer would account for. If I contract with the farmer and do the sampling, the farmer can never be blamed if something goes wrong. It is always my fault. I sit down with the farmer with confidence in my sample. The next thing I tell him is, "Don't tell me about all your soils, but if you have one soil that is extra good, maybe one small spot in the field that I may not be able to find, tell me where it is. I will pull a sample there for you." The objective is to compare the highest producing soil to the rest.

The closer I can get to the soil that does the best, the closer I can bring those other soils to doing the same thing.

I had a farmer from Kansas call me one day. He said, "I have an 80-acre field and one end of it never makes good grain sorghum, but the other end always does. We spend more than we make on the bad end. I would like to send you a sample and have you tell me what is wrong with it."

I said, "I would like you to take a sample out of the poor end and take a sample out of the good end, and send them both, but don't label them in any manner that would tell me what is good and what is bad. You code them so that you know which one is good and which one is marginal or bad. I ought to be able to tell you which is which over the phone."

I have even had fellows pull samples and tell me one was good and one was bad on purpose. They knew the "good one" was the bad one and the "bad one" was the good one. They did this to see if I could pick them out. If you have a spot that always does the best it will be the closest to right. There are some exceptions. If you grow wheat, the best wheat land will not necessarily grow the best corn. There are things that make wheat do well, but they do not really affect corn. In southeast Missouri, the soils that are highest in manganese—many barely have enough manganese—will do great with wheat, and the wheat can really be a little short of the ideal calcium level. This one particular area can grow good wheat, but can't grow good soybeans on some of the same area. The reason farmers can't grow good soybeans is that calcium is short. Wheat, being a shallow feeder type of crop—though I know the roots go deep—doesn't have to have the same relationship with nutrients that soybeans do. If you look at a soil that grows the best soybeans, and all the nutrients are in the right proportions, it will also grow the best wheat. Sometimes you have one thing that affects a crop more than another. If you have extra calcium in a soil, well, naturally, the legumes are going to do better because they can take the extra calcium. Weeds that like extra calcium will do better, too.

I once consulted with two brothers in North Dakota who had been certified organic for years. The problem was, bindweed was taking over their farm. They told this one fellow—who was a client of mine—that they were just going to have to go out of organics and lose their certification. Their fertility program was manure, and that is all they used. They didn't have enough manure to put it on every field every year, but they had tremendous quantities of manure for their farm. I have never been on their farm and haven't met the fellows to this day. Our connection has been the telephone. I asked, "Do you have some fields that are really bad and then some other fields that aren't so bad?"

They responded, "We have one field that is 90% taken over by bindweed and we have another field that is probably only 10% gone." There was time to take samples from the fields. Leaves from the bindweed were sampled. Two different labs were used. One lab was used to do soils, and a second lab analyzed tissues. The lab receiving the tissue never saw the soil samples, and the lab that got the soil never saw the tissue samples. Now if I tell a farmer he needs boron on his corn, and he fails to supply the boron, and he will take a leaf analysis, it will show up immediately, provided the tissue analysis properly gives every limiting factor. In short, I use the tissue to balance out.

In the case of the bindweed, the soil and the weeds were analyzed. The results were as expected. They revealed that too much manure had been used, and the potassium levels had gotten extremely high. Bindweed loves low calcium, high potassium soils. This weed has the ability to forage for its needed calcium. Bindweed showed no deficiency of calcium. Other crops, however, exhibited a shortage of calcium.

Bindweed releases an exudate into the soil. This plant's acid dissolves enough calcium to supply its own needs.

Hands-On Agronomy

Weeds—Guardians of the Soil

The German farmer did not consider many of our common weeds harmful in themselves. According to him, the harm came from the farmer's failure to control the weeds which were growing in his fields. The German had a most efficient, simple method of handling barnyard manure. The manure pile was under continuous construction, and as the manure came from the barn or corral or roadway, it was stacked with layers of manure or litter alternating with layers of weeds. By this method of manure-pile building, the farmer explained, the amount of the final fertilizer was markedly increased through the addition of the food-filled weeds; and fire-fanging of the manure was prevented because the weed layers permitted proper aeration.

I examined one pile of this fertilizer that had already gone through the processing. The stack on the outside looked like any typical manure pile now and then seen in American barnlots. Inside, the pile resembled true compost somewhat, but was really just mellow, well-rotted manure of a superior quality. I have since wondered if this German farmer could not have been employing a fertilizer-making process handed down from the Romans. The Catholic monks in Europe a few centuries back were known to have employed in their very efficient agriculture some of the teachings of Cato, who had lots to say on this subject.

—*Joseph A. Cocannouer*
Weeds, Guardians of the Soil, 1950

Bindweed also loves potassium, and with extremely high potassium in some soils, bindweed thrives. The remedy was easily discerned. So I recommended liming to correct the calcium level. In turn, the calcium would help to control the excessive potassium. As a consequence, the bindweed couldn't thrive anymore.

Top-producing soils have a specific nutrient relationship, but so do poorly producing soils. A soil sample, properly done, will tell you where you ought to be, and the closer you can get to the prescribed numbers, the better the soil system will produce.

When I started out as a consultant in 1973, I think it cost $1.50 to do a soil test in southeast Missouri. I charged by the acre, and if you had a large enough farm it cost $1.50 an acre. Dr. Albrecht sent a letter to me when he sent me my certificate. He said, "Neal, you really aren't an agronomist. You have just shown that you have the ability to go out and become an agronomist. An agronomist is the fellow who goes out in the field and does it. When you get out there and actually are working with the farmers, that is what will make you an agronomist." He also said, "You are not going to get any of the good soils because when you charge that kind of money the guy that doesn't have any problems doesn't want to spend the money. The fellow who is going to spend the money is the one who has the problem. He may not tell you it is a problem, but it is."

I had three good friends. I got their farms on a consulting basis because they were pushing me to hurry up and get done, and basically they didn't have big problems. They just wanted to find out what to do and they were sort of following along as I was learning what to do. I still remember another man who gave me a 210-acre farm to sample. He farmed 1,500 acres, but he picked out this one 210-acre irrigated farm. He said the reason he was calling me was that his brother-in-law had good results with me. After I did the soil testing and came back from the area, before it was ever sent in to be analyzed, he looked at the map and was amazed. He said, "You have sampled that farm and every problem area that's in there, you have it drawn on this map within 100 feet." I always put everything to scale. Then he said, "I hired a specialist who came down here from Ohio, and I paid him $8.00 an acre to help me grow corn. I lost money. Then I didn't learn my lesson, and I hired another expert to come in from Missouri. I paid him $10.00 an acre and I lost even more money. I really wouldn't have you come except I know what you have done for my brother-in-law. This is my worst farm. In the very best year on this 210-acre farm, put to grade, furrow irrigated, I have made 23 bushels of soybeans. There have been years when I didn't make a ten-bushel crop."

He followed through and did what was called for. The next year he called me and said, "I want you to do that 210 acres again, but it is not my worst farm anymore. I have another 160 acres, and now it is my worst farm." Eventually he put in all 1,500 acres, a step at a time. In the beginning, I really didn't realize how much of an advantage it was to be able to work with problems because, as a result, being exposed to problem after problem after problem, you finally learn that as long as you follow the chemistry, the physics and the biology, you are going to solve the problems.

Dr. Albrecht explained to me once, "If I could have any soil I wanted, it would be pure humus." He literally started his career with the isolation of humus from the soil. He extracted enough humus to run a soil sample on the humus, and he did this time after time. He reasoned that the most fertile productive soils must resemble the makeup of humus. Albrecht evaluated humus and, sure enough, that is what he found. What the most fertile soils have in terms of nutrient balance is also what the humus has in terms of nutrient balance.

I am not suggesting that we can take a clay soil and turn it into humus. I am merely suggesting that the closer we can match up our soil to the components of humus, the more productive it becomes. Soil will always be clay if it's clay. You can never make humus out of clay by taking clay and correcting the fertility load. There is a difference between clay and humus. Humus has been alive at one time and clay has never been alive.

What is humus? It is the completely decomposed remains of plants and animals. If you take an average of what remains after the complete decomposition of living organisms, plants, animals, whatever, doesn't it seem likely you would get back to the same thing? It seems logical to me that we could determine the average nutrient makeup of living organisms by looking at the soil, and we could also determine the average makeup of the soil by looking at the makeup of living organisms. Back in the middle 1970s, a consultant in California asked me to come out and work with some citrus and nut growers, as well as cotton people. He said, "I want to introduce you to a good friend of mine. He is a medical doctor and I want you to do a soil sample on his garden. He has one part of the garden that does wonderfully well and the other part has problems growing anything." He insisted because the physician had helped him solve a daughter's health problem.

The medical doctor lived as much as possible out of his own garden. His wife was a nutritionist. The two were allergy specialists. When he was around age 55 he expanded his practice and started working more with nutrition to solve health problems. I took samples from the poor and the good garden soil. About a month or two later, I came back to California to deliver the results. He asked me over "this afternoon," because he had only about 30 minutes since he and his wife had to attend an important meeting. I explained that the calcium level ought to be 68% saturation. He said, "That's the same thing you and I need in our bodies to have the right calcium balance." When I told him what the magnesium should be, he said that was what he and I needed, and the same thing with potassium. He had 1,500 patients and they paid him to tell them what to do so that they would not get sick. His patients were movie stars and athletes and politicians from all over the world. They came twice a year for checkups and so forth, and he would tell them what to do.

That man was 70 years old when I met him and he came to the office six days a week at six o'clock in the morning, and he didn't leave until six o'clock at night. He said, "I can see very clearly what you are telling me. If we could straighten out the soil so that we have the right nutrient relationships, that would translate to the plant." It does. Dr. Albrecht showed that with feeding tests with animals. "That means a lot of the problems we are having to deal with as doctors should be solved by agriculture. This would leave time to concentrate on things like birth defects and other degenerative diseases."

If we analyze humus, which comes from all living organisms, that humus and the most productive soil analyze to be the same. What makes us the healthiest is exactly what we have inside us as far as mineral content is concerned.

What did Dr. Albrecht find when he analyzed humus? He found the same thing as that little old pie chart in the textbook. Every soil textbook shows you an ideal soil and it will show 45% minerals, 5% humus, 25% air, 25% water. What he found when he analyzed humus was 50% minerals, 25% air, 25% water, the very same makeup as the most fertile soils. The only problem with that pie chart is that the texts do not tell how to get it. In your mind's eye, italicize this sentence—*the basic makeup of the plant and animal kingdom as it decomposes and becomes humus matches the nutrient makeup of the most productive soils.* That is one of the reasons why we say that the nutrient balance we use is the basic foundation of soil fertility. The closer you get to what the soils should have, the more problems you solve.

Lime Your Soils for Better Crops

The science of the soil has done much for our better understanding of how the soil and the plant roots interact to make the crops grow. From better understanding, some principles have resulted for better guidance of our farm practices.

Liming the soil is one of those practices improved through science. We formerly encouraged liming as a struggle against soil acidity. It is now practiced to put calcium into the soil for nutritional service to the crops. It helps them in their synthesis of proteins and other complex compounds of higher food values to man and beast.

Calcium plays its role as a small part of the material of construction. It is recognized more readily in the ash. In animals and man, calcium is recognized easily as bone. In all life it is far more important than merely a part of the final structure. It serves as the tool in many life processes. It is a necessary tool for fashioning the different proteins that only plants can fabricate from the elements. It seems to be associated with the processes by which livestock assemble these plant proteins into choice animal products of great nutritional value. We have long been liming for legumes and we have connected livestock with legumes. But we have been late in recognizing this basic principle of the interaction between the calcium of the soil and the roots of the crops. As a matter of fact, it is the working principle of this food creation assembly line.

Calcium serves, in the growth of plants, to mobilize other essential chemical elements into the plant more speedily. It puts a higher content of the ash elements into the forage. It is always associated with the crops that we say are better feed for young animals. It is associated more with feeds for growth and reproduction than with those for fattening only. It is associated with the soil's microbial processes that build up soil nitrogen. It is also effective in making green manure and other organic matter decay more rapidly and release their fertility for crop production. All life, from the lowly microbe to man himself, is dependent on a good supply of available calcium in the soil.

Liming the soil is one of the contributions to the better nourishment of all that grows on our farms. This soil treatment must, however, be judiciously connected with other treatments. It must not, therefore, be used excessively. If wisely used, this farm practice—as it is now undergirded by the science of the soil—will bring about better understanding and use of the other necessary soil treatments. This better knowledge should conserve not only the body of the soil, but also its fertility or internal strength by which all life must be fed.
—*William A. Albrecht*
The Albrecht Papers, Volume III, 1989

Clay won't ever become humus even though we provide the exact amount of each nutrient to achieve top fertility. The same basic nutrient relationships are there, though. The same amount of calcium, the same amount of magnesium, the same amount of potassium—and if you think about it, it does make sense.

Whether it is a farm situation with corn and alfalfa, or whether it is a case of lawns and trees, the laws of physics, chemistry and biology make sense. We may be dealing with potted plants in southern California. It may be a greenhouse, or palm trees in the Caribbean. No matter what kind of plant you are talking about, the same laws of science apply. These laws are our common denominator. As long as we use these laws, we can work with someone all the way on the other side of the world. As long as we have our road map, which is our soil analysis, the program is clear. The laws that affect soil fertility do not change for Missouri, for the east or west, or for some other country. Those laws are just as certain as the sun and the rain.

I do a lot of work in northeast Arkansas as well as southeast Missouri. I live 60 miles from the Arkansas border. I cross the Mississippi River and I am in Illinois. But when you go to Arkansas, you don't cross a river. You drive until you find a marker. It says, ARKANSAS LINE. There is a gravel road, and here's a field, and there is a field next to it. The farmers in Arkansas are told, "This works for Arkansas soils," and the farmers in Missouri are told, "This works for Missouri soils." Yet there is just a gravel road separating them. People farming on separate sides of the road are told to use different advice from different people. Cross the Mississippi River and go into Tennessee. What the people in Arkansas say about growing cotton with foliar nitrogen supposedly does not apply in Tennessee.

As long as we stick to the basic laws of chemistry, physics, and biology, we can work with soils anywhere. Those laws will work when the weather is frigid. We might have to use a four-wheel drive vehicle with a drill and auger bit to sample the soil, but those laws will work. The same nutrients have to get into those plants, wherever they grow. The laws of nature work on banana trees just as well as on spruce or evergreens. There are some government plantations down in the Dominican Republic where I've done fertility work for bananas, coffee, milo and cotton. Whether up in the mountains where they grow coffee, or down on the plain where they grow bananas, the principles are still the same. I have worked in deserts. The principles work just as well in desert soils as they do in soils with a tropical setting and a lot of rainfall.

You have to work around each situation, but in terms of measuring fertility, the lessons are the same and in place. When you get the numbers right, and the plant is suited to the environment, results will follow.

I had a client on-line in British Columbia. He had a problem. The operation "came out in the red every year we've ever done any work on our soils," he said. He grows carrots and all kinds of vegetables. He tried to grow enough to take care of his own needs and still sell produce into the market. He worked on my program for one year. He reported back to me at the end of the year. "This year is the first time we have ever made money."

I received some samples from him again. The program works and will work. It works for trees. It works across the board for the basic crops.

I have a client in West Germany who owns 4,000 acres of timber. He grows blue spruce for the commercial market. Customers come in and buy a block at a time at a certain height. He had some blocks of trees on which they could never get the proper height. He had other blocks of trees that grew beautifully. His forester wondered how anybody could come from the United States and tell him what to do for blue spruce trees in Germany. I suggested the forester take samples out of those lots, following a set of instructions. The forester pulled the samples according to instructions and sent them over. I had them analyzed and took them back to Germany. I sat down with him and the owner and went over them. They had sent 14 samples and they were going to choose one area where they would follow through on a fertility program. The forester couldn't speak English and I couldn't speak German. With an interpreter it took almost a half day to communicate. At the end of the half day, the forester said something to the owner in German and the owner smiled and said, "My forester said that he would like to do 14 tests instead of one test because he said you put everything in order from the best to the worst."

All I can do is follow the numbers. This was heavy, black, muck soil right on the then East-West German border, which, in fact, split the farm in two.

There are two or three professors over there who feel that they can solve the acid rain problem in the German forests by correcting the calcium level, and I believe they can. The only problem is some are trying to correct the situation with gypsum (calcium sulfate) instead of high-calcium lime. The correct liming program works on trees and it also works very well on turf grass.

A turf grass farmer not too far from Little Rock, Arkansas, has one of the most balanced soils that I have ever seen, albeit not because of me. It was there when I came. He takes all the grass clippings and dumps them over on the edge. If anyone picked up those grass clippings and composted them, he or she would have one of the most balanced composts possible. I mentioned this, and the fellow just said, "We sell sod, we don't sell grass clippings."

Most sod farms are not well-off because they keep on taking the sod away. But on this farm, one end is terrific. At the other end of the farm, grub worms are eating up the profits. It shows in the soil analyses.

Chemically speaking, if you analyze the soils and rocks in an area, they will have the same makeup. In southern Illinois, we have several high-calcium limestone mines. Around those mines, the soil will be high in calcium until you get down into the river where the water has eroded the soil away. I have a client in southern Illinois whose corn wasn't doing well. He was raising good corn at first, and then he said his yields kept going down. He had a calcium limestone mine right in the middle of his farm. His calcium had gotten too high, and he had neglected magnesium. Every time he needed lime he put on limestone from the available quarry. He corrected the pH, but he forgot the limitations that walk hand in hand with pH. The nearest dolomitic limestone mine was 130 or so miles away. He had to send a truck out from his place. Neighbors called him crazy. The very next year his corn harvest came right back to where it was before.

Everything I use answers a formula. Nitrogen recommendations answer a formula, but nitrogen is one thing you can count on least because of the volatile nature of nitrogen in the soil. You can check it today and get a big rain, and suddenly part of it is gone. Chemically speaking, the soils and rocks in the same area will have the same makeup. If there is calcium in the rocks, there will be calcium in the soil. If there is plenty of magnesium in the rocks, there will be plenty of magnesium in the soil. This is an important point to remember. If the soil has not been moved in or out by erosion, rocks and soils in a given area remain blood brothers. Potassium soils in Scottsdale, Arizona, just south of Phoenix, are close enough to the potassium mines to be influenced by this proximity. Still, area farmers think they have sodium toxicity problems.

I worked with one farm near Scottsdale where the operator used a moldboard plow and a crawler caterpillar to break the soil, turning it over 22 inches deep every year. If you have any kind of openness in the soil, sodium and chloride are the first two things to leave. An open soil with plenty of calcium and plenty of water will not permit sodium to accumulate. This farmer thought he had sodium because his pH was high. His problem was potassium and magnesium, and his potassium was so high it was tying up his trace elements and hurting his crops.

You can start across Arizona and go into southern California. Some of those farmers in the mountains say they have a sodium problem. They are not down in the Imperial Valley where the creeks and rivers meander across the landscape. Their problem isn't sodium at all. It is potassium. But they never get a detailed analysis that enables them to discern this fact. On the other hand, in the Red River Valley in North Dakota, farmers have extremely heavy soils that hold a heavy payload of potassium. Because they don't audit the ability of the soil to hold potassium, they simply look at how many pounds are there. The heavier the soil, the more ability that soil has to hold fertilizer, and the more ability it has, the more it takes to saturate the soil with the proper amounts of nutrients. Some testing facilities tell those farmers that they have so much potassium that they do not need any.

The first time I went into the area, I discovered that many of those soils needed potassium. I was telling the farmers to put on potassium and one guy spoke up and said, "Well, you know, the university tells me that I don't need any potassium. Yet I can tell exactly where I use it on my crops."

What I am looking for in terms of a soil program is getting the right amounts in the right place at the right time. If you have too much or too little of any nutrient, it is going to hurt you. The rocks and soils in a given area tend to have the same nutrient content, and certainly scientists tell us that our soil comes from decomposed rock. Consider this, for rock to become fertile soil, it would have to break down from rock to gravel to sand to silt and finally down to very fine clay—to the finest clay particle possible. You actually

The Land

Henry George, United States economist and land reformer (1839-1897) discovered that the value of land is measured by the number of people who passed the front gate each day. If one came by, your place might be worth $1,000; if 100 came by, it could be $100,000. Even your gold mine might be worthless if no one could possibly travel past your land.

"So," he said, "the people give you the value of the land, and the people may take it away. Blessed are the people."

"Also," he said, "landowners are only custodians. They are the users of the land. If they use it well, they may keep it. If they use it poorly, the people should take it back again, and let a good custodian have it."

The feudal kings, using a similar theory, granted fiefs of land to chosen feudal lords. The people who lived there were also given to the lords, as serfs. But again, there was a string attached. The lord was only a custodian. He could retain the land and the serfs only as long as he cared for them as well. If he abused the land or failed to feed the serfs and give them social security, the king could reclaim the fief and give it to a better lord.

God, as the partner of feudal kings, approved these transactions.

Do not smile. Feudalism worked as well in relation to its original ideals as democracy works in relation to our Bill of Rights. Remember, in the ancient ceremony of knighting the feudal lord, a lowly serf hit him across the face with a glove, to remind him all over again that he must serve the whole community, caring for the land and feeding the people, or lose it all.

Are we so proud? Who cares for our land? Who cares for our people? Who intervenes when bad farmers pollute the land and hurt the communities? The farmer's eye should fatten the cattle. His dreams should sow the crops. His mind should fertilize the soil. His love should attend the harvest. Where have America's farmers gone? Will they ever return?

—*Lee Fryer & Dick Simmons*
Earth Foods, 1972

don't get any nutrient holding capacity from sand. Sand doesn't hold any fertilizer. The only two things that hold fertilizer in soils are the clay colloid—the very smallest particle of clay—and the humus, including the very smallest particle of organic manner. You have to measure how much of each there is in order to know how much fertilizer that soil needs.

It is good to have *luxury amounts* of potassium, but it is not good to have *excessive amounts*. Potassium ties up boron, which is what builds the grain, and it crowds out the manganese, which causes the grain to be set in the first place. Admittedly, soil is made up of sand, silt and clay, even though clay basically holds the nutrients. Still, the soil makeup is the amount of sand, silt and clay. We call the mix *soil texture*. Soil texture is important in two ways. Soil texture defines the amount of sand, silt and clay as it affects water holding capacity. A fine sand has the ability to hold about an inch and a half of water. A silt loam could hold two inches of water, and a silty clay loam might hold three inches of water. A silty clay loam can hold twice as much water as a fine sand. In other words, if you get two inches of rain, silty clay loam—dry to start with—could absorb the whole load. That fine sand would never hold the water. Fine sands also hold the least amount of fertilizer and heavy clays hold the most. There is one difference, and that is if the water isn't there, you'd better be able to supply it from somewhere. You can take a fine sand that has the proper nutrient relationships, and get enough water into it, and take a silty clay loam that has the same nutrient relationships, and you can grow just as much corn on that fine sand as you can on that silty clay as long as you have enough moisture. If you have the same amount of fertility, the difference is the water. I have clients on fine sands who will raise 190 to 200 bushels of corn and then go right on to their heavier soils without the proper nutrient relationships and they will raise 175 bushels of corn, all on the same farm. Yet some would tell all those willing to listen that heavy soils always out-produce sands.

There is another advantage to sands. Problems can be corrected faster. If sandy soils are out of balance, it takes less money and you can get a faster response in terms of production than you can with a heavy soil. On the other hand, once you get those heavy soils corrected, you can make all kinds of mistakes, and the nutrient load will last a long time. Sand keeps calling for help. It does not have the nutrient holding ability of clay. Only the clay particles hold nutrients in the sand. It isn't the pounds of fertilizer that produce the crop. The pounds of fertilizer merely tell how to get the proper nutrient balance in the soil.

An-i-on / ˈan-ˌī-ən / *n* [Gk, neut. of *an-ion*, prp. of *anienai* to go up, fr. *ana* + *tienai* to go] **1** the ion in an electrolyzed solution that migrates to the anode **2** a negatively charged ion **3** an acid forming element **4** opposite of a cation

Cat-i-on \ ˈkat-ˌī-ən \ *n* [Gk *kation*, neut. of *kation*, prp. of *katienai* to go down, fr. *kata-* cata- + *tienai* to go] **1** positively charged base elements, either alkali metals or alkaline earths **2** migrate to the cathode in an electrolyzing solution **3** the opposite of an anion

2

Cation-Anion Connection

NEW WORDS ARE NOW COMMANDED ENTRY into the farmer's vocabulary, *cation, anion, exchange capacity, base saturation,* and strange new nuances that attend the use of a soil audit must be mastered. But all have to do with the clay of the earth and the electricity of nutrition, and how nutrients, or the lack thereof, govern everything from crop production to weed control. I will proceed to expand this outline in this chapter.

In buying a farm, some people seem to prefer space and location to prime land. Land in the Missouri Ozarks—often seemingly quite useless for crop production—sells for more than prime land in the Little Dixie area of northern Missouri. There are some yellow, clay soils in the Ozarks of Missouri. I went up there to sample a farm on one special occasion, and I was really pleased. This fellow wanted to develop his farm, but the soils were extremely poor. They grew scrub oak, not much more. As we were pulling the samples, I discerned a nice yellow clay soil, and I thought this was great because it could be built up easily. When I received the analysis back, it was immediately evident that the soil had no more ability to hold fertilizer than a sand dune in Florida. It was a yellow clay, but it had not been broken down into a fine colloidal soil. There were no fine particles in it.

A soil colloid is a piece of clay that has been broken down to where it can't be broken down further. Such a clay particle and humus carry a negative charge, much like the negative post on a storage battery. Fertilizers must have a positive charge to be held to the soil colloid. Calcium and magnesium from lime compounds comply with this requirement. So does sodium. Hydrogen, as a gas, also has a positive charge. Negative sites on a clay particle will attract and hold positives, according to our scientific conceptualizations. The more clay colloids in the soil, the more negatives there are to attract positively charged elements, much like a magnet. Positively charged elements are called *cations*. Negatively charged elements such as nitrogen, phosphorous and sulfur are called *anions*. Negatives do not hold to the clay colloid. The bottom line is that clay has a negative charge and the element being held on that clay has a positive charge. Most of the chemical reactivity of soils is governed by clay colloids. These colloids are extremely small, and can't been seen with the naked eye.

I always like to point that out because there are some laboratories that will not measure the amount of clay in a soil. Some operators put it between their thumb and two fingers and rub it around as if to say, "Well, that feels like so much clay," and so they put that number down. If you start getting good, round numbers on a soil test, you can just about say, "Well, they are just estimating the exchange capacity." That is a standard practice in Europe. It is a

Hands-On Agronomy

standard practice for a lot of soil labs over here. Obviously, if you cannot see the colloid with the naked eye, how are you going to determine how much of it there is unless you involve sophisticated instrumentation? Colloids are plate-like in structure. These plates lie down on one another, very flat, forming the clay soil.

Colloids come from clay and organic matter. In other words, there are a humus colloid and a clay colloid. Both have a negative charge. They are very small, much like dust or talcum powder. These smallest pieces of clay—along with humus—attract and hold nutrients, but they are also easy to lose. If you could collect the dust that wind moves across a field and analyze it, you would find that it has the highest fertility of any part of the field. The most fertile part of the soil always leaves first, via either water or wind erosion. The longer erosion continues, the worse it gets.

When I pull soil samples, a lot of farmers think I overdo it. Take a flat field. Basically, if I can find out which way it drains, I will sample the low end and the high end. The biggest area I ever recommend being put in a sample the first time around is 20 acres. The low end will almost always have the highest nutrient content because the lion's share of nutrients are held on the clay particles, which are that light dust. On upland soils, whatever way the water drains, the fertility goes that way, too. Soils can be built up. They can also be torn down. In the area where I live, soils that are considered the worst soils—the ones that nobody really wants, the ones that are sold for horse pasture—were considered the most fertile soils in southeast Missouri when my grandmother was a child. Growers farmed it and farmed it and let it erode away. They would raise wheat year after year and burn the stubble, then plant something else for a second crop. Nobody really wants to try to raise crops on it nowadays. Much of this land is blow sand.

The first thing to do for your land is to correctly measure the amount of clay and humus the soil has in it. Nothing less than a detailed analysis will answer the questions. The procedure I rely on is atomic absorption. Technicians use a flame and actually measure the atoms, and how much the atoms will absorb in terms of color. This test shows a different color for each nutrient. That measurement has a name—*cation exchange capacity*, or CEC. As mentioned earlier, cations are nutrients with a positive charge. *Exchange capacity* is merely a measure of capacity of plant and the soil to exchange nutrients. Whether the CEC is large or small, it affects the colloid's capacity to hold nutrients such as calcium, magnesium and ammonia nitrogen, and it also affects the quantity of the nutrient needed to change its relative level in the soil. A light soil will hold less of everything. Consequently, it doesn't take as much fertilizer to get the right nutrient balance for total saturation, but the nutrient load can be lost. If you have an exchange capacity of, say, 5, that is a sandy soil for certain. It is not going to hold very much fertilizer. Another soil may have an exchange capacity of 10. It will hold twice as many pounds of nutrients as the soil with a CEC of 5. I do not use the term *cation exchange capacity* on my soil tests. I like the nomenclature *total exchange capacity* much better. Cation exchange capacity means that the laboratory is measuring a certain part of the cation capacity. It may be measuring all, and it may not. I put *total* on the form because I want to assure the farmer that I am measuring all the cations that could have a major effect on the soil analysis.

A lot of soil tests do not measure the sodium content in the soil. If you get a soil test that doesn't measure sodium content, it does not measure the *total exchange capacity*, and therefore the exchange capacity will be wrong. The exchange capacity is not something you measure and then fill with nutrients. The exchange capacity is developed because the soil could hold a certain amount of calcium, magnesium, potassium and sodium. Each of these nutrients must be measured, or a valid answer will not be forthcoming.

Hands-On Agronomy

Cation Exchange Capacity

The first order of business for the soil colloid . . . is to hold nutrients—nutrients that can be traded off as the roots of a plant demand them. Thus the first index from the laboratory—the energy of the clay and the humus.

Almost all laboratories report cation exchange capacity, and they do this in terms of milliequivalents, or ME. If it helps, you can think of an electrician measuring in terms of volts and amperes, or a physicist measuring magnetic energy in terms of ergs and joules. The soil laboratory has its own lexicon. It measures colloidal energy in terms of milliequivalents of a total exchange capacity, since soil colloids—composed of clay and organic matter—are negatively charged particles. Negative attracts positive. Cation nutrients are attracted and held on the soil colloids. Since anions are not attracted by the negative soil colloids, they remain free to move in the soil solution or water.

ME represents the amount of colloidal energy needed to absorb and hold to the soil's colloid in the top seven inches of one acre of soil 400 pounds of calcium, or 240 pounds of magnesium, or 780 pounds of potassium, or simply 20 pounds of exchangeable hydrogen.

—*Charles Walters & C.J. Fenzau*
An Acres U.S.A. Primer, 1979

There is a category called *other bases*. It covers cations not usually singled out in terms of how many pounds are available in small amounts. So I use the term TEC or the total exchange capacity instead of the CEC. The TEC shows the measured amount of holding power of the clay and humus in a soil.

Let me illustrate the point. Potassium has a single + beside it, meaning a single positive change. So do sodium and hydrogen. But calcium and magnesium exhibit a double plus charge, thus a ++. The latter are strong-arm elements. They have the capacity to push every other element aside.

Hydrogen is at the bottom of the pecking order, and then come sodium, potassium, calcium, magnesium. Certain nutrients obtained from the use of lime and manures and fertilizers, called cations, with their positive charge, are attracted to the colloid because it has a negative charge.

As mentioned, the clay colloid has a plate-like structure. This plate may be hexagonal, square, chunky or blocky, but it basically maintains a plate shape of some type. All of these get attracted. For every plus there is a negative.

That is great as long as we have enough negatives, but when we start saturating a soil to achieve pH 7, no negatives remain, and therefore nutrients can no longer be positioned on the soil colloid.

Adsorbs is a term that needs to be added to every vocabulary, with special emphasis on the "ad." It means *held on the surface*, in this case on the surface of *the clay particle*. When a plant root puts off its acids, an exchange between hydrogen and a cation nutrient takes place.

Sand has a low exchange capacity and holds less nutrients than other soils because it contains smaller amounts of clay and humus. Gumbo, on the other hand, has a high exchange capacity. A Florida sand used to grow leather leaf fern probably has a 3 or 4 exchange capacity. Some soils have a 40 to 50 exchange capacity, or ten times the ability to hold nutrients. If you started out with nothing in either soil, it would take ten times more fertilizer to balance the high exchange capacity soil compared to the low capacity soil. That is why we have to measure the soil and mark the nutrient equilibrium, or lack thereof. High TEC soils therefore hold much larger amounts of fertilizer and moisture because it contains higher amounts of clay and humus.

In a Mississippi survey, 82% of all farmers questioned said that they thought soil tests should be taken on farms to determine how much fertilizer should be used. Only 28% of the surveyed farmers actually used soil tests. Many farmers do not believe in soil tests.

Virtually all of my clients come to me by referral. I cannot convince anyone in an hour or even in a day. Most farmers do not really trust soil tests. If you start reading all the literature on soil tests, it might seem appropriate to ask, "Why should they?" At a meeting in Illinois, the head of the state Extension Service was on the panel with me. One of the farmers asked if it was possible to use a soil test to determine the fertility of a soil. The head of the Extension said, "No. You only use a soil test to determine roughly how much fertilizer to put on to feed the plant." I said, "I tell every farmer that from the analysis I do, I can sit down with him—not knowing what his soils will do—and rate the samples from the best to the worst."

I have had farmers tell me the reasons they do not trust soil tests. One fellow, in his early sixties, said he hadn't used soil tests for years, but in a sense he had. He said way back when the AAA program was in effect, and the government paid for the limestone, he had some very good pasture and some very poor pasture. He went out and took soil samples and he said, "You know what? I noticed the poor pastures needed two tons of lime and the good pastures also needed two tons of lime. One day I was digging post holes and got down to some old yellow clay, and I thought, "I wonder if I had soil like that how much it would need." The next time I sent in some soil samples, I reported that the yellow clay was from one of my pastures. It came back needing two tons of lime just like the rest of them. I decided, why should I walk all over these fields and take these soil samples to get the government to pay for the lime. From then on, I just kept a bucket of soil in my barn. When I thought I needed to put on lime, I put some of that soil in the sample bag and sent it in. They would tell me I needed two tons of lime."

I recall another farmer. His fertilizer dealer called me. He said, "We have a major problem in this area." This guy had overlimed his fields. He took a soil sample one year and sent it in to the university. They told him to put on two tons of limestone. He took a sample the next year and sent it in to the university. He didn't tell them that he had put lime on the year before. He thought that they ought to be able to pick that up. The recommendation came back, two tons of lime. He got so much lime on his fields he tied up the other nutrients, and his yields dropped. The fertilizer dealer said he took a soil sample from another client's land and split it up into three parts. He did this because he said, "Always, if a sample comes from the northwest part of the county it needs three tons of lime. If it comes from the northeast part of the county, it needs two tons of lime. If it comes from the south part of the county, it only needs one and a half tons of lime." He just wondered if it really made any difference.

One day, some few years ago, I went to see a possible client in Oklahoma. We walked over his ranch for a good half day, and he asked a lot of questions. He was a psychiatrist with a farm, actually. When we got back to his ranch house, he looked me straight in the eye and said, "Neal, you don't really believe that they run every one of those soil analyses like you are leading me to think? You don't really think they are meticulous about putting all those numbers down accurately, and that the report really reflects what is there?"

Hands-On Agronomy

Reciprocal Relationship
of Soil, Plant and Animal

What is soil? Soil is basically fragmented rock ground down by the action of streams, by erosion from rain, by wind, by the mechanical breakdown from animal life, by the chemical action of growing elements within it, by the expansion and contraction of freezing and thawing, by the action of energy from the sun, by the trituration of rock by glaciers, by growing vegetation, by the action of bacteria and molds, by the acids and bases that are created by growing organisms, by the minute root systems that help to break it down, such as the micro-rhizomes that find their way into the smallest crevices of rocks to cleave them by the force of growing and dissolve the exposed surfaces by the chemical elements which they contain.

Good soil is teeming with fungi, bacteria, protozoa, earthworms, beetles, crustacea and larvae of insects, as well as reptiles, and even small animals. The root systems of our crops and their productivity are actually altered as the population within the soil changes. Man alters these by the addition of organic and inorganic elements, by governing the moisture, varying the temperature, and controlling radiant energy.

What does man remove from the soil? Man removes plants and animals and their products. He removes much of the plants, the animals and the excrements without returning them. These are considered of organic nature. Of what do they consist? Primarily they are proteins, fats, carbohydrates, minerals, and water. Plants and animals are produced from a living soil. Their return to the soil constitutes the completion of the ecological cycle. They are basically made from inorganic rock, the water of the ocean, the gas of the air, and the energy of the sun.

Some students of ecology argue that only the proper combination of the mineral elements need concern us, for water is obtainable, air is all about us, and radiant energy can even be produced artificially. Others hold staunchly to the theory that it is the return of organic elements to the soil that is all important to the production of the most beneficial crops for man's use. They further believe that true plant and animal health comes only with a large return to the soil of the organic wastes, manure, garbage, carcasses of animals, and the plants themselves that have been broken down into humus by the action of bacteria, molds, and the earthworms.

Though hydroponic solutions of water, inorganic elements, air and radiant energy, produce plants, they ask, "What is the effect of consuming such plants as food on the optimum development of animal life, not only for the present, but for the generations of future animals?

There are those who feel that there is the middle ground where soil not only needs the mineral element, but that activators from organic material returned to the soil enhance plant growth, either through making the mineral elements more readily available or also by actually being incorporated into the new plants. They recognize that the leaf is a great chemical factory for transforming water, mineral, organic materials from the soil, gasses from the air, and radiant energy from the sun into the nutrients for growth and reproduction of root, stem, flower, leaf, and seed.

The ecological cycle has always been variable. The plant and animal population, including man, has been physically modified as natural forces have altered environment. The simple factor of rainfall is continually changing. The rainfall may be gentle, evenly stretched over the so-called rainy season, or it may fall all at once in the space of a few hours leaving catastrophe to animal, plant, and soil. When rain comes as a deluge, the total precipitation for the year may be high, but because of the short space of time involved, the summation of the effects may be similar to those found in years of serious drought. There are years of cyclonic winds, sometimes accompanied by driving rains in a given area, altering the ecological pattern. In other years, not only may the rainfall vary but variable humidity may be experienced; or a dust storm may be tragic to one area where the soil surface is eroded, yet may be a blessing to another where the soil is deposited.

The effect of weather on the living elements in the basic soil of a given region may alter its water retention and fertility. In turn the pattern of vegetation may be completely changed, the wild life pattern redistributed. The large animals may migrate. The lesser may die off in large numbers and those remaining become scrawny. It may be years before the former environmental factors return, if ever.

Man has been pointed to as the perpetrator of the greatest disasters to fertility and potential agricultural resources by ignoring the relation to each other of forests, soils, and the animals that dwell in them.

Marco Polo recounts the abundance of forests and animal life of China, but by modern times these have largely disappeared. Lack of conservation practices in the water sheds of the Tigris and Euphrates destroyed the fertility of the valleys and their civilization. In the desert areas of North Africa where shifting sands have swallowed the fertile fields of past civilizations, the adventurer finds the olive press and other evidence of human habitation in a vast sea of waste, again credited to the misunderstanding of total ecology by the men of that day.

Similarly, extensive areas of our own country have been transformed as the ecological pattern of soil, plant, animal, and human life have been altered.

Students of bionomics find today that the primordial life cycle from the soil to the plant, through the animal and back to the soil is frequently disrupted. Man fails to return to the soil much of his crops, his animals and excrements, thus breaking the natural cycle of life. So, in striving to maintain his economy, man must artificially return to the soil that which he removes.

—*Francis M. Pottenger, Jr., M.D.*
Missouri Agricultural Experiment Station's
Research Bulletin 765

I said, "It is not a matter of believing it, I am certain of it."

He said, "Well, you will never convince me. I don't believe it." He then related the following story.

"When I was getting my doctorate in California, I got a job working for the university running the soil tests. At the beginning I was really meticulous. I would run those tests and did all the numbers just right. It would then go into the agronomist and he would make the recommendations, and I really didn't know what was going on. One time I told the agronomist that I would like to take a look at the soil tests. I went in there and pulled out the soil tests and the recommendations. I noticed that if the farmer reported that he could grow 150 bushels of corn, the analysis didn't make any difference. If it was 150 bushels of corn, the amount of fertilizer was the same every time. He just took out of the textbook what it said for 150 bushel of corn." It didn't make any difference where the phosphate was or the potassium. He said, *We will feed the plant and we don't worry about the soil.*

The Oklahoma client concluded, "I thought to myself, 'Why do I need to worry about running soil analyses if they are not even going to be used.'" He said this incident came up in the springtime. Finals were coming and soils were pouring in. He knew basically what was going to happen from one area to another, and if anybody ever checked up on him, he knew they wouldn't do anything. He concluded, "According to the area, I just started writing down numbers. There were so many, I couldn't catch up and keep up with my studies. You know, it didn't change the fertilizer recommendations a bit."

Right in the area where we lived, there was a fellow who graduated from Purdue University. He wanted to have a soil test made. It didn't have anything to do with Purdue at the beginning, but in the end it did. Anyway, he wanted to have his soils tested, but he also went out and pulled sam-

The Importance of Calcium for Large Yields

To talk intelligently about soil fertility and crop yields, we must understand about soil and plant colloids and base exchange phenomena. Nutrient ions necessary for plant growth must be in solution so that they can be absorbed into the roots. Soil and plant colloids help to store these nutrients in the soil and in the plant. They make possible the base exchange phenomena, which make it possible to apply large quantities of lime and fertilizer to a soil, which can then hold it in readiness for the plant when it needs it.

When we apply limestone and mix it with the soil, we have a mixture which is only partially ready to support a good crop. Not until the calcium and magnesium in the limestone have disintegrated and become part of the colloidal complex in the soil through base exchange reactions does the growing crop benefit from the calcium and magnesium in the limestone. If limestone is applied to the soil and the ground remains dry, the limestone remains ineffective. If the limestone is too coarse, it may not be effective very rapidly.

—V.A. Tiedjens
More Food from Soil Science, 1965

ples and sent them to the University of Missouri. The soil test results came back from the University of Missouri. It revealed that the pH was something like 5.0 or 5.6. The results came back from our lab. The pH was around 6.5. He said, "Everywhere I look, I am a point to a point and a half lower on the university tests compared to the tests that you people do. How do I know which one is right?" So he sent samples to Purdue. When those levels agreed closely with our lab tests, he was satisfied.

University of Missouri uses salt pH tests. The tests we use are water pH tests. There is an important difference. The salt pH test will generally read a point to a point and a half lower, maybe sometimes a half point lower. Herbicide instructions call for a pH of such and such, but that is not for a salt pH test. It is for a water pH readout. So if your pH shows a 5.5 on a salt pH test and I show 6.5 on a water pH test, it could affect the herbicide program, if there is such a program. It is important to know which is which. In farm periodicals, they almost always fail to tell you which one is being used.

There are several different ways to run trace element tests. There are different extracting solutions. Even if the same extracting solution is used, and the same shaker from the same company to shake the solution is employed, if one worker shakes it fifteen minutes and another shakes it thirty minutes, the results are going to be different. A higher concentration will result for the one that was succussed longer.

The laboratory that I use feels that you get a more accurate reading if you shake it longer. They don't cut down the time of shaking in order to get more samples processed. The question is, how do we get the most accurate readings, the ones most helpful to the farmer and the fertilizer dealer? The laboratory I use buys the most expensive extracts because it wants to do the best job. There's a lab close to where I live that runs three times more samples in an eight hour shift than the lab I use could run with three shifts a day. They supposedly measure all the same things. They just cut down on all the time involved.

I have clients who have been with me since the mid-1970s. I have seen a soil look great one year, and the next the bottom falls out. There seems to be no explanation. It doesn't fall out on every field. It's not the rain. It just happens. I don't know what the scientific explanation is. If I don't catch it, and there are crops that really benefit from calcium, the yield will suffer. Calcium is the one thing that I notice most of all, but there will be other nutrients—phosphates, for instance.

I have one client—still one of the best I have ever had—who decided to use our testing services. It was late in the spring when the samples went in. It got dry early that spring. He said, "Look, we need to start to work, and this field is the driest, and we can go ahead and get it ready for cotton. Would you use this test from this other lab and tell me what to do? I know you can't tell me that you know exactly what to do, but at least that is better than what I am going to do." That particular lab simply said he needed two tons of any kind of limestone, etc. Although Dr. Albrecht always cautioned, "Don't do it," we sat down and used the formulas. We went through and calculated out how much limestone was needed. According to the formulas from the numbers on his lab test, he needed high magnesium limestone. Magnesium deficiency is basically not a problem in most soils, but some of the lighter soils do need it if they have never had it. His had never had it. When our sample came back, it turned out that he didn't need high magnesium lime. He should have used high calcium lime. I did him a disservice. I can't use somebody else's numbers and know the right thing to do. I have to use the soil test I understand, and not one from another lab.

Now, why should anybody believe that my service is better than anybody else's? For one thing, I try to find out what is the next limiting factor, and then try to review the principles of physics and chemistry in order to answer the questions. I know that all of these things have an effect—sand, insects, disease, variety, drainage, placement, weeds—but increasing the soil's fertility does more to take care of problems with yield than anything else. It helps to moderate some of these other factors.

The answers contained in what I call *The Albrecht System* are based on over 40 years of practical experience in the field. Not my 40 years, but 40 years that this system has been applied.

Let me recall a California company that hired me to consult on 100 acres of lemons because they had problems with the trees. While I was on the job, the farmer said, "We have 35 acres of grapes and we would like you to do our grapes, as well." I told him that I had never done any grapes before. But I called and talked to a fellow who had worked with grapes for years in the mid-1970s. He told me, "You just go ahead and have them do the same thing they would do if they were growing a good crop of corn. That is the first step. After they have followed the recommendations, have them increase the potassium level as high as you can up to 7.5% saturation of the soil." Later on, we were at a conference together and he told me how he had learned to work with grapes. "We treated those soils as if we were going to grow corn, and then raised the potassium levels. I learned that in France. I went to the managers of various vineyards and asked to take a soil sample from the very best area each had, and told them I would send each a copy at no charge. In every case it came back just the way Dr. Albrecht said it should be, except the potassium was on the high side." If we don't have any idea of how to grow a crop, there is always a first time and what you do is contact the people who already work with the crop.

There are 75,000 acres of rice in southeast Missouri. I met with a rice producer and sat down to tell him what to do. It was almost exactly opposite to what all the literature says to do to raise rice. The literature says, "Don't put on lime if you are going to grow rice." The reason they give is that it will create a zinc problem or an iron problem. That is what happened to a lot of central Arkansas farmers when they started growing rice. They had borderline iron and zinc problems, and when they put on the calcium they tied up those elements, and it has been assumed that this happens everywhere. In the southeast Missouri area, certain farms have excellent zinc levels and tremendous iron levels, and you can put on all the required lime you need without tying up either.

There were two brothers who grew some of the very best rice in our area. At that time a-140 bushel rice crop was almost unheard of, yet one of their fields produced 140 bushels per acre. They also had other fields where areas didn't deliver a crop. All I did was sit down and show them the differences. I started having rice growers put lime on their rice acres. As soon as the soil's calcium levels were corrected they started receiving premiums at the mill because of the crop's milling quality. Several received a 50 cent premium per bushel.

A good soil test is dependent on a good soil sample. Sampling instructions are more than mandatory. They are bible text. I always insist on a composite sample from each area. I do not want more than 20 acres in a sample. If I have a twenty-acre field and it is level, and the farmer says there is no difference, I will take 20 probes of soil and put it into one sample. The first time over, I take one probe of soil for every acre. If it is a huge farm with 160 acre fields, I may— if it is level—fudge a bit and take one for every one and a half acres. Then I put those together but no more than 20 probes, or 20 acres, to make one composite sample. If a farmer has an area he is concerned about, and it is big enough to fertilize separately, I will sample it separately. Composite samples must be well mixed. If 20 probes are taken, a half gallon or a gallon zip-lock bag should be used

The Soil Audit

A soil audit requires a map.

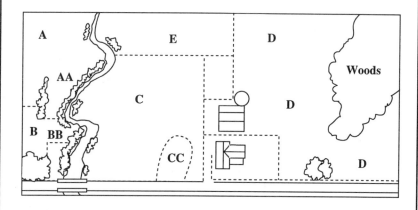

Areas obviously labeled differently require special probes. Several rules rate consideration in effecting proper sampling.

1. After making a soil map, divide fields according to soil types and conditions, past fertilizer treatments, and take samples from each area large enough to permit separate management. Composite samples should not include more than 20 acres under most circumstances.

2. Avoid sampling unusual areas or spots such as old fence lines, dead furrows, eroded spots, fertilizer spill spots, field depressions. These areas will not be representative of the whole field. Such areas should be sampled separately if tests are desired.

3. Individual samples can be taken with a clean spade, a sampling tube or an auger. A sampling tube will provide the most accurate composite since it tubes a uniform core of soil the full depth of the aerated topsoil. If a spade is used, be sure the sample is uniform in profile to represent the soil from the surface to the depth being sampled. The proper depth should include the major feeder root zone for the crop being grown (the top 6 to 8

inches for most crops and soils). Subsoil samples and other special samples desired should be taken according to special needs.

4. Collect an adequate number of individual samples of uniform depth to represent each area and mix them thoroughly in a clean pail to make a composite sample for testing.

5. Record sample locations on a map to help you or your consultant interpret the tests and make proper recommendations.

6. Package and label samples correctly to avoid breakage and mixups. Include adequate information such as name, field number, sample identity, depth of sample, date, crops being grown, etc., to insure complete and reliable results.

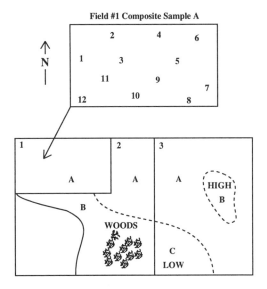

This diagram illustrates the points being made. One composite soil sample usually covers a five to ten acre area. Note how 12 probes were made in the section designated as 1-A. Certain obvious conditions made this area distinct. The soil seemed consistent. Its history required it to be treated as a unit—on and on. It is well to build a history of each field the way real estate companies build an abstract of real property.

—*Charles Walters & C.J. Fenzau*
An Acres U.S.A. Primer, 1979

to contain the soil. The probe with soil can be placed right in the bag. A hit with a large screwdriver will cause the soil to fall into the bag. Probes should go six to seven inches deep in any soil being worked.

Avoid unusual areas for a soil sample. Don't sample where an old bale of hay was split open for feeding. Don't sample in an eroded area. Stay away from old house sites. If a house burned down on an acre, stay away from that spot. The zinc content there usually will be four or five times higher than surrounding soil.

For soil sampling, divide the fields into areas. Draw a map that shows where the samples came from. Use proper sampling tools. You can take a sample with a trowel or a spade. First of all, be sure you get all the rust off by running it into the ground a few times. Just remember, you want to have uniform sized cores of soil. What I use is an old low-priced t-probe with a cut-away side. I use that cut-away side because then, when I pull it up, I can start looking at that soil and see its profile. If I have a soil that is extremely hard, I put a pull pin through the top and use a three pound lead weighted polyurethane mallet to drive the probe into the soil.

Always number and record the samples. The main problem I have with people sending in samples is that they don't pay enough attention to the numbering. Sometimes I get two samples that carry the very same numbers or identification letters on them. On the other hand, I have farmers who send me the worksheet that lists samples by number, what crop is going to be grown, what the crop was last year, what the yield was, and I always have some who will write, "My fertilizer dealer has these fertilizers available, and if I can, I would like to use them." I will not make that recommendation if there is something else that is better, without stating so.

If I know what a farmer is trying to accomplish, I can do a much better job for him. At least if I know what crop was

Hands-On Agronomy

there last year and what is to be grown this year, that is a tremendous help.

When you pull your samples, pack them tightly in a box, especially if you are going to send them via U.S. mail. Make sure they cannot move around.

A number of people have asked me what I considered to be an ideal soil. I would respond, "There is no need for me to talk about an ideal soil because everybody has to work with what they have." But for a meeting a few years ago, I put together on paper my ideal soil. The exchange capacity would be 12. An exchange of 12 would mean quite a bit of clay, a good nutrient holding capacity. Also, if there is a problem with a big deficiency, a farmer would not have to spend too much money to correct it. The pH would be 6.3. When everything is right in a soil, the pH is going to be between 6 and 6.5. Organic matter would be at 5.1%. This would provide approximately 100 pounds of nitrogen release from organic matter over a growing season.

Fungi in the soil like more of an acid-type condition, so the further soil pH gets below 6, the more the fungi will operate. On the other hand, bacteria like a high pH, so the higher the pH gets, the more bacteria will function as a force. When the pH is between 6 and 6.5, the numbers denote an environment in which the bacteria can do well, and so can the fungi.

I believe the soil I have described is the one I would best like to take my chances with. Others would do just as well though, if we work to balance what we have.

Now let us consider anions. Anions do not hold to the clay particles. Humus can hold them, but they won't be held otherwise. Humus can actually hold nitrogen, sulfur and another anion, boron. Clay will not hold any of these.

On a standard soil test, we start out with the total exchange capacity. That is the first thing we need to know. Then, after we know the capacity of the soil to hold plant nutrients, there is another portion of the test that goes hand-

When the Soil Has Been Overlimed

When a soil is overlimed, more than 80% of the capacity of this soil is saturated with calcium and magnesium. pH of this soil is higher than 7.0 and the farmer says that his soil is alkaline or sweet. According to the location, the climate, and other conditions that cannot be controlled by the farmer, the soil may be naturally alkaline not only because of the excess of calcium and magnesium in it, but also because of the accumulation of sodium and potassium in the same. Southern salty soils are usually very alkaline with pH 8.0 to 9.0.

The irrigation in a dry climate or in a dry summer makes the upper layer of any kind of soil more alkaline because the evaporating water drains the soluble salts upward into the upper layer of the soil. Where special cultures are raised, such as blueberries, a seemingly normal soil is to be made more acid once in a while, i.e., the calcium and magnesium base saturation has to be brought down to 50% and pH to 5.0, or even lower than that.

How to reduce the alkalinity of the soil is quite a frequent question. To correct an acid soil, namely, to increase the pH of a soil is definitely an easier and cheaper task than to correct alkaline soil or reduce the pH of the same.

To make a soil more acid we have to wash out or to neutralize chemically some substances in the soil that make it alkaline. This is a very complicated chemical process in which not only the substances that we apply and those that we want to wash out or to neutralize are involved, but almost all the plant food elements and the whole chemical and physical complex of the soil take part. Therefore, when the project of reducing the alkalinity of a particular soil is under way, a close chemical control is a must in order to avoid undesirable side reactions.

There are several methods to reduce high alkalinity in soil.

1. *The application of mineral acids*, an example is sulfuric acid. Such an acid will turn the alkaline substances into neutral and water soluble ones. The alkaline substances that exist outside the colloidal system of the soil, will turn into sulfates, namely, into neutral salts and will be washed out if there is sufficient water. The application of strong acids, however, is not very popular

because of practical inconveniences with diluting the same and with getting the liquid into the soil. This material may be used on small areas and in special cases only.

2. *The application of acid salts*, namely, salts that have been composed by combining strong acids with weak bases; such salts are: iron, aluminum or manganese sulfates. The strong bases in the soil push out the weak bases in the acid salt and occupy their places; thus, the strong bases turn the acid salts into neutral salts. By this procedure the strong active element from the soil is pushed out of the action, and, consequently, the alkalinity of the soil is decreased.

—*Rudolf Ozolins*
private papers, *Acres U.S.A.* collection

in-hand—the base saturation percent. The reason it comes second is because you can never establish the base saturations unless you know the exchange capacity. Base saturation teaches us that in each soil there is a specific percentage of nutrients that grows crops best, and that it is not the soil that receives the most pounds per acre that always delivers the best crop.

The longer a farmer works with my program, the more this will become plain. Anatomically, you use the pounds to get the percentages, and percentages tell how a soil is going to perform. Yield and quality are determined by the percentages, not the pounds. Thus our bottom line: base saturation percentage tells us what the soil is composed of in terms of cations—calcium, magnesium, potassium and sodium. It also tells us that the availability of these nutrients to plants generally increases with their percent saturation.

Magnesium and manganese are exceptions. A higher percent saturation of magnesium in a soil does not necessarily mean that this nutrient is more available. It is possible to get to the point where the percent of magnesium—as it goes up—actually makes less magnesium available to the plant. Here are the optimum percentage base saturation of cations for most soils. The cation calcium should be 60 to 70% of the saturation of the soil. In other words, 60% of the mineral content of that soil should be calcium. That is on a light, sandy soil. On a heavy clay soil, 70% would be optimum. The number for magnesium is 10 to 20%. On a heavy clay soil, it would be better at 10%. The ideal is for calcium and magnesium to total 80%. In a high clay soil, 70 + 10 = 80, and in a light sand 60 + 20 = 80. Light sands have to have more magnesium in order to spoon-feed the plant. Heavy clays do not need that magnesium.

There is another side to this story. The nutrient side is not the important side. The other side is the effect that calcium-magnesium have on the physics of the soil. A heavy clay soil needs to have more calcium. A light, sandy soil needs to

Hands-On Agronomy

have more magnesium because magnesium tightens the soil and pulls it together. The higher the magnesium content in the soil, the stickier it will be when wet, and the harder it will be when it is dry. Sodium can cause hardness but magnesium is basically what gives stickiness to a soil. On the other hand, the higher the calcium, the looser it becomes even to a point—if you overlime your soil—you can actually account for so much space in a soil that the water gets away. The lighter the soil, the more important it is not to overlime and not to get too much calcium in from whatever source.

Potassium should be at 3 to 5%. On grapes, cotton or woody plants, a better number would be around 7.5%. When you are at 7.5% potassium, the load will cut down on the available hydrogen in that soil. In short, there are trade-offs. A soil with a deficiency is also a soil with too much of something else. We have to realize that if we build the potassium up to 7.5%, and we have 10% magnesium and 70% calcium, something else has to make room. This will be the weakest link in the chain, namely hydrogen. Hydrogen should be between 10 and 15% of saturation. Hydrogen gives a bit of acidity to the soil so that it can keep phosphate, potassium and other nutrients more available. These nutrients tend to tie up. With hydrogen, some acidity can be maintained for the plants to use them.

The other bases are 2 to 4%. We concentrate on these in the trace minerals tabulation rather than as a base saturation percentage. They are needed in minute amounts. No one I know has concentrated on them long enough to say, "We need this much of aluminum, or this much iron," and so forth.

The above inventory of figures (the base saturation percentages), then, tell a farmer how productive his soil is. If you have a heavy clay soil with 70% calcium and 10% magnesium, and the rest of the numbers fall in place, and you have a second soil with, say, 60% calcium and 20% magnesium, the 70 + 10 soil is going to outproduce the other one every time. The 70 + 10 equation has more of what contributes to the ideal situation for a clay soil—more calcium to keep it loose and less magnesium to hold it together, because clay soils are naturally tight. They have very small pore space. Basically the problem in a clay soil is generally too much water. In a sandy soil, the problem is generally too much air. Thus we increase the magnesium in the sand in order to get the pore space out, and pull the particles together, and increase the calcium in a heavy clay to push the particles apart, causing them to aggregate in clumps in that soil.

True soil balance means determining and adding the proper amount of each nutrient. Fertility is the balance between elements. Not only is each element necessary individually, but a balance of all soil elements is necessary collectively. Every one works on every other one in an interdependent way. Adding too much of any nutrient means complexing some other nutrient needed for proper plant nutrition. Justus von Liebig is the fellow who gets credit for the concepts of N, P and K, meaning nitrogen, phosphate and potash. He determined that there was a Law of the Minimum. He said that if you don't at least have this minimum, then your crop is going to suffer. That applies not just to N, P and K, but to all the other nutrients.

Andre Voisin, a member of *de l'Academie d'Agriculture de France*, distilled his years of research into the Law of the Maximum. It means that if you put on too much of a given nutrient, it is going to tie up something else that is needed. He found that if you put on too much potassium, it ties up boron. If you put on too much phosphorus, it ties up zinc and possibly copper. If you put on too much nitrogen, it ties up copper and sometimes some of the other elements, even zinc. If you put on too much calcium, it could tie up all the other nutrients, depending on their presence.

Hands-On Agronomy

Thus our lessons fall into place. When the pH is 7 or higher, the exchange of hydrogen will be zero. As you come down the scale from a pH 7, then hydrogen begins to increase in direct proportion (as long as a water pH test is used to measure the phenomenon). If pH goes from 7 to 6.9, exchangeable hydrogen will go up by 1.5. If pH goes from 7 to 6.8, exchangeable hydrogen will go up by 3. For every 0.1 that pH is dropped, exchangeable hydrogen from pH 7.0 downward will go up by 1.5%.

When micronutrients are present in the soil in adequate amounts, and the soil has the right base saturation percentages, then they are most available, but not necessarily in adequate amounts. At the right percentages of calcium and magnesium—if the micronutrients are in that soil—these are going to be present in their most available form. Still, there are a tremendous number of soils that can be balanced in terms of all major nutrients, and be missing micronutrients in bare minimum amounts. They are in the deficient category even after we have done everything we can to balance the soil. It is not correct to say *balance the soil*, and micronutrients will take care of themselves. Some soils simply do not have them. But if they are already there and just tied up, they will be released.

Cal-ci-um / ˈkal-sē-em / *n, often attrib* [NL, fr. L. *calc-, calx* lime] **1** a silver white bivalent metallic element of the alkaline earth group occurring only in combination **2** chemical symbol:

3 a plant nutrient that should occupy between 65 and 70% of the positions on the soil colloid in terms of the exchange capacity **4** at the proper saturation, improves soil texture, makes phosphorus and micronutrients more available, and improves the environment for microorganisms **5** helps plants form better root systems, stems and leaves for efficient use of sunlight energy, water, carbon dioxide, nitrogen and mineral nutrients **6** most important fertilizer element **7** essential for building normal bones and teeth, important in blood coagulation, and lactation; enables heart, nerves and muscles to function; regulates permeability of tissue cells

3

A Hands-On Approach

SOILS ARE PUT TOGETHER IN PLATES. Some soils are colloid or sub-angular. They have a prism shape or one best described as long triangular. In any case, it all boils down to plates, one sitting atop the other. The ideal soil in terms of a textbook example is 45% minerals, 5% humus, 25% air, 25% water. The question poses itself: how do we get the minerals to be 45 to 47%, and specifically how do we get 25% air and 25% water into soil if it does not already have it? The answer is less complicated than the question. In fact, when you get the mineral balance in its correct equilibrium, you will have achieved the right mix of air and water in the soil.

The chemistry of the minerals also affects the physical structure of a soil. Therefore, the only way to deal with the textbook mandate is to first correct the minerals. If the mineral component is imbalanced, it is never possible to have the right amount of air and water. The mineral balance, in turn, depends on base saturation percentages and humus. This complex determines how much air and water space a soil will permit. When a soil audit reveals a correct mineral balance, any air and water problem will be minimal.

Obviously, poor soil structure means too little space in the soil. Heavy equipment compacts the soil by restricting the amount of space between soil particles. Either air or water has to give way. To construct the proper environment for plant roots and soil microorganisms, minerals in the right amount in effect govern the physical structure. Therefore humus which has 25% air, 25% water and 50% minerals is based on mineral building blocks in the first place

There are at least four ways to influence soil structure favorably. One of the ways is to use manures, composts, mulches, microbial stimulants, anything that puts microbes into the soil and supplies them with food. Deep tillage—rippers, plows, chisels—all can create a temporary effect by breaking up hardpan and plowpan barriers, but this physical approach cannot be considered basic. A third way is to use a soil conditioner. And finally, soil structure can be influenced by proper fertilization of the soil, namely supplying nutrients in the right amount as determined by soil tests.

Our objective is to remove compaction so that roots can not only grow in the topsoil, but also penetrate subsoil layers as deep as required to pick up water. In a non-productive soil, roots simply cannot get through any of several barriers. The best ripper in the world will not cause hardpans to melt away unless a correct mineral balance has been constructed first. A proper mineral balance, therefore, is the precursor to lasting success, whatever the hands-on approach.

For an ideal soil, humus would be a big key. Also, humus is the big key to water holding capacity as well as fertilizer holding capacity in terms of the amount that is in the soil.

The Organic School

A controversy of much interest is the attack on commercial or chemical fertilizer by the proponents of organic fertilizers. "Fertilizer kills the earthworms, it sours the soil, it burns out humus," the organic school keeps repeating. Such statements have mighty little to back them up. The USDA Beltsville Experiment Station reports, "Earthworms thrive and do a better job of soil building on well-fertilized land—more benefit is obtained from fertilizer when earthworms are present."

There is some question, however, whether our researchers are ever going to be able to set up comparative tests. There is the problem of the difference in rate in which the fertilizer elements become available from chemical fertilizer and organic fertilizer. The nitrogen and phosphorus may be released very slowly from the compost. This will result in differences in the growth and maturity of the plants at any particular time. The vitamin content may as a consequence be different whether the plants are harvested the same day or at the same stage of maturity on different days. Comparisons of this kind, therefore, become useless to the scientific investigator.

Yet we all know that we need vast quantities of organic material in the soil. Organic material is the crux of the whole soil building program. Ample supply gives us a soil in which roots can find food. It means a favorable environment for the molds, fungi, bacteria and earthworms. All these play an important, if poorly understood, role in connection with our own health.

As Roger Bray of the University of Illinois has put it:

"Nutritious food depends on the chemical properties of the soil. This means that either we have to fertilize plants scientifically for the production of food adequate for survival, or we reduce our world population by the slow process of starvation, until finally we reach a balance with nature's way of doing things."

—*Jonathan Forman*
The Land News [Friends of the Land], 1950

Most farmers think that they would love to have a soil that is all humus. Soils that are high in humus always serve up copper deficiency problems. Peat and muck-type soils generally mean production problems because of copper deficiency. To illustrate the value of humus, take 100 pounds of dry soil, 12 x 36 x 6 inches deep with 4 to 5% humus, it can hold 165 to 195 pounds of water. That is equal to holding a four to a six inch rain. On the other hand, take a similar block of soil, 1.5 to 2% humus, it can hold only 35 to 45 pounds of water, which is equivalent to 0.5 to 1.5 inches of rain. A soil with a good humus content, say 4 to 5%, can hold more than double the amount of moisture the 1.5 to 2% humus soil can hold. We live with 0.5 to 1.5 inch rainfall in our area because most of our soils are below 2.5% humus. Below 2.5% humus, nutrient elements leach out because it is easy to lose nutrients with a low humus soil. Also, a soil with 2.5% or less humus keeps microbes on a starvation diet. Most people think they would like to have high humus, but Albrecht's work on humus revealed that even balance cannot completely annihilate all the problems.

The term *humus* is not used on my soil audits, but just below the pH there is a designation, *organic matter percent*. Really, that term *organic matter* in that position should be *humus*. *Humus* and *organic matter* are used interchangeably whenever I am talking about my soil test form. Humus is made up of decomposed residues which have been completely broken down in the soil by microorganisms. The *organic matter* or *humus* terms notwithstanding, when I am talking about a reservoir for nitrogen, phosphorous, sulfur, boron and zinc, I am not talking about undecomposed residues. I am talking about the humus that is completely decomposed, otherwise the reservoir function wouldn't happen.

Why does not clay hold nitrogen, phosphorus, sulfur and boron? Because humus is "stronger" than clay. When you take a handful of clay in one hand and a handful of organic matter in the other hand, and measure the nutrients, humus holds three times more nutrients than clay.

Organic matter contributes to soil productivity in many ways. It improves the physical structure of the soil. It increases water infiltration. It improves tilth, decreases erosion, and supplies plant nutrients. Let's take the beneficial properties of soil humus.

One, it releases plant nutrient element fertilizer. It releases the nutrients slowly out of the humus over a growing season, cafeteria style. We can speed that up or we can slow it down. The speed up is geared to overuse of nitrogen, basically.

Two, it improves the physical properties of soil. It helps hold water better. It certainly adds to the tilth and friability of soil.

Three, it aids in micronutrient nutrition of plants through chelation reactions. It turns loose microorganisms in the soil as it also serves as a good source of food for microbes.

Four, it aids in solubilization of plant nutrients from insoluble minerals. This means that it helps break down fertilizers that are on-scene in the wrong form and tied up or complexed.

Five, it has high absorption or exchange capacity for plant nutrient elements. That is one of the reasons humus has three times the holding capacity of clay. It can grab and hold the nutrients right on the outside, *adsorb*, if you will. Albrecht made a classical study of the holding capacity of humus. He and his associates isolated humus and subjected it to the strongest acids in order to knock loose the nitrogen. Nothing worked. But the exudates from plant roots did the job. Plant roots could unhinge the nitrogen easily. Microbes can, we can't!

Six, humus increases a soil's buffering capacity. Farmers who have high organic matter or humus content soil can make many more mistakes without paying for them immediately. Maybe the grandchildren or great-grandchildren will pick up the costs, but for the moment humus permits mistakes. I have clients in northeast Iowa who have 7 and 7.5% organic matter in their soils. Some soils around Ames have 5% organic matter. The buffering capacity of such soils is tremendous. The term *buffer capacity* requires explanation. Excessive nitrogen applied to a light sandy soil will ruin that soil system rapidly. The same application can be made to high humus soil and it still might last for years. *Buffer* means that you can make a lot more mistakes without seeing ill effects immediately. Buffer capacity is also an index for water holding capacity. The farmer who has to work with small amounts of water gets into trouble faster if he does not have the needed buffering capacity.

Seven, the dark color of humus favors heat absorption and permits early spring planting. A dark color also permits the soil to dry out faster for more timely field entry.

Eight, certain components in humus may exert plant growth-promoting effects.

Nine, humus supports a greater and more varied microbial population favorable to biological control, but it also favors a microbiological contribution to fertility.

Ten, humus reduces toxicity of certain substances, both natural and man-made. To illustrate the point, let's look at zinc excess and copper excess in Florida citrus groves. These groves have levels capable of killing 50 year old grapefruit trees. Often they have double that level in soils still used to grow trees. Over the years they have also supplied the other nutrients as indicated by balance. The real stock answer to combat toxicity has been to increase the organic matter in the soil. Florida growers do not like the term *manure*. They call used cow and chicken feed *organic*.

Eleven, humus increases the soil's water holding capacity. Humus can be built by increasing the efficiency of microbial decomposition of plant residues. And humus can be destroyed by working soils that are too wet.

I have a client with the prime goal of building up the humus content of his soils. He grows legumes. He uses microbial materials. He does everything possible to encourage microbes, and he is strict in following proper tillage practices. He farms heavy gumbo soils. One year—after he had been working on this program for three or four years—conditions stayed wet and wet and wet. The very day he could get a disc from one side of the field to the other without it balling up too much, he started working the soil. In his case, I pull soil samples in the summer. Accordingly, I pulled the samples in late August. This farmer started out on a 210-acre farm that had 2 to 2.5% humus content. In a matter of three or four years, he built his level up to 4%, with some acres a little above that figure. It looked good for a couple of years. Then suddenly he was back to 2.5% humus again. Then, as I started looking at the soils, the percentage kept climbing until finally about half the acreage still had 4%, as it had before. Finally the picture emerged. I called the client and asked whether he worked the driest field first. He said, "Yes," and then I named another field and he said, "Yes," he'd worked that one next. Then I named another field. I could name the fields and the sequence in which he worked them. The first one lost humus back to the starting point. By the time I got to the ones in the middle, it became evident that it didn't rain after he started working those fields and until he got the entire farm planted. By the time he got half the fields worked, all the land had dried out to the point where he wasn't working his soils any wetter than he had before. Where he worked the soils wet, he lost all the humus he had built up in three or four years.

A lot of the old timers still say, "If you work a clay soil wet, it will take a year to get it straightened out." The why and wherefore is not difficult to understand. Working wet soils annihilates air and water spaces. Removal of the air space destroys the environment that microbes need. Without air, the aerobes cannot break down residues in the proper way.

There is a set way to achieve this transformation if humus is to be built. Basically, you need a carbon to nitrogen ratio of 10.4 to 1 in order to build humus. The finished product will be more than 10 to 1. Most corn, soybean and crop stover computes to 60+ parts carbon to 1 part nitrogen. If there is not enough air to permit microbes to increase and multiply, the quality and quantity of humus simply evaporates. Unfortunately, there are years in which a 2,000 or 3,000 acre farmer will have to work some fields wet, or he is not going to get his crops planted. But in agriculture, proper tillage practices—as well as proper nutrient balance—is required if top results are to be achieved.

Withal, farming does not lend itself to single factor analysis. Growers who worship at the altar of pH need to understand that good pH does not guarantee a balanced soil. Illinois farmers I know say they want a pH 7. The reason is that a pH 7 on a water pH test gives an assurance that the calcium level is exactly right for them. There are some exceptions. If you take some cornbelt soils of Illinois, at pH 7, no calcium deficiency will show. It just so happens that the closer the Illinois farmer aligns his operation to pH 7, the better his crops. But farmers relying on a salt pH test must know that this higher reading translates to pH 6. Some growers say they don't want pH 7 or even pH 6, but pH 6.5. No matter what the pH readings are supposed to be, does a good pH assure a balanced soil?

The answer is "No." pH is influenced by four major cations. Calcium influences pH, as do magnesium, potassium and sodium. Extremely high sodium will deliver a high pH. Potassium influences pH even more than calcium and magnesium.

As the boxed material clearly points out, magnesium, pound for pound, can raise pH up to 1.4 times higher than calcium. A soil high in magnesium and low in calcium can test above 6.5 and still be entirely inadequate to grow alfalfa. Of prime importance are calcium and sodium—sodium, because it must be buffered or removed, calcium, because most of the time it has to be supplied. It is an Albrecht axiom that once all the nutrients required are supplied, the pH will be right.

Most farmers have seen a slide conceptualized by The Fertilizer Institute. It depicts *desirable* pH ranges for some few crops, the term *desirable* being somewhat incorrect. It really should be *tolerable*. Blueberries are shown to tolerate a pH between 5 and 6, but the best blueberries grow in the 6 to 6.5 pH range, provided all the required nutrients are present in the proper amount.

Back in 1979, I was hired to go to Pennsylvania to see two brothers who were operating a pick-your-own truck farm and nursery and greenhouse. They wanted me to evaluate

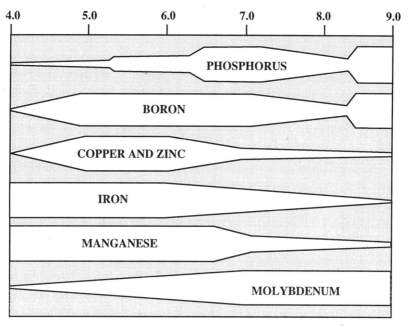

SOIL pH AFFECTS NUTRIENT AVAILABILITY

their soils, the best to the worst. The very best soil was right in line. One of the brothers said, "How would that soil do growing blueberries?" I gave the explanation I related earlier on grapes. I said, "Well, I have never worked with blueberries, but my experience suggests that blueberries ought to do better on this soil than on any other soil you have in spite of the fact experts will tell you that you have too much calcium, and blueberries do not like calcium."

He said he wanted to show me something. So he pulled out a soil sample from a major state university and a letter that said, don't plant blueberries on this soil because the calcium is too high and they will die. He said, "Now what do you say?"

I repeated the same thing I had already told him.

The farmer went on to explain, "By the time we pulled our samples and got them back, the blueberry plants had arrived and we decided to plant them on the very spot I asked you about. They turned out to be the best blueberries in the area, certainly the best blueberries we had ever grown. Not only were they the most productive, they were also the largest and sweetest."

A watermelon planted in a 5 to 6 pH soil doesn't mean it will grow well, regardless of what agricultural institutions say it will. A heavy clay soil without much silicon will not produce a good watermelon crop. On the other hand, a heavy clay soil that has been balanced will often produce great watermelons, sometimes not. It depends on the amount of silicon in that clay soil. Silicon is one of those elements we call *way out*. Watermelon has the best nutritional silicon. It concentrates silicon. That is one of the reasons it does so well in sand. If you don't have enough silicon in a clay soil, you can have all the balance you want and still not get the crop. There is a problem with this. We do not measure the silicon content of soils. When someone asks me if he can grow watermelons in a clay soil, my answer is, "If you balance it out and there is enough silicon."

Silica*

It is a proven fact that silica plays an important fertilizing role in the plant kingdom. Tests have shown an improvement in cultivation following the addition of silicates. Silica also functions as a vital element in protecting plants against mold penetration, and it has been found to influence the use of other ingredients useful to plant metabolism. A rich supply of natural organic silicates can be found in *Equisetum arvense*, the source of vegetal silica.

Better known as horsetail, spring horsetail, or scouring rush, this perennial grows wild in all temperature zones of our planet. It belongs to a small group of plants known as pteridophyta, which is distinguished as nonflowering and non-seed-bearing. Horsetail thrives on clay-like sandy soils. It occurs mainly in marsh lands but can be found in woods and forests, moist fields, meadows and along the sandy shores of creeks and streamlets. Some varieties have adapted to other environments, living along roadside and stony ground. Horsetail has such an awe-inspiring history that a short trip into the distant past is fitting.

Silica deficiency may exist if your diet consists of too many refined foods. Silica is abundant in the shell of brown rice, in leafy greens and bell peppers. When food is processed, silica is unfortunately removed. Fiber is usually the first to be cut or washed away, and along with the fiber, the silica. Stripped cereals and other processed foods have decreased silica supplies. This massive loss of natural silica has been paralleled by an increase in degenerative diseases.
—*Klaus Kaufmann*
Silica, 1990

*silica—silicon dioxide, SiO_2
silicon—

14
Si
28.0855

Unfortunately, silicon is something we do not know how to measure properly. Sand basically contains silicon.

The very best alfalfas do not have to be in soils above pH 6.5, although pH on the high side will create an environment that alfalfa can stand, more so than the other way. The alfalfa crop thrives on soils favoring bacteria. Bacteria work best in the top few inches of soil. Withal, microbial life can cover over some of the problems that are created otherwise. A good environment for microbial life often depends on manures or humates or biologics to supply many of the things we do not know how to measure.

Crops and plant species each have a story to tell, if we have the wit to learn. Take the rhododendron, for instance. The rhododendron and azalea both have a reputation for requiring acid soils. Yet, the very best rhododendron and azaleas do not grow on acid soil. But they do grow on a well-balanced soil. It is true they can endure acid soils and still grow, albeit not with the same quality. If one nutrient is out of kilter, the rhododendron will have trouble. A rhododendron can stand a low pH soil and high magnesium. It can *endure* low calcium and high magnesium.

The sensitive nature of balance can be illustrated with reference to one of my clients in Nevada, where boron is often a problem. Boron above 2 ppm is excessive, yet I encountered boron at 20 ppm. There are plants that will grow with boron at above 20 ppm, but not golf course grass, which is what my client wanted. There is a multiplier in dealing with soil pH that is best expressed in logarithmic terms. If you have pH 7, it is neutral. If you have pH 6, it is ten times more acid. Going down to pH 5, acidity is one hundred times greater.

Plant removal of basic cations such as calcium and magnesium hardly has any effect on pH because so few pounds are removed in relation to the amount in the soil. A 150-bushel corn crop takes roughly twenty-eight pounds of calcium and 28 pounds of magnesium. The lightest,

The Secret Life of pH Management

The pH of a soil is affected and influenced by four elements: calcium, magnesium, potash and sodium. How much of each is present in a soil must be known before an appropriate lime and fertilizer program can be designed.

Magnesium, pound for pound, can raise the pH up to 1.4 times higher than calcium. A soil high in magnesium and low in calcium can test above 6.5, but will be entirely inadequate for the growth of alfalfa or the growth of legume bacteria, and above all for maintenance of an environment necessary to decay organic crop residues into humus.

It is more essential to manage the factors that construct the soil pH as determined by present soil tests than it is to be concerned with the calculated amounts of nitrogen, potassium & phosphorus. Why?

• The conversion and availability of mineral elements are related to and regulated by the system of decay in the soil. The proper decay processes are initiated and determined by usually full levels of calcium and reasonable levels of magnesium.

• A balanced equilibrium of calcium and magnesium creates a soil environment for bacteria and fungus activity for the proper decay of organic residues into CO_2, carbonic acid and a host of many weak and mild organic acids, all necessary to convert and release mineral elements in the soil system.

• An imbalanced equilibrium of calcium and magnesium permits organic residues to decay into alcohol, a sterilant to bacteria; and into formaldehyde, a preservative of cell tissue. The symptoms of this improper decay system can be observed when previous year's stalks are plowed back up just as shiny and fresh as they were when turned down.

• Under these circumstances larger and increasing amounts of nitrogen and fertilizer minerals will be required just to maintain normal crop yields. The soil system is not complementary to release the minerals nor the other soil essentials for optimum growth.

• And remember also that large applications of nitrogen consume larger amounts of calcium as well as "burn-up" crop residues and humus. You can get increased yields for a few years from this stored-up wealth of humus, but eventually you will have to account for this withdrawal.

• Without an active organic matter system in the soil you cannot grow any crop at all, no matter how much nitrogen, potassium and phosphorus you add. The soil is a living, complex system that not only holds the 12 necessary minerals needed for plant life, but also is the factory that produces carbon dioxide, digests lignin into humus, provides nutrition and energy for desirable bacterial and soil animal life, and is the container for both water and air. Can you germinate and grow a plant in subsoil material without humus action present?

• In the absence of a system of organic matter management and calcium it will soon be essential to consider buying dry-ice (as a source of CO_2) and propane gas (as a source of additional carbon). Both are sad excuses for our ignorance and mismanagement of calcium and magnesium and at the same time a dear price to be paid for our continued disregard of this important and vital soil equilibrium.

• A soil program with managed levels of calcium and magnesium will allow the nature of the soil to function complementarily to the process of life and in many cases actually diminish or even eliminate the causes of many problems we can't explain or do much about ourselves. Some of these benefits and affects are:

1. More efficient photosynthesis.

2. Maximum use of heat-degree days—a natural time clock of the life systems of plants.

3. Create and maintain root and stem capacities for optimum use of sunlight energy and thermal efficiency by the leaves of the plant.

4. Thereby the plants can use water, CO_2, nitrogen and mineral nutrients with greater efficiency.

5. A healthy and normal functioning plant can maintain an adequate hormone and enzyme system so vital to resistance to insect and disease hazards.

6. A balanced soil equilibrium will regulate and manage the quality and availability of all mineral elements needed by growing plants.

7. Excesses of minerals during the early growth stages often plug up the vessels of the stem and are the frequent cause of early death. A dead plant system cannot mature or ripen itself.

8. An excess of magnesium as well as nitrogen in the soil initiates the processes which prevent the crop from growing dry and nutritionally ripe which is a major goal of every farmer.

9. Carbon dioxide availability is more important to high-yield potentials than nitrogen or any mineral element. The supply in the atmosphere could sustain life for not much more than 30 days, and depends on the soil decay system to replenish its supply. Without the beneficial effects of calcium in the soil system and its effect on soil structure and tilth, the processes are retarded and inefficient.

10. Clay soils high in magnesium and low in calcium cement together tightly, are subject to compaction and clodding, crust over easily and prevent the insoak of water and the recovery of capillary water during the dry periods of the season.

11. Soils in such poor tilth and structure increase the effects of the many weather hazards that annually impair normal plant growth. With a managed calcium-magnesium equilibrium we would not have to lean on the many poor excuses of weather we use every year to explain away our ignorance and personal mistakes. We cannot do much about the weather, but we can use the experiences of our mistakes to create a more integrated soil management system that would tend to diminish or even eliminate the many variable hazards of the weather.

> —C.J. Fenzau
> "The Management of Calcium for a Wholesome Soil and Crop System," *Acres U.S.A.*,
> November 1971

sandiest soil often will have 800 to 1,000 pounds of calcium in it. It would take years and years for crop removal of these nutrients to cause acidity. The chief culprit is leaching of basic cations by rainfall. Water simply takes them away. But this is still not the key. We have to consider nitrogen fixation by bacteria on legume roots. If nitrogen is not securely held, as water moves through it takes some of that nitrogen and carries it away. Ammonia will take sodium, but so will any type of nitrogen that moves through that soil. By the time ammonia has traveled through the soil, it has changed chemically to nitrate. It takes either sodium or calcium as a passenger on its trip to the sea. Nitrogen with water will not take magnesium, however.

Bacterial conversion of nitrogen compounds in the soil—whether from manure or compost, from commercial nitrogen, whatever—is the key to lowering soil pH. When the nitrogen moves out, it takes certain cations with it. That is why overuse of nitrogen takes out cation nutrients, especially if they have been recently balanced.

In short, imbalance can create other imbalances. The weakest link in the chain is going to affect the yield. In many soils the weak link is not nitrogen, phosphate, potash, not even calcium. I have had clients whose soil tests show they do not need calcium. They used at least as much phosphate and potash, and invariably they were using too much nitrogen. But sulfur and micronutrients were limiting the yield. I have four clients in southeast Missouri who raised their corn yield in three years by 30 to 40 bushels per acre when they started using sulfur and micronutrients. That's the only change they made. When I started suggesting certain things they could do to save money, they spent it on micronutrients. Yet micronutrients only make a difference when everything else has been corrected. If there is a magnesium excess, loading on micronutrients will not help. Magnesium deficiency is also a limiting factor. So are defi-

Hands-On Agronomy

ciencies of calcium, nitrogen, phosphate, sulfate and potassium.

In any long range program, calcium comes first. Its status has to be discerned via laboratory test because calcium deficiency seldom shows up visually in the field. Secondary effects—such as high soil acidity—usually limit growth first. High soil acidity makes it possible to get manganese, aluminum and iron toxicity. Academically, the reason calcium deficiency seldom comes up is that usually there are hundreds and even thousands of pounds in the soil, and it is never likely that more than 50 pounds will be used by the crop in any one year.

Calcium is essential. If not enough is available, it means that there won't be the right amount of air and water, and there won't be the efficiency needed to get other nutrients into the plant. When I say that 60 to 70% saturation of calcium is required, I am not talking about the whole soil. The saturation referred to here is actually in the clay colloid and

---

FREQUENCY OF LIMING DEPENDS ON:

- **Soil texture.**
- **Nitrogen fertilization rates.**
- **Calcium and magnesium crop removal.**
- **Amount of lime applied.**
- **Soil pH range desired.**

---

soil water. At 60 to 70% calcium around the plant root hairs, microbes do well, and the exchange of elements also works well. In the absence of calcium, more potassium ions are required around root hairs to get the same amount of that nutrient into the plant. It also takes more nitrogen around those same root hairs to effect uptake into the plant. As the calcium concentration is increased, so is efficiency in getting other nutrients into the root. This means less nitrogen to do the same job, and less phosphorous and less potassium. Conversely, the lower the calcium in the soil, the more nitrogen etc., is required to get the same crop yield.

I work with some 75 farmers in eastern Iowa. If you take the calcium/magnesium relationship in their soil—and they tell me how many bushels of corn they grew over the last four or five years—I can closely calculate how many pounds of nitrogen they used. Actually, I prefer they tell me how much nitrogen they use. Then I can compute the average corn yield. However, if something is way out of line, this computation isn't possible. Iowa cornbelt soils generally are in tolerable shape to start with. Yet almost all have a calcium shortage, too much magnesium, not enough sulfur and not enough boron. Every other nutrient has to ride on the back of calcium to get into the plant. Calcium puts the starch into the leaf. Calcium activates several enzyme systems. It increases yield by reducing soil acidity. Its use as a fertility agent increases calcium availability. Moreover, calcium improves microbial activity. I always look at calcium first because it makes every other fertilizer nutrient more efficient.

Common sources of calcium are calcitic limestone, which has 31.7% calcium, and dolomitic limestone which has magnesium as well! 215 to 225 pounds of magnesium and 425 to 450 pounds of calcium will usually be the analysis for the top dolomitic limestone.

Gypsum is a source of calcium, but it can be used only when the calcium connection is close to right. Marl rock

Hands-On Agronomy

rates consideration. On the east coast they use a material called aragonite, literally marine deposits ground up in the islands. It is high in calcium. There is also hydrated lime and burnt lime.

Basically, when I mention lime, I am referring to calcium and dolomitic limestone or gypsum. Hydrated lime or burnt lime may be useful if the soil is barren. Frequency of liming depends on soil texture and nitrogen fertilization rates because nitrogen drives out calcium. Nitrogen will drive out sodium first, but if there is a paucity of sodium, it will take out calcium. Frequency of liming is hardly influenced by the removal of calcium/magnesium by the crop. The frequency of liming depends on the amount applied. Frequency of liming also depends on the soil pH range desired. But you will recall that when the nutrients are right, the pH will be right.

There are some advantages to liming acid soils. The process lowers toxic levels of aluminum and manganese. It also

---

ADVANTAGES
FROM LIMING ACID SOILS:

- **Lowers toxic levels of aluminum and manganese.**
- **Increases some microbial activity-decomposition.**
- **Overcomes the potential for calcium or magnesium deficiencies.**
- **Increases symbiotic nitrogen fixation in legumes.**
- **Increases availability of phosphorus and molybdenum.**

---

governs iron release. However, too much can lower the level of iron and cause iron chlorosis. Finally, lime increases microbial activity, manages decomposition and overcomes the potential for calcium or magnesium deficiencies. It increases symbiotic nitrogen fixation in legumes and it increases availability of phosphorus.

We analyze limestone for its calcium and magnesium content, and the fineness of grind. Nutrient and particle size analysis is necessary, particularly the latter, because the finer the particles, the more available the calcium. Agricultural limestone on an eight-mesh screen means 100% goes through. Only 90% goes through a 20-mesh screen, and 60% through a 60-mesh screen. I tell farmers that if 60% will go through a on100-mesh screen, there is no need to worry that the grind will not be fine enough. For limestone applied in the fall, a third of the calcium will become available the first year, another third the second year, and another third the third year provided there is enough moisture. This suggests full utilization on irrigated acres. Without enough moisture, it may take four years to see the full effect, rather than three. Lime reacts in one to three years when the particle size is at least 60% through a 100-mesh screen. On a four- to eight-mesh screen, this means only about 10% breakdown occurs in one to three years. From an eight- to a 20-mesh size, there is a little over 40%, from 20 to 50, about 75%. From a 50- to 100-mesh screen, then as far as the particle, if 50 to 100% of it goes through a 100-mesh screen, it means 100% availability over three years.

Basically, limestone is calcium carbonate or a mixture of calcium carbonate and magnesium carbonate. Most areas require calcium carbonate. Few locations require a calcium magnesium carbonate. Water treatment plants that take their water from the river use calcium carbonate for filtration. Often they just throw it away afterwards. Power generating plants that burn high sulfur coal also use calcium carbonate. This by-product is often useful for crop acres.

Hands-On Agronomy

Sugar beet refineries use calcium carbonate to filter beet juices, the calcium becoming a waste product. We have used them all in one area or another to supply calcium.

Calcium carbonate pH can run as high as pH 8.2 to 8.4. The small amount used in relation to the soil mass will not create an adverse effect, however. Some few short range pH problems can result, but basically limestone application to answer a calcium requirement and to buffer excessive magnesium will result—within three years—in the pH going down, not up. Calcium actually controls a part of the magnesium, and magnesium causes pH to be higher than calcium.

Molybdenum will remain available at a pH close to 7 because of the effects pH has on that element. For the most part, pH 6.5 will keep phosphorous available. A pH 7 or below—all the way down to 5—will keep boron available if there is any in the soil. As pH 6 comes into view, the amount of copper and zinc available is decreased. At pH 6.5 the caution flag goes up for each of the above named nutrients. pH 5 heading to pH 6.5 will unfold deficiency.

Iron availability starts to decrease between pH 6 and 7, meaning trouble if there is barely enough iron. As the calcium is raised, the iron level decreases. Manganese, on the other hand, gets to about 6.5 before it starts to decrease. Therefore soil pH does affect nutrient availability. This is one of the reasons that a lot of crops thrive at low pH levels. Blueberries thrive at low pH levels because this acidity means plenty of iron. Alfalfa thrives at a high pH because it always gets plenty of phosphorous and molybdenum in the higher range. But alfalfa has a problem without boron. At pH 7, boron availability starts to drop off, and most soils don't have enough boron to begin with.

All things considered, calcium carbonate should provide a 100% neutralizing value. But we rarely look at *neutralizing value*. We look at how to add calcium. Dolomitic lime, calcitic lime, oyster shells, burned oyster shells, basic slag, gypsum—all those products have calcium in them. Gypsum, meaning calcium sulfate, does not neutralize the soil. The pH will not be adjusted by gypsum because the sulfur and calcium content offset each other.

I determine the advantages of liming and how much lime should be used by measuring the amount of clay and humus in the soil. I measure the CEC, but I do not determine limestone needs on the basis of pH. Even at a classical pH, it is possible to still need calcium, and if that calcium is not supplied, crops are going to suffer.

I had a client near Fallbrook, California with pH 8.2. He still needed calcium, and he put the calcium on his soil, a ton of gypsum and a ton of calcitic lime. He grows for Sunkist, and they had told him at last report that he had the best fruit of any grower in the valley. His pH went from 8.2 to 8.4, after I told him to apply lime. This caused no problem because his other nutrient levels were adequate. I never look at pH to determine when to lime or what kind of lime to use. I look at the deficiencies in the soil. Liming materials must be evaluated according to the calcium-magnesium content and according to the fineness of grind. The limestone test I mentioned earlier is not expensive, only about $20 a sample.

I use a formula developed in the 1950s, even though few consultants use it.

Breakdown of limestone depends on the fineness of grind. An extremely fine grind will move into soil quickly. On legumes such as soybeans and edible beans, the ease of solving a calcium deficiency can be detected with a special observation plot. Beans can be planted and allowed to grow 12 inches tall. Calcium, as shown to be required by a soil analysis, applied to 12 inch high beans will permit a timely test. Although the following would be difficult to detect using only the soil, calcium deficiency will also show up in the leaves promptly. After liming it will be necessary to wait until it rains an inch, or to irrigate. A leaf analysis should be

Hands-On Agronomy

taken on each following day. By the third day, a leaf analysis will reveal the optimum calcium in the leaf. It isn't necessary to apply calcium in the fall in order to get it into a legume.

Why is it possible to have hundreds of pounds of calcium in the soil and still show a calcium deficiency in the leaf until we get to 60% base saturation? So far that answer has proved elusive. Not so elusive is the fact that tissue analysis reveals that it takes application of an inch or so of water and three days, after which the calcium is there.

But be careful with calcium levels. The day you get calcium up to 85% base saturation, 90% of the available iron will generally be complexed, locked up as in a vault. With base saturation below 80%, greater limestone availability is the measured result. Calcium can tie up magnesium, potassium, boron, zinc, and copper. It does this because it affects pH. pH swings tie up various nutrients. Calcium does not tie up nitrogen as it saturates available sites on the soil colloid. Soils that have 80% calcium saturation allow a farmer to paint the field green with easy nitrogen uptake. But this high calcium content helps construct a weak stalk, the mechanism being easy nitrogen access into the plant. This ties up the copper nutrient so necessary to stalk strength.

Any time there is a shortage of potassium, manganese or copper, a weak stalk will be the observed result. High potassium ties up manganese. High nitrogen ties up copper. High calcium ties up potassium. Each and all can cause a weak stalk, but calcium is the culprit if everything else is available in adequate amounts, and a high calcium level prevails. It does not take a great flush of nitrogen to get an excellent yield. My approach to high calcium is simple in the extreme. I start backing calcium down until everything else is there in equilibrium. High calcium doesn't have to be a detriment, but it almost always is because it is allowed to tie up nutrients the plant requires.

A Hands-On Approach   79

There is another rule. The higher the calcium, the easier it is for moisture to leave the soil. This fact annihilates the old saw that you can't get too much calcium. In fact, you can get too much calcium. I consulted on a corporate farm owned by two families. They had 2,300 acres, and they were told that they couldn't put on too much lime. They applied six tons to the acre because the location was southern Illinois and there was lots of acidity. They had one field that couldn't be treated because there was a ditch there. They piled the lime on one side of the ditch. They couldn't get over to the other side until spring. In spring, naturally, they didn't get it spread. I came on-scene that fall to analyze soils. Where the limestone was piled, you couldn't tell it was intended to be applied to the other little field. When I saw the results I knew why they had hired me. All of that soil was 81, 82, 84, 85% calcium. Magnesium was tied up, potassium was tied up except for one little field behindthat woods, which was right on the money. Actually none of those acres needed limestone. They told me that soybeans was their best crop, and they were taking yields of 45 to 50 bushels of soybeans per acre before that fatal limestone application. Within two years after applying the limestone described earlier, they were down to 30 bushels of beans per acre. The reason yield dropped was they had tied up magnesium and potassium. Once this was understood, work was started to get that calcium out, and now the farm has returned to superior yields.

It all depends on the numbers. Some people in the northeast say that they need 80% of saturation for calcium, not 68%. Every lab has to have a model soil to calibrate machines, and that model soil is not something that is decreed by the government. It is something that each lab determines. Each morning the lab to which I send my samples sets its machines according to its soil model. If they run a lot of samples that morning, they will do it again at noon.

Depending on the number of samples, they may do it three or four times a day.

Every lab has a different numbering system. Some 80s are like our 68s. Two brothers up on the Ohio-Michigan border heard that I worked with people who had used too much lime in their soils. One of them said, "Our Dad was convinced that we needed to get our soils up to 80% calcium. Our soybean yields have declined by one-third or more." The brothers realized what they had done. It was a mistake. It took about four years to get them straightened out. When you start looking at the numbers and percentages, don't take unknown figures and try to transpose them to your operation because it won't work.

Mag-ne-si-um / mag-'nē-zē-em, -zhem / *n* [NL, fr. *magnesia*] **1** a silver-white light malleable ductile metallic element **2** chemical symbol:

3 occurs abundantly in nature as an alkaline earth **4** used in many industrial processes, including photography, pyrotechnics **5** MgO used in fertilizers, cements, insulation **6** in medicine, the magnesia is an antacid and mild laxative **7** in soils, magnesium has 1.666 times more exchange capacity than an equal amount of calcium **8** high magnesium and low calcium permits organic residue to decay into alcohol, a sterilant to bacteria **9** it should occupy between 10 and 20% of the soil's exchange capacity **10** in the human body, it is essential for nerve and muscle activity and in bone structure, aids in growth promotion

4

Calcium, Magnesium and Tillage

CALCIUM AND MAGNESIUM GO HAND IN HAND. Magnesium is a constituent of chlorophyll. In fact, chlorophyll and photosynthesis rely on its presence and availability. Magnesium aids in phosphate metabolism. And it activates several enzyme systems.

For the moment, we are required to understand the functions of magnesium in a crop, but we also must comprehend the functions of magnesium in a soil.

Magnesium, in conjunction with calcium, is the key to air and water in the soil. Magnesium helps hold the soil together and tightens it up. Too much of this wonder element hardens the soil when it is dry, and makes it sticky when it is wet. In my area, the soil we call gumbo becomes so sticky it builds up to three or four inches on the sole of your boot before you can kick it off. This boot test suggests 30% base saturation, perhaps more. Ideally, that number needs to be 12, meaning that 30% is 2.5 times more magnesium in that soil than ought to be there. I have to deal with more soils that are high in magnesium than any other problem. In addition to the influence of magnesium on soil structure, there is also the nitrogen connection. Magnesium has more of an influence on soil pH than calcium. If I could hold enough calcium in one hand to raise the pH by one point, and I took the same amount of magnesium in the second hand, the last would raise pH by 1.4. It is therefore a 1.4 to 1 relationship. Any time you have more magnesium in a soil than calcium, the pH is going to be extra high. If I can get magnesium out or complex it with sulfur, I will have a far greater effect on dropping pH than if I take calcium out. Magnesium in the soil will be a carbon copy readout of rocks in an area. Deficiencies occur most often in coarse textured, acid soils. Soil extremely high in calcium can actually tie up the magnesium to the point that we get a magnesium deficiency in the plant but excessive magnesium still exists in the soil.

Magnesium occurs as a cation with a ++ charge, which is strong. When it gets on a colloid, there are not very many things that can get it off. Calcium can tie it up, but calcium generally won't be a factor unless over-saturation occurs.

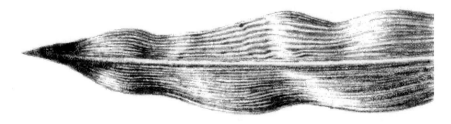

Magnesium deficiency causes whitish strips along the veins and often a purplish color on the underside of the lower leaves.

Too much magnesium in a soil prevents the plant from getting enough. If the magnesium level in the soil is extremely high, a leaf tissue analysis on corn will often reveal a magnesium deficiency. That is one reason I always caution farmers to use a tissue analysis for short-range evaluation, and use a soil analysis for long-range analysis. Let's recap. Using our tests, target figures are 60 to 70% calcium, 10 to 20% magnesium. With an exchange capacity of 6 or less, the target begins to rise from 12% magnesium. The lower the exchange, the higher the percent of target magnesium up to 20%. An exchange capacity of 7 or higher, means the ideal magnesium level should be 12% or less. The magnesium problem is easiest to illustrate on corn. Less than 10% saturation of magnesium will cost at least ten bushels of corn per acre. Magnesium above 15% saturation on soil with a CEC that is 7 or higher will cost ten bushels of corn per acre because the plant simply won't get enough. Most state universities are never bashful in telling farmers to spill on nitrogen. At one land grant university test farm with 40%

SOME ASPECTS OF MAGNESIUM IN THE SOIL:

- **It is contained in minerals such as biotite, dolomite and chlorite.**
- **Deficiencies occur most often in coarse-textured, acid soils.**
- **It occurs as a cation (Mg^{++}).**

Calcium, Magnesium and Tillage

magnesium and 45% calcium base saturation, they order up 240 pounds of nitrogen to grow a 175-bushel corn crop, which it does. They do not explain that once you get above 20% base saturation in terms of magnesium, the cost of the error will be at least 15 bushels of corn per acre. If magnesium can be reduced from 20 down to the high teens—the reduction is going to make you five bushels of corn per acre. Below 15, the reduction will deliver another ten bushels of corn per acre. If base saturation falls below 10% magnesium, then the formula does not work. To compute nitrogen for corn, the old rule of thumb is that it takes 1.5 pounds nitrogen to produce a bushel of corn. Depending on magnesium levels, it doesn't happen that way. The first order of business is to see whether magnesium is above 10 and below 15. If we have 68% calcium, 12% magnesium, plenty of phosphorus, plenty of potassium, it only takes one pound of nitrogen to produce a bushel of corn on fertile soil. At magnesium base saturation 13 or 14, it takes 1.3 pounds of nitrogen to produce a bushel of corn. Above 15, it takes 1.4 pounds of nitrogen. At 18 and 19 base saturation magnesium, it figures out about 1.4 or 1.45, and above 20 it takes 1.5 pounds of nitrogen to produce a bushel of corn.

This is not to suggest the purchase of that much commercial nitrogen. But it does take into account nitrogen released from humus and organic matter. After you compute the above, then the rest must be supplied. In a corn-soybean rotation, I compute three-fourths of a pound of nitrogen per bushel of beans. As a practical matter, this will be a safe assumption. On the average, soybeans do not provide a pound of residual nitrogen per bushel of beans. On the average, beans put in escrow approximately three-quarters pound of nitrogen per bushel of beans for the next crop in the rotation. In a poor growing season, it can be as little as a half pound of nitrogen per bushel of beans. Dupont has researched soybeans for years. Their studies have revealed that, in an average year, soybeans only take 50% of their

Calcium and Magnesium

Calcium and magnesium are considered as elements of secondary importance in the industry and market of the commercial fertilizers, but the truth is that for the soil and for the plants calcium and magnesium are primary in importance both quantitatively and also for their bio-chemical significance.

A deeper look into every living body, including the human being, discovers the fact that nothing can live without calcium and magnesium. The skeletons of human beings and those of all fully developed animals are built of tri-calcium phosphate. The immense world of microbes and all the bio-chemical processes require certain amounts of calcium and magnesium. There may not be a green plant without the action of magnesium, for magnesium controls the development and the bio-chemistry of the chlorophyll molecule; subsequently, there is no photosynthesis, namely, no food for other forms of life without the work of magnesium. Every agricultural product contains certain amounts of calcium and magnesium, and logically a fertile and productive soil must contain calcium and magnesium—in fact, it holds very large amounts of both of these two elements. It is necessary to have 1,000 to 36,000 pounds of the so-called exchange calcium and 200 to 3,000 pounds of the exchange magnesium per acre to satisfy the colloidal adsorption capacities of the different soils.

It has been proved that calcium is the most important element among all the plant food elements. Therefore, before any kind of fertilization project is worked out upon soil, it must be seen that the percent of calcium and magnesium base saturation as a part of the total exchange capacity of the particular soil has been established, as for instance, 65% for calcium; 15% for magnesium for the common kinds of the cultivated plants. And it is as important to eliminate the deficiencies of these two elements as it is to avoid the excesses of the same in the soil.

—*Rudolf Ozolins*
private papers, *Acres U.S.A.* collection

nitrogen from air, and under adverse conditions as little as 25% of the nitrogen is taken from the air. Textbooks say that legumes take 70% of their nitrogen from the air, even so, they still have 30% they have to pick up from the soil under excellent growing conditions. The point here is magnesium, not nitrogen. The higher the magnesium above 15% base saturation, the more problems in terms of corn and grass type crops such as wheat, oats, barley—but that is not true of legumes. The problem with legumes such as soybeans shows up when you start coming from 10 base saturation. The same is true when you start coming from 10 on alfalfa. When you get to 12 you already have too much magnesium to get optimum production out of alfalfa. If you are growing soybeans or alfalfa and you have 18% magnesium and everything else is right, it doesn't work like corn. With corn we pull it from 18 down to 15, and we use less nitrogen and get a yield increase. If you start pulling alfalfa land down, you won't get any increase at all if you go from 18 to 14. If you go from 14 to 13, you won't get an increase until you get down to less than 12% base saturation of magnesium.

A client in Illinois grows red clover for seed. In his area farmers consider two bushels of red clover seed per acre an excellent yield. The year we got his magnesium down below 12%, he doubled his red clover seed production to four bushels per acre. His soybean yields increased by ten bushels an acre over a three or four year period. He had some old alfalfa seed. He really didn't know how good it was. He just happened to find it somewhere, and he seeded it in his wheat that February. It came up as a solid stand and he kept that stand for about three years. I asked him, "Did it run out faster?" He said, "No, it was messing up my rotation so I finally just worked it in." Ohio research has revealed that certain legume yields start to decrease once you pass 11.75% base saturation magnesium. The study was undertaken to disprove the validity of using cation exchange capacity for making fertilizer recommendations. The results failed to substantiate the looked-for results.

Any cation, whether it is calcium, magnesium, potassium or sodium, can tie up any other cation. In extremely light soils high potassium will tie up magnesium. This is even more the case in sandy soils. In high clay type soils, it is just the opposite. Magnesium gets so high that it starts tying up potassium. As the percentage of magnesium drops, the pounds of available potassium actually go up. If we take that ideal soil, 68% calcium and 12% magnesium, and use a product with pure calcium in it, and take it from 68 or 69% base saturation, but put no magnesium on it to counteract the treatment, the application will drive magnesium down 1%. Every time the percent of calcium is increased by 1, the magnesium goes down by 1% also. The exception is a magnesium source that also has calcium, such as dolomitic limestone. Remember, the numbers say calcium and magnesium should total 80%. When calcium and magnesium together total more than 80%, and calcium goes to 68%, the result will still be too much magnesium. What difference does that

---

SOME FUNCTIONS OF MAGNESIUM IN CROP GROWTH ARE:

- **A mineral constituent of chlorophyll.**
- **Actively involved in photosynthesis.**
- **Aids in phosphate metabolism.**
- **Activates several enzyme systems.**

---

make? Really, it makes the most difference on the other side. If you have 80% calcium in your soils and 5% magnesium, this means too much magnesium in that soil because the two added together total 85. The high calcium percentage is tying up the magnesium. If you bring that calcium from 80 down to 70, magnesium will jump from 5 up to 15. This means we have to release magnesium before we see the effect. We would bring the calcium down and raise the magnesium up in order to feed the plant. Otherwise we have to buy magnesium for foliar feed application or use enough sulfur to acidify it and kick it loose. On the other hand, even though a soil shows 5% magnesium and 90% calcium, the physical effect is a heavy, tight soil because the magnesium is still there working on the physical structure. But it is not available for the plant to use. A lot of people will say, "Well, you tell me that magnesium keeps the soil tight, and I only have 6 or 8% magnesium in this soil and it is still hard and tight." If you have 6 or 8% magnesium and an 80 to 90% calcium level, the calcium is masking the true picture. If you brought calcium down to 68 from 90 base saturation and you had 5% magnesium, this means we brought it down 22 points. We must now add 22 points to the magnesium value. If we get the calcium down to 68, the magnesium then will be 27. When calcium is driven out of the soil by too much nitrogen, magnesium remains unless sulfur is used to buffer the magnesium. Every time you put nitrogen on these soils that total above 80 calcium-magnesium, the process takes calcium down, magnesium up, and magnesium is never going to be neutralized or taken out unless sulfur is used to complex the magnesium.

An excess of cations—calcium, magnesium, potassium or sodium—brings the major element in excess into conflict with the weakest link in the chain. It is not bound heavily on that soil colloid. So, when we put sulfur on a high calcium soil, it is going to work on the calcium. If we put sulfur on a high magnesium soil, it will work on the magne-

Influence of Calcium on Magnesium

Numerous observations lead to the following conclusions:

1. Besides their own physiological functions, the magnesium salts exercise poisoning effects on all plants, including the higher algae and higher species.

2. This poisoning effect by magnesium rests mainly on the displacement of calcium from its important place in the cell nucleus.

3. The poisoning effects by magnesium are wholly prevented by the presence of ample amounts of calcium salts.

4. A distinct excess of calcium salts lowers the function of the magnesium which manifests itself in reduced plant production.

5. The nuclear substance of the lower algae and fungi is calcium-free.

From the very beginning it was very clear that with respect to the calcium factor in practice we are dealing with mainly pronounced differences in calcium and magnesium contents of the soil. If the magnesium exceeds the calcium, which is prominent in the subtropical and tropical regions (deserts excluded), then the calcium fertilization shows itself more important. But should the calcium content be noticeably higher than the magnesium, accordingly the latter as application may well be tested. It may be a question of needing a magnesium sulfate fertilizing which in yield production surpassed all other magnesium fertilizers. According to our researches in Tokyo, there are 4.8 parts crystallized magnesium sulfate as capable for work as 100 parts pulverized magnesite for barley culture. But when magnesium sulfate is applied as top-dressing, one part is sufficient. At the research station of North Carolina it was observed that calcium-rich soil with 0.4% magnesium showed symptoms of magnesium deficiency by tobacco. But an application of 20 to 30 pounds magnesium sulfate per acre could remove the symptoms of magnesium deficiency. Often it is convenient to combine the magnesium with the potassium fertilization. The potassium-magnesium-sulfate has established itself brightly in this case.

—*Oscar Leow*
Die Ernahrung der Pflanze, 1931
private papers, *Acres U.S.A.* collection

sium provided there is enough calcium. It will also work with sodium. After calcium and magnesium are under control, sulfur will start working on other nutrients. Free lime is not considered by atomic absorption tests. North and South Dakota and several other states have calcareous soils, but do not take special notice of free lime. In effect, we do take notice, but the free lime we consider is only what the plant can use. Consequently, we are merely measuring what is available for the plant to use during a growing season. If it is there and tied up, we do not need to know about it until it is released for plant use. It is having no effect on the physical structure and it is having no effect on the mineral balance. People who measure free lime say they need no calcium because they have all this free lime, yet it is in the wrong form. It is not in the form that the plant can use. Once we get it into that form, it will show up in a test.

When both are deficient, we have to buy calcium and magnesium. On a soil just under 80% saturation of calcium and magnesium combined, where calcium is deficient, if you correct calcium to 70%, low magnesium can be the result. Below 10% means a magnesium deficiency. You can always tell the correction factor by adding the percentage of calcium and magnesium together because they have a direct effect on each other. If the combined total is above 80%, you always use only calcium. If the total is less than 80%, then calcium and magnesium are indicated in order to get the correct amount. It is absolutely mandatory to have the right calcium-magnesium ratio in order to have the right amount of air and water in the soil. A typical sample tells its own story. Let's say we have 53.07 calcium and 40.38 magnesium. One way we can get magnesium out of the soil is to use sulfur. But there is another key to getting magnesium out of the soil. Magnesium will never leave a soil, even if you pour on the sulfur or sulfates until calcium saturation is above 60%. One reason for this is that 60% or higher calcium gets the soil loose enough to permit the movement of the water. Without water movement through the soil, sulfur simply accumulates. As a consequence, before we would even try to take magnesium out of this typical sample, we would correct the calcium at least to 60%. Based on the total exchange capacity of this soil, it would take two tons of calcium per acre to correct the situation. Enough lime to bring calcium up to 68% means an increase of 15%. Our objective is to bring magnesium down by 25% for a 68/15 position. The calcium reaction will take three years because calcium breaks down about one third per year unless an extremely fine grind material is available.

The lowest priced source of magnesium—in a calcium/magnesium compound—is dolomitic limestone. Magnesium oxide is not generally a good source of magnesium because it breaks down so slowly. Magnesium sulfate is expensive. When potassium and magnesium and sulfur are required, Sul-Po-Mag or K-Mag (potassium-magnesium-sulfate) might be indicated, that is if only small amounts of magnesium are needed. Dolomitic lime and potassium-magnesium-sulfate are the two I normally like to use. Other materials are either not very effective or more expensive. It might be possible to pulverize magnesium oxide and build it back into a prill, to make magnesium available. The market does not favor the seeker in this case. Remember, when you apply calcium to a soil when potassium is in excess, this will have a pretty big effect on the potassium. If you have a normal potassium level and you apply a ton of calcium lime, generally it will have little effect on the potassium. Application of calcium controls magnesium, and the magnesium increase ties up the potash and a decrease releases potassium back out. This is a trade off situation. Trouble usually arrives when we overuse calcium or overuse magnesium. Too much of either ties up the potassium.

To correct compaction, you need to get your calcium levels to at least 60% saturation. That means the right chemistry and the right tillage. It may not be necessary to get calcium to 60 if a soil conditioner is to be used. Parenthetically, my clients have done some amazing things with soil conditioners. But how do we get soil to respond in terms of soil chemistry at 60% base saturation of calcium? In terms of breaking up a hardpan, tillage alone may not work. Tillage and fertilization go hand in hand, but for a tillage program to work properly, you have to have the proper balance in terms of the fertility.

After the soil has been limed properly, then some type of a ripper or deep tillage tool—a sub-soiler or even a chisel plow to penetrate through any hardpan or plowsole—recommends itself.

The first order of business, of course, is to establish whether a hardpan in fact exists. The instrument of choice is a soil compaction tester. It has a gauge that measures up to 300 pounds per square inch pressure. The one I use is made by Dickey John at a cost of between $175 to $200. In a field situation, we see how far we can go before we hit 300 pounds per square inch pressure. That is where roots will stop growing. The drier the soil, the easier it is to hit the 300 pound barrier. I never probe a very dry soil to find the resistance to root growth. I test in a soil that is relatively moist.

A simple soil probe test is often of merit. Push the probe down, right in the crop row. Then just lay it down flat on the soil with the cut away part towards the top. Start with your thumb and press directly down on the soil until you feel resistance. If you feel resistance within a half inch, it will be safe to say the magnesium level is in the 20s and maybe in the 30s. If resistance is reached at 2.5 inches, then the magnesium level will be below 20, but above 15. If you get down to four or five inches, it is going to be below 15. The right balance will be indexed when you have a good, crumbly, aerated soil for at least four or five inches.

I visited a farm in Red Oak, Iowa and they didn't know anything about soil balancing, but their corn always did

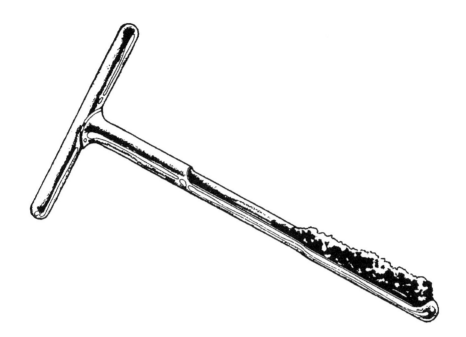

well on one 40-acre field. I took a soil probe into the field. Testing as described here, I could go all the way to the handle. That farmer had 68/12 on calcium/magnesium from the beginning. All the people around there said that if you raise any more than 150-bushel corn, you are a liar. Yet, that field produced 172-bushel corn on the whole field. There was no irrigation, just dry land, and it wasn't a heavy soil. It was an upland soil. There aren't very many soils like that.

Most of the time you will hit resistance before you get to a 12 inch depth. After you determine where it is, the next thing to determine is how much of a compacted layer you have. Most of the time it will be between an inch and two inches thick. Generally, a ripper pulled at 12 to 14 inch depth, will break through a hardpan. But before you even think of using a ripper, certain rules have to be followed. Let's say the hardpan is evident, and let's say its residence was at nine inches, at which depth three inches of hard soil were registered. That defines the critical area at 12 inch depth. The objective is to just barely penetrate the 12th inch.

Calcium, Magnesium and Tillage

If you rip 18 inches deep, the procedure defines the depth the soil will pack the next time. In other words, the shallower the soil can be worked, the more successful will be coping with hardpan.

Again the first order of business is to correct your calcium. I have to deal with this because of the demands made by modern agriculture. Often farmers bring in big earth moving machines. They level soils for the purpose of planting rice. They raise rice for two years, then they raise soybeans for a year or two, then back to rice. They flatten the terrain out, flood the rice, furrow irrigate the beans or the grain sorghum. I sampled soils during August for in-depth analysis because they wanted to grow a crop that fall. I have seen soils that were packed to the point that it took a three pound weighted mallet and 75 blows to get the probe six and three-quarters inches deep. These data represent tremendous compaction problems that must be dealt with. The first thing, always, is to lime the soil. If that calcium level is not at least 60%, and rippers start working the soil, magnesium will make it runny and sticky, and the soil will slurry right back together. The Soil Conservation Service says on Sharky clay soils—which are the type soils we have to deal with along the Mississippi River—it does no good to rip those soils because of the propensity to slurry together again. Needless to say, there are arguments between farmers. One will say he has ripped the soil and it didn't run back together. Another will say he ripped, and it closed up like slurry cement. The determining factor, always, is the calcium level. At 60% calcium or higher, the ripped soil won't run back together. The only problem with most growers is that they look at pH rather than calcium. So one farmer will have plenty of calcium, the other won't.

From my vantage point, it is necessary to determine where the compaction layer is. The next rule is go over the field one time when the soil is dry. Pull your equipment, tillage tool, ripper, whatever, at least four and a half miles per hour. For most soils, you should only do this one time in the fall. If you go over it twice, you put so much air space between the soil particles that sometimes it won't settle back out. Too much air space, and you will lose part of your moisture next spring. I have a client who has a 60-acre wheat field along the Missouri River. He wanted to rip it because it was compacted, but it never dried out. It was always wet because of the water table. His solution was unique. In January or February he set his alarm at midnight. That was the time when it got cold enough to freeze. He then would start ripping until the tractor started to spin in the morning.

His grandfather once made 50 bushels of wheat on that field years ago, but most of the time—because wheat doesn't like wet feet—20 or 30 bushels of wheat became the norm. The year he ripped the frozen soil, water wasn't a problem, and he made 64 bushels of wheat per acre.

Break through the deepest compaction layer. Work to the depth it takes, generally 12 to 14 inches. The required depth can be determined with a soil probe or a soil compaction gauge, or even with a crowbar. Use narrow shanks set wide apart. If you don't have a ripper and you don't have extremely tough soil, and a chisel plow with narrow shanks is available, set those narrow shanks at 30 to 40 inch centers. If you have them on 12 inch centers, take off two, leave one, take off two, etc. Let's say you determine you need to go 14 inches deep and you can only get to 13 inches, don't go over it again. Next year it will be easier.

Generally, it is not a good idea to subsoil in the spring because too much air space is permitted in the soil. Each year the procedure ought to be easier. After about three years, it will be possible to stop for two or three years, unless something is being done to compact the soil again. It is absolutely mandatory to keep the compaction layer broken up by minimizing traffic over a field. Travel over the same tracks if possible.

We have what is called a ripper-hipper in our area (sometimes a hip and ridger). It can rip right under the row in order to get the cotton root to go straight down. It will rip and hip a row right on top, and make a bed on that row to plant on it. I tell the farmer to rip right under the row if possible. In terms of corn production, a ripper between the rows, especially in the area of wheel tracks—it is an excellent procedure to get more air back into the soil the last trip over, when the corn is not too tall.

I had one client who failed to follow instructions. I told him only go as deep as he could pull. I told him to take off a number of shanks until he could pull, but he failed to do that. He kept all of his shanks on, and he put the ripper down as deep as it could go. The next time I was up at his place he said he was upset because he put that ripper on his tractor and burned out his tractor motor. Obviously, a fair measure of uncommon good sense must be invoked at all times.

I had one farmer client who had the biggest Massey Ferguson the market had to offer. He had about nine shanks on the back of it, and he was running 15 inches deep to get his hardpan broken up. He hit a stump and pulled the whole back end out.

A tillage tool that requires both understanding and tender loving care is the disc. In my book it rates special attention for use on lighter type soils. If you have a finishing disc and the cutting side is shiny all the way up to the axle, that is fine. But if you have a shiny blade all the way up the other side as deep as it is cutting, you are just packing your soil back. The disc blade on the cutting side should be shiny, but on the outside it should only be shiny about an inch or two. If you have light sand, it becomes elementary to determine whether a disc packs or not. Some areas are very sandy. An inch of rain might fall at night. By noon the next day, all the water is gone. Often the farmer has it in mind that if the disc doesn't ball up, then conditions are not too wet. They

　　　　　　　　　　　　　Hands-On Agronomy

assume light soils are not subject to compaction. Actually, compaction can be delivered not just by the tracks of the tractor, but also by a lot of farm equipment. Most discs do pack back. To deal with this propensity, we try to keep root and water avenues to the subsoil open by using a sub-soiler. We try to keep our humus and tillage up. In terms of management, there are some things a farmer can do. Sometimes the farmer who does what we say is all wrong is the person who will come out ahead in the short run. One specific situation is *wet conditions*. Sometimes the farmer who plants under wet conditions will have a soft enough place to get the roots through. Once roots break through that compaction layer, the plant will start building its root system below because it can feed down there. I have clients who raise rice. They often get into their rice field with big equipment, and they disc the rice stubble in while the water is still standing on the field. They do not get compaction when they do that. As long as water is standing on the field, this traffic won't compact. But when equipment rolls across the spots that are muddy, that is when the farmer gets stuck and starts compaction with a vengeance. When all that space is filled with water, buoyancy will hold up the equipment. When the soil starts drying out and mud becomes evident, that is when water leaves the air spaces, and that is when smearing can cause a problem.

I am not suggesting that soils should be worked this way.

I admit that I used to think that rice farmers were going to tear their soils to pieces, but they don't. Some of my clients farm in Germany using large equipment, too. The money crop is sugar beets. They will bring the moldboard plow into play, and they don't wait until it is dry. They work the soil wet. They harvest it wet. And they plant it wet. They do everything wet if they have to. Because of this they buy machines that will "out-pull anything." Because of the sheer size of many operations, harvest often runs into wet conditions, with much resultant packing. Wet conditions contribute mightily to the creation of hardpan in a soil. If the crop is planted and roots get past the compaction level before the soil dries out and gets hard, the plant will feed. In such a year the farmer who works his soil wet will get ahead.

I am not suggesting that this is the way to do it. But I am saying that sometimes the farmer who works his soil wet is going to have a crop that looks better than the farmer who plants under dry conditions. The key is getting those roots through the obstructing barrier. Nutrients and the water must move down, water being a prime concern. If the water can penetrate, so will roots.

A lot of growers believe that freezing and thawing take care of hardpan. Dr. Al Trouse has gone as far north as Minnesota and into Canada. He will testify that freezing and thawing will not take care of hardpan. One researcher at Rutgers raised 120 bushels of soybeans to the acre on a test plot. He dug out the soybeans to determine the journey of the root system. I have seen pictures of them. The mass looked like a woman's hair, only the soybean root ran six feet deep. He said, "If you want to grow top yields, you have got to get those roots down. If you don't get those hair roots down, you simply don't get the yields."

Another side of the picture can be developed and printed with a soil conditioner. Many clients use soil conditioners but it may take three and four times before a compaction breakthrough barrier takes place. The heavier the soil, the more likely it tends to be that way. The reason is—and this is going contrary to what a lot of people say with soil conditioners—that often it is not possible to use enough conditioner economically to do it. A case report should illustrate the point. I have used conditioners in lawn and landscape work in California, Texas and the Midwest. I had one client in California who reported soil as hard as concrete. His thumb could get only as deep as his thumbnail, and it was hard from there on. They have extreme amounts of sodium and chloride in many western soils, including this area. Until they are removed, it remains impossible to do anything. They put on an ounce per 1,000 square feet once a month for three months. This computes to roughly one gallon per acre, which is not a recommended practice. After that treatment, it was possible to take a finger and run it all the way down in an adobe type soil.

In a landscape situation, this is possible, but problems can develop when the soil becomes too lapse. I have some clients who tell me that they never get a soil opened up with soil conditioner used as recommended until the third or fourth application. That is why I suggest sub-soiling first. If a soil conditioner will do the job, use that—but if the soil conditioner falls short, then consider a deep tillage implement.

Farm talk is often quite elusive. I can relate a personal experience, one prompted by a soil conditioner discussion. At one time I responded to a question with, "I don't have clients who use it. I have never heard about how they work." A farmer told me, "You ought to give them a try because they work pretty well." I went to one of my very best clients, a fertilizer dealer with five farms, and asked if he had heard of or used soil conditioners. He stopped and took a deep breath. "Well, I never told you, but I've used soil conditioners for a number of years." He would rip where the soil was hard, but he used soil conditioners to keep pore space open. He said, "You know that 160 acres with that low swag in it down there at the Weeks Farm?" I said yes because I sample it every year. He said, "Well, about three years before you started working with it, we put soil conditioner on that soil. They never grew a crop in that swag, because water always stood there. Ever since using the soil conditioner it has grown a crop there every year. I never tell anybody that I use soil conditioner because a lot of people don't think it works and I sell fertilizer to a lot of guys."

I tell everybody about soil conditioners because I don't sell them. I will give you alternatives. You can use the mineral balance, the ripper or the soil conditioner with a ripper. I became convinced by an old friend by the name of Jake Weeks. Jake sold chemicals for years. A new company took over when he was in his 60s, and they fired him. He couldn't get a comparable job anywhere. He found out about Agri-SC. He talked to some of the farmers he had known for years. He asked them to try the soil conditioner. One of the farmers put the soil conditioner on a heavy black soil. He put on four ounces to the acre and marked it with a flag. Six weeks and two inches of rain later, he got the farmer to bring out his backhoe. They dug a trench right across the place where they had applied the product. From down in the trench it was not possible to see where the flag was. One fellow got into the trench with a knife. He started to cross the trench with that knife. When he got to where that flag was, he couldn't pull it past that point.

The fellow on the backhoe was a Doubting Thomas. He started to cross with that same knife. When he got to where that flag was, he literally shook trying to pull that knife through untreated soil but he could not do it. In a month and a half, the effects were to be seen three and a half to four feet deep.

I cannot look at a soil or a soil report and tell whether a soil conditioner will work the first time or the second time or the third time. One farmer once told me, "Use it at the four ounce rate until you know it works, and then cut back to the two ounce rate." Apply in a spring, fall, spring sequence. The heavier the soils, the more this observation holds. A good soil conditioner can be expected to increase permeability to water movement, decrease bulk density and enhance water holding capacity. Used on a lawn, roots go deeper, water stays longer and grass remains greener.

I have mentioned Dr. Al Trouse. He came to the Herman Warsaw farm. He dug a trench to see if there were compaction layers. The findings depend on the definition of a compaction layer. When Trouse digs a trench he takes a brush and a trowel. He can pick out the wheel tracks, the press wheel tracks of the planter, and he can pick out where the chisel plow shank ran. He can identify where a moldboard plow ran, or where a disc passed over. He will identify every one of those little places in those trenches.

I once attended a seminar in Indianapolis where he spoke. One day he spoke on root development and compaction. He said, "Now in the morning at nine o'clock—if you will be out here in this corn field—I will have a trench dug." At 6:00 a.m. the next morning he and two assistants dug a trench. He took us into the cornfield, showed us the trench, and said, "Now this is unusual. The corn roots in this field go deeper than is normal. What I am going to tell you is that this is the first year they have ever grown corn here. In fact, from looking at the soil, I would estimate that it was in pasture until two years ago." The owner wasn't there so who was to verify it? While we were standing there, this pickup truck pulled up and two guys got out and walked over to us. One of them said, "I thought I better come over here and see what is going on in my field."

Al Trouse, as if it were a normal, everyday occurrence, said, "I'm sorry to cause you a problem, but I didn't know whom to ask and I needed to dig a trench. I hope you don't mind. I'll fill it up when I'm done but while you are here, I'd like to ask you a couple of questions. Could you tell us the history of this field?" The farmer said, "Well, until two years ago, it was in pasture. Last year I grew soybeans on it and this year is the first year it has been in corn." Trouse asked about tillage practices. He had already shown us the moldboard plow layer and pointed out where the chisel plow and the disc had been used. The farmer proceeded right down the line to tell us what Trouse had already related. The point is that there is no soil without some compaction.

Ni-tro-gen / 'nī-tre-jen / *n, often attrib*
[F *nitrogène*, fr. *nitr* + *-gène* -gen] **1** colorless, tasteless, odorless gaseous element that constitutes 78% of the atmosphere by volume, stacking up 75 million pounds over every acre of land **2** chemical symbol:

7
N
14.0067

3 focal element in the nitrogen cycle by which nitrogen passes through successive stations in air, soil and organisms to achieve fixation **4** a governing factor in the decay of carbonaceous materials **5** amino nitrogen takes up 6% of compounds **6** every cell in plant life requires nitrogen in the right form **7** 5% of organic matter in soil is present as nitrogen **8** nitrogen joins carbon, hydrogen, oxygen as a main constituent of the animal body, other than the skeleton

5

Using the Nitrogen Cycle

AFTER THE REQUIREMENTS AND LOGISTICS of fertility management have been determined, some questions arise soon enough. When is the best time to put on fertilizer? If the crop to be grown in the spring is corn, when is the best time to put on phosphate and potassium? Is it better to supply phosphate and potassium in the fall, or would spring application better serve the purpose? Farm magazine ads and fertilizer company pitch sheets want fertilizer sales in the fall. This counsel has the benefit of avoiding a spring rush for the suppliers.

Our soil analyses clue us in on what to buy. The shape of the soil figures, and may, in fact, be the determining factor in considering phosphate and potash for fall application.

In any case, nitrogen must rate first attention because it is the hardest fertility assist to deal with. It is also the most difficult to recommend properly. Clashing philosophies govern terms used, the chief division being the difference between feeding the plant and feeding the soil. The concept of feeding the plant is flawed, of course, if the shape of the soil is unknown. Mere application is no assurance that the plant is going to assimilate the fertilizer anyway.

Essential elements for plants are several. Basically we get carbon, hydrogen and oxygen from air and water. Nitrogen, phosphorous, potassium, calcium and magnesium will command a great deal of attention in this book. I will cover at great length sulfur, and then go into trace elements—particularly boron, copper, iron, manganese, and zinc.

High yielding crops with adequate fertility use water more efficiently. In one case I often illustrate with slides for farmers, the fertilized area produced 118 bushels of corn, and the unfertilized area produced 80 bushels. The fertilized plot made 7.6 bushels of corn per inch of water, and the unfertilized soil made 5.3 bushels of corn per inch of water. Most farmers are familiar with a normal corn leaf, a nitrogen starved leaf, a phosphate starved leaf, and a potassium starved leaf. I call attention to such signs and symptoms because many farmers will say they need more nitrogen on their soil. They might be putting on 200 pounds of nitrogen, but they still think they are not getting enough. All you have to do is walk into the field when corn is already past tassel to tell if this is true. Nitrogen deficiency starts with a V in the leaf at the bottom. A potassium deficiency also shows up in the oldest leaves. You can tell the difference easily. Still, most farmers see the leaves that are showing a potassium deficiency, and they think they have a need for more nitrogen. A nitrogen starved plant will exhibit its sign at the leaf tip and move down in a V shape. In a potassium starved plant, the edges of the leaf begin to die off, the damage moving inward. Almost all of southeast Missouri soils have potassium deficiencies. It is seldom economical to put on the amounts our tests show as deficient. I recom-

Hands-On Agronomy

mend that farmers at least put on a maintenance level when such deficiencies are shown.

On many farms in our area, if you walk into the field after the corn starts to silk, you will see those bottom leaves with a brown edge on them. If you start to see the leaves die from the outside in, that means a potassium deficiency, not nitrogen deficiency. Some studies in the 1970s revealed that the higher the potassium in the ear leaf at silk, the higher the corn yield is going to be. As long as you don't get that potassium level to exceed the point where it starts tying up something else, you have the ability to take the potassium in and get a good high level at the time of silking. We grow a lot of popcorn in our area. Popcorn shows potassium deficiency very quickly. If you can keep the potash in the plant, you can get the yield. Potassium has a lot more to do with yield than a lot of people think.

On the average, a plant contains 2 to 6% nitrogen. We can get large quantities of nitrogen from the nodulation on legumes. In an excellent situation, 70% of the nitrogen comes from the microbes. Under medium growing conditions, you only get about 50% from that source. Under poor conditions, you get about 25%. As far as I am concerned, the better we can influence the chemistry and the physical structure of the soil, the more efficient we make those microbes. If we have a normal year and we have the soil in the right shape, the microbes are going to be able to do a better job. Therefore we don't decrease their efficiency as much as we would in a soil that doesn't have proper fertility. Non-legumes absorb NO_3 or nitrate nitrogen and NH_4 or ammonium ions from the soil. That nitrogen is used to form chlorophyll, proteins, amino acids and nucleic acids. In particular, we look at it for greenness. If a plant doesn't have enough green, we say it doesn't have enough nitrogen.

If you have corn or any kind of a grass crop and you don't see the tip of the oldest leaf show yellow, it is not necessarily nitrogen. It can be something else, because the yellow of nitrogen deficient plants will show in the oldest leaves first. That has to do with the greenness of the chlorophyll. That pale or yellowing plant can be needing phosphate, sulfur, or even boron. Nitrogen is needed to build proteins. If we want to have protein in our alfalfa, we need to have enough nitrogen. If you don't have enough nitrogen and you have enough calcium and sulfur, you still won't get your protein. If you have a situation wherein microbes are only 50% efficient at taking nitrogen from the air and putting it into the plant, then alfalfa is not going to do its best. I see situations in which there is plenty of calcium and sulfur, and still there is a shortfall of protein in alfalfa.

If we can get the ammonia form of nitrogen into the plant, we can help build amino acids in the late period of grasses. If you can get ammonia into the corn after it already has silk, it will actually take that ammonia and build amino acids with it. That is one of the reasons why putting on ammonia forms of nitrogen late in the year will actually show an increase in amino acids in the plant—provided, of course, you don't overdo it.

Nitrogen is essential for plant growth and is a part of every living cell. There are three major forms of soil nitrogen. Organic nitrogen is a part of organic matter, or humus, and it is not readily available. It makes up 97 to 98% of total soil nitrogen, and it is held there, albeit in a form the plant cannot use. When we measure manures, we measure organic nitrogen. When you measure organic nitrogen in manures, you have to cut in half the amount it contains before calculating the nitrogen you are counting on for the crop that year. Ammonium nitrogen is another form of nitrogen in the soil held by the soil colloids. The NH_4 attaches to the clay particle and is less available than nitrate. Less than 1% of the total soil nitrogen is generally in the form of ammonia in a natural system. Nitrate nitrogen and other soluble compounds are also available in the soil as 1 to 2% of the total soil nitrogen.

Hands-On Agronomy

Application of Fertilizer

It goes without saying that it is often desirable to feed growing crops. In such cases the best practice is to apply small quantities of the fertilizing materials at each application and then make the applications often. By following this plan, on an active, living soil the biotic workers will be able to complete the necessary conditioning very quickly and all soil operations will go right on harmoniously.

In our farming and gardening our aim should forever be to obtain normal growth, for normal growth and quality are synonymous. A quick, falsely-stimulated growth may be pleasing to the eye, but that growth can easily be deceptive.

Remember our reference to Sir Albert Howard's *Health Highway*? The establishment of that highway in our food-producing soils should be our chief aim. And this desirable situation, as we will recall, obtains only when the beneficial soil fungi are actively on the job. When new stuff is added to the land, though it may be of the highest quality, considerable conditioning of the materials will be needed by the soil bacteria as well as by the molds themselves before that "protein flow" will be at its efficient best.

By applying the "soil food" well in advance of planting time, or a little at a time to growing plants, as suggested above, the soil workers will be able to condition it and that "soil machine" discovered by Sir Albert Howard will not fail to function smoothly— which means no obstructions in our health highway.

How important it is not to be deceived by the appearances! We should strive to know what is going on down in the root zone of our crops. One question should constantly be in each of our minds: Am I getting normal growth, or is this largely false stimulation? An over-stimulated crop will usually be far more attractive to the eye than a crop that is growing normally. It will, that is, unless you are able to detect the true quality signs. When a crop is growing on a dynamic soil, the quality indicators will be there, one of which is a darker and more velvety green in many crops. Over-stimulated crops often have a metallic green. One can learn to detect normal, quality growth if he is observant.

—*Joseph A. Cocannouer*
Natural Food & Farming, 1961

We can take a measurement of nitrate and ammonia in the soil. This test measures the soluble nitrogens in order to tell where we are in terms of the crop cycle. Crops take up large quantities of nitrogen. Eight tons of alfalfa requires 450 pounds of nitrogen by dead reckoning. The crop has to get this nitrogen from somewhere. If it gets 70% of the nitrogen from the air, 30% still has to be accounted for. That means 135 pounds of nitrogen have to come from somewhere if there is to be an eight ton alfalfa crop. This does not mean we simply put it on. It does mean that we have to make the soil operative so that more than the nodulation on the legume supplies nitrogen. All those microbes in the soil can have a fantastic effect because more than the *Rhizobium* genus of bacteria supply the nitrogen. Algae supply nitrogen, and there are various types of other soil life that also supply nitrogen. This supply chore is usually accomplished by working on organic matter. Huge amounts of nitrogen seem to be available based on a measurement of total nitrogen, but most of it is tied up in humus. There has to be some operative principle that makes it available. If we have a 5% organic matter soil, we already have roughly 100 pounds of nitrogen that is available for that year's crop. Put that 100 pounds along with the other 70%, and we now have to account for 35 pounds of nitrogen from somewhere else. This is not a tough job for the microbes as long as we give them the right environment. That is why it is so important to get the chemistry and the physical structure of the soil just right. By dead reckoning, a 150-bushel corn crop requires 200 pounds of nitrogen. Actually, it all depends on where the calcium/magnesium levels are. It depends on the soil's balance.

Soil high in magnesium means that a 150-bushel corn crop will require nitrogen calculated at 150 times 1.5. In other words, 200 pounds of nitrogen will be short, based on such an extremely high magnesium level in the soil. And yet in a good fertile soil, it is routine to get 150 bushels from 200 pounds of nitrogen or less—pounds taken up in the total crop. Thus the 200 pounds represents the total amount taken up in the crop either from the soil's organic matter or via application. In the Missouri bootheel, we do well to get 60 to 80 pounds of nitrogen from organic matter. This information is provided by soil test. When we consider the nitrogen which is reported on the test as pounds per acre, we are not talking about any nitrogen from a commercial source that may have been applied or any nitrogen from any manures that have been put on. Every time we have 5.1 humus (termed organic matter on our soil test) in a soil, the nitrogen figure will be 100 pounds. Every time we have a 2.3 humus reading, nitrogen is going to be 66 pounds. This is nitrogen to be released from the soil humus over the growing season. Subtract the amount that is shown sourced from humus, and add the required rest.

Do we add that by growing legumes? Can it be added via *rhizobium* on soybean roots? If a corn or grass crop is to be produced, where is the rest of the nitrogen coming from? That is what we have to look at.

I have clients who have used what I call biological stimulants between 1975 and the present for this job. If the soils are worked correctly, I have seen these products work on the same fields year after year. But if the soil fundamentals are not correct and in place, you can get into all kinds of trouble relying solely on biologicals.

In 1977 and 1978, a company that makes a product called Agrispon hired me to do all their troubleshooting east of the Mississippi River. In two years, I visited over 13,000 acres, not because these acres represented all applications made, but because some few of these acres (about 7%) had problems. No one knew much about field application at that time because such products represented a brand new concept. The first problem surfaced in southern Illinois, which was close to where I was working. The company asked me to go up one day and look at a farmer's corn. I took a look at it. Right to the row where he used anhydrous ammonia, that corn was tasseled out and looked the best. Where he used the biological and no anhydrous or other type of nitrogen at all, the corn had hardly tasseled except in the low spots. That had been soil conservation land for ten years. He had plowed weeds as tall as his head under with a moldboard plow the previous fall. There was little rain during the winter. As a consequence, decay faltered, and the undecayed weeds were still there when he planted his corn. Where he knifed in anhydrous, the extra nitrogen broke down those plowed down weeds. The undecomposed materials in areas without nitrogen application were still there to compete with the crop for an inadequate amount of nitrogen. Though by August the corn without anhydrous looked like it had come out of the problem, it cost the farmer about 25 bushels of corn per acre in terms of yield because he starved his plants early in the season.

As a result of that consultation, they sent me to farms spread from Missouri to the east coast. Over a two-year period I visited over 13,000 acres treated with these products to supply needed nitrogen. Out of these 13,000+ acres, 93% of the crops were properly represented and were as good or better than what the farmer had been doing. Only 7% had problems. I took a lot of pictures of the problems because I wanted to document them. There is always a logical explanation for problems. If this explanation can be discerned from the record, it can save a lot of money.

I know farmers who have never heard of biologicals. They won't hear about them from me because they have trouble just staying up with what they are doing right now. I don't try to come into an operation and say, "Look, you are doing this the wrong way and you need to do it like this." What I have learned by hard experience is to sit down with the farmer and say, "What do you want to accomplish? We will help you accomplish that with your soils as best we can. You will have to decide what approach you take."

Hands-On Agronomy

I have farmer/clients who are completely organic, and I have clients who are completely commercial. The people who really work with natural systems can come out ahead of the guy who is commercial, but some farmers just don't have the mind-set it takes to work with natural systems. There are some clients I simply instruct, "Under the situation you are operating in, you are not going to do well with biologicals." Thus some companies don't want me talking to their customers. The further out of whack the soil is in terms of chemistry, the more that is true. On the other hand, I have clients who say they would like to try a little bit. Accordingly we work into it slowly. Some clients use biologicals on the whole farm. Usually I don't ask who is using what. I just come in and start talking about their program. Nothing is said or done to come in sideways or tell a farmer to do his job some other way. I just want to recite the basics. In terms of biologicals, the closer the chemistry in the soil is to being "right," the better they are going to work. If the chemistry is not right, then extra steps must be taken first to see that the basics are more perfectly in place.

I have clients who grow alfalfa and use ammonium sulfate, and I have other clients who grow alfalfa and use the biologicals. I have still other clients who grow alfalfa and do not apply either one. It all depends on the basics and the concepts a farmer understands. It is not my objective to govern the approach. But I will tell the farmer who is doing neither if either one would benefit his alfalfa, and which would likely do best for his circumstance.

A few years ago, in southern Illinois, the alfalfa weevil absolutely ate up not only the first cutting, but also the second. A farmer who attended one of my meetings had never heard of the biological approach. But his fertilizer consultant called me and said the farmer wanted to plant some new alfalfa in the spring. He wanted to use Agrispon, and wanted me to tell him—based on his soils—whether it was going to work. I said, "Not only will I tell you, but you

Microorganisms and Soil Structure

Flocculation and sedimentation of soil particles in an aqueous suspension, as a result of a change in charge of the particles, can account for the bringing together of primary particles of colloidal size (less than two microns). However, flocculation and sedimentation are of limited importance in aggregation under natural conditions in the soil. Drying of a wet soil tends to bring primary particles together, since the attractive charges are brought closer together when the water films between the particles are reduced. On the other hand, drying of the soil may result in the development of unequal stresses which may break the soil into particles. Other physical forces, such as freezing and thawing, also may cause fragmentation of the soil mass into smaller units. Tillage may break up the soil mass into various units such as clods, fragments, crumbs and granules. Plant roots certainly tend to push primary particles closer together to form aggregates or structural units in the soil, as do the mycelia of certain fungi. Earthworms, crayfish, ants, and many insects form aggregates and, in many cases, may stabilize them. Certain bacteria, through the production of gums, may have similar effects. Burrowing animals, such as moles, separate the soil mass into units. Thus in nature there are numerous ways in which lumps, granules, clods and other aggregates are formed from the soil mass into the many-sized units that are found in the soil.

Once the soil units are formed there are numerous ways in which they may be stabilized. Inorganic cementing materials, such as iron, may give extreme stability such as occurs in the Latosols. Also colloidal materials, such as clays and organic matter, through their chemical and physical effects stabilize the soil units.

Microorganisms, during the decomposition of plant and animal remains, produce numerous organic compounds and release inorganic substances that affect stability of the soil units. Some of the compounds produced and released exert a tremendous effect on stability. Other compounds have little or no effect. Some of the natural products produced by microorganisms are more effective per unit weight than are the synthetic stabilizers that have been produced. In addition to the foregoing microbial effects, the physical influence of certain fungal mycelia in holding together the soil units should be mentioned. Microorganisms vary greatly in their ability to stabilize the soil.

The soil fauna is also important in influencing soil stability. For example, the earthworm secretes slimes that render the cast several times more stable than the original soil. Under some mulching treatments, as much as 40 tons per acre of earthworm casts were produced and deposited on the surface of the soil. Thus there are many factors involved in forming soil structure units and in stabilizing them. The kind of soil structure will depend upon type of soil and all aspects of its chemical, physical, and biological makeup.

—*T.M. McCalla and F.A. Haskins*
Missouri Agricultural Experiment Station's
Research Bulletin 765

have the best chance because you have excellent soils. If you put the product and an insect repellent together, then you are going to be able to get that alfalfa right through." I knew he could because I have seen other people do it. He planted his new seeding of alfalfa and the insects never touched it, even though they consumed his established crop that did not receive the Agrispon and the repellent.

There are other farmers who raise alfalfa in the same area. I wouldn't think of telling them to do the same thing because they do not have the proper foundation. Admittedly, these few remarks are getting far removed from commercial nitrogen, but some understanding of the topic is necessary. So, back to the numbers on basic crops. Soybean production factors out as follows: a 50-bushel crop takes 280 pounds of nitrogen. Some texts tell you that a 60-bushel crop requires 295 to 300 pounds of nitrogen. The same general rule governs both soybeans and alfalfa. For ease of computation, I like to think in terms of 300 pounds of nitrogen and 60 bushels of beans.

In a normal growing season, you are going to get 50% efficiency from the nodulation on your beans. If it takes 300 pounds of nitrogen to grow a 60-bushel soybean crop, and you are getting 50% efficiency, this means another 150 pounds of nitrogen must be accounted for. What if you have 2.3% organic matter? That factors in another 66 pounds of nitrogen. Subtract 66 pounds from 150. This leaves another 84 pounds of nitrogen to be accounted for. Without that extra nitrogen, you will not grow 60 bushels of soybeans per acre.

The first clue for a decent production level is calcium in the 60% range. If the soil colloid does not have a proper calcium level, nitrogen will not deliver a top yield. Once you have your basics in place—60 to 70% calcium, 10 to 20% magnesium—then and only then do you start looking at nitrogen as a factor in growing high yield beans. There are very few farmers on my program who raise 60 bushels

Hands-On Agronomy

of beans without obtaining some extra nitrogen above the amount supplied by the soil and nodulation.

A typical farmer question runs approximately as follows. If a grower wants to raise a 60-bushel bean crop and he is at a 60% calcium level, how many pounds of extra nitrogen would he have to add, the organic matter level being 2.5%? At 2.5% organic matter, such a farmer will have 70 pounds of nitrogen supplied by the soil. He will need 150 pounds of additional nitrogen in a normal year, after accounting for the 50% supplied by nodules. Again, if you have 70% efficiency from your beans, that goes up. We are considering a 50% efficiency factor right now because it is easy—and expected in a normal year. In other words, 150 pounds of nitrogen generated by bacteria goes into production. We have another 150 pounds to go. Take that 70 pounds from 2.5% humus off the equation and we have to come up with another 80 pounds of nitrogen from some other source. All this assumes that we have a good fertile soil and that there is a proper phosphate and potassium level.

It is not discussed generally, but there is a vicious nitrogen cycle that you can get into just by pushing nitrogen. And there are other things that can contribute to crop production for which nitrogen gets the credit. All things considered and all things in perspective should be a norm. We say legumes can get nitrogen out of the air, but we have to add that they don't get it all from the air. At least 30% has to come from another source, and that 30% either has to be supplied by microbial activity in the soil or by a commercial source. The farmer can choose either one, but when the choice is made, he or she has to deal with the consequences.

If you choose commercial nitrogen, that act will start making that soil more and more reliant on commercial nitrogen. If biology is the choice, everything else has to be right and in place, else the biological activity will turn out to be the limiting factor. Before microbiology works, chemistry and physics have to be in place. Albrecht's percentages are what really make the microbes work. I have clients who do not know about microbial products and still can raise 60 bushels of beans without commercial fertilizer, but that is not the general rule.

Manures are an excellent source of nitrogen. I work with farmers who use a lot of manures in some areas, and I have other areas under consultation where there is no livestock for thousands and thousands of acres, and nothing organic is applied. A real saving factor in my area is a broiler production facility that generates 15,000 tons of manure a year. All of it is moved out to farmers.

Most of the farmers in southeast Missouri didn't know the value of manures when I settled in the area. It was generally not available to those who had gone out of the livestock business. In time some of us sat down and worked out some figures. One farmer tried it on 400 acres and another one tried it on a few less acres. Now the man who contracts for disposal of the manure has no trouble at all finding someone who wants it. In fact, my clients want it all.

Several items merit front burner consideration when applying manures. Number one, the manure content will vary from fall to spring, depending on the feed content. Manures are nitrogen rich. Once you know what your nitrogen content is, divide by two to compute the nitrogen potential.

There are tremendous differences between poultry, cow and hog manures, and there is even a difference between layer and broiler manure. Layers are fed extra calcium to strengthen the egg shells. Broilers generally do not get this ration.

I had a client who had 26,000 layers and farmed 160 acres. He had me analyze his soils because his fields weren't producing good crops any longer. He had put so much layer manure on his farm and pushed the calcium level so high, it started tying up all his trace minerals. He was destroying his farm with the manure. It took about five years to get that problem solved because he didn't choose to buy sulfur for remedial application.

His son raised turkeys down the road. The son needed calcium and was putting on turkey manure and his dad was putting on too much calcium using layer manure, so I had them switch. They both solved their problems.

Manures will drive calcium out of the soil except where calcium is highly supplemented, such as for egg production. The problem is that magnesium will take the calcium's place. The farm mentioned above didn't have excessive magnesium. In fact, it had basically the kind of magnesium levels needed. By the time we got finished with the switch, both were a little on the high side, but not extreme. When the calcium got high, it tied up his iron and certain other trace elements. This was what kept hurting his crops.

Every soil is different. You have to analyze what is going to happen to the several nutrients. When you analyze soils, you have to remember that just because a certain program works on one farm, that doesn't mean it is going to work on the farm down the road. Every time the numbers change, a new set of circumstances come into view, with a new set of possibilities and potential problems.

If you use manure to take out calcium, and magnesium goes too high, in the end you are going to have to use some sulfur to get magnesium down to a reasonable point. You might as well start with sulfur in the first place, especially if calcium levels are low and magnesium levels are high. This inventory of facts should prompt us to remember that manure will take out some calcium. Manures will supply extra nitrogen, phosphate and potash to be certain, and is always a better source than physical measurements suggest. Nevertheless, an analysis gets you into the ballpark.

I work with a ranch in Texas that began using legumes to supply all its nitrogen for pasture grasses. In the 1960s, the Extension Service said this couldn't be done because it wouldn't work properly. In 1973, when oil prices went up, the dialogue became, "How do you do this?" Within two to three years, an extension specialist in livestock management at Texas A&M was telling a veterinarian from Stephenville, Texas that this very ranch's program was an A&M idea.

Legumes will supply nitrogen. Regardless of the legume you are using, don't forget about what type of year it is. If you have a good year and growing conditions are right, then count on legumes to supply quite a bit of nitrogen. If conditions are terrible, you are not going to get more efficiency from the microbial than you get anywhere else. The more you work with the microbial population in the soil system, the better they are going to do in a poor year. The bland remark that in a poor year you are only going to get 25% efficiency from legumes in terms of supplying nitrogen isn't true. But if you have poor soils and a poor year, most likely you will not get much. If you don't know for sure and you want to get some general ideas, do a nitrate and ammonia analysis. You can go three feet deep. But if you go that deep, at least take the top six inches separately. Put that in one sample bag. To look at the next increment, go down 12 inches. Put that in another sample bag. For corn, you can stop there. For cotton, in some areas roots go down 18 inches. Ask for a nitrate and ammonia analysis, and look at how much nitrogen is calculated for each sample.

I had a client who made 45 bushels of beans. He had a lot of rain through the winter. Come springtime, he planted corn. A little later he became concerned about his nitrogen stores. We had an analysis run for the area where he grew beans the year before versus where he grew corn during the same time frame a year later. He had 65 pounds more nitrogen on the side where he grew soybeans than on the side where he grew corn.

Several things could contribute to that. Generally, if you are growing soybeans in a place, you are only going to get about three quarters of a pound of nitrogen per bushel of soybeans for use by the corn. You can't just say, "Well, we

120   *Hands-On Agronomy*

Quality Produce Demands
Proper Composting

Today we still notice that cabbage, cauliflower, broccoli and kale can give off very intensive aromas while cooking. This, too, depends on the fertilization of the soil.

The reason is that breakdown products contained in the manure, such as skatole, indole and other phenolic compounds (to the layman, that which stinks) are not further decomposed. They enter the soil, are absorbed by plant roots and migrate into the plant tissue. These breakdown products have been excreted by the animal or human organisms, are toxic wastes of their metabolism and imprint their history on the soil and the growing plant.

Night soil is particularly undesirable in this regard, but even sewage sludge contains many toxic compounds, unless properly decomposed by an aerobic composting process. The difficulty is that these byproducts are rather stable and can survive for a long time. Returned in food to the human upper digestive tract where they do not belong, they can cause many symptoms of indigestion, flatulence and maybe even allergic reactions.

Biuret is a contaminant or byproduct of urea and urine. It is extremely stable. In greenhouse and field experiments at Purdue University it was demonstrated that it was toxic to growing corn plants. It caused leaf chlorosis, hyponasty and it severely stunted, twisted and deformed plants with their leaf tips rolled together. All fertilizer salts, when placed with the seed, resulted in decreased length of primary roots. The ability to survive germination damage was severely reduced by increasing the biuret content. The rate of growth and the yield were reduced.

—Ehrenfried E. Pfeiffer
speech presented to Natural Foods
Associates Convention, 1961

are going to get one pound of nitrogen per bushel of soy-beans produced." It depends on what you are doing to influence the microbes that build nitrogen in that soil.

I had a client near Moses Lake, Washington call me one November. He said, "They tell me that you have been working with this 'biological' product which helps supply nitrogen, and I want to try it on some land, but there is no need for us to put a fall application on because our ground freezes up. You can't tell me that if I put it on in November that it is going to do anything from now until next March." I responded, "There is one thing you need to consider. When the very top surface of the soil warms up to 28 degrees, certain microbes start to work. It doesn't have to be a case of putting a thermometer in the soil, and the whole thing being thawed out. When the sun is shining on the soil surface, a certain number of microbes start to work right then."

He said, "Well, I don't really believe it, but I will take this 30-acre field and split it into three parts. On ten acres I will put an application right now, and on the other 20 acres I will not do anything. Next spring on that first 10 acres I am going to make another application. Then I am going to put an application on the middle ten acres and use the last area for a control."

He was producing carrots. He made the application on ten acres, first taking samples for analysis to determine the nitrogen levels. The readout was very low. I already knew that during the winter it was common to cause an accumulation of 30 to 40 pounds of nitrogen by applying the "biological" in the fall. The Moses Lake client hardly made the application before it froze up. He called in the spring and asked me to come out there and put on a meeting. He said, "By the time you get here, I will have a nitrate and ammonia analysis because the soil is thawing out." When I got there he was really excited. He said, "You know, we have 35 pounds more nitrogen on this ten-acre treated plot than we do on either one of the other ten-acre plots."

If such a program is not begun in the fall, and you want to use this type of program, you must have at least 40 pounds of nitrate nitrogen in place, or else you have to come in with an equal nitrogen supply. A nitrate and ammonia analysis can tell you what you need to know.

I have farmers growing corn and they don't know if they have enough nitrogen a week before silk. They need to pull special samples and have them analyzed. Almost any laboratory can provide a nitrate and ammonia analysis because that test is pretty well standard. One lab seems to be just as good as the next. A nearby laboratory can make a nitrate and ammonia test easier on you because the lab needs it within 12 hours. If you can't get it there within 12 hours, take the sample into the house and spread it on waxed paper. Put a fan on it and dry it out and then send it to the lab.

With reference to nitrogen, it is most difficult to properly recommend management because five things can happen to it.

1. It can be used by the crop, which is great.

2. It can become part of the soil complex, which means it can be *adsorbed* on the clay colloid or get incorporated into the humus. When it is on the clay colloid it is not too hard to get hold of, but when it is incorporated in the humus, microbial activity and chemical balance must attend its release.

3. It can leach down in the soil and be transported away from the production with drainage water.

4. It can be eroded away no matter what form it is in.

5. It can volatilize and escape as a gas.

When nitrogen from any commercial source suffers from water standing over the crop for three or four days, a big portion of it will be lost. After four days you probably will have lost almost all of it.

The Nuances of Nitrogen   123

I had a client who put 90 pounds of nitrogen on his corn at planting time. A 14-inch rain followed when the corn was 12-15 inches tall. Even though the land was put to grade, one 20-acre field was covered with water on the low end for four days. A nitrate and ammonia analysis revealed that the ammonium sulfate—a stable nitrogen form—held on the end where the water hadn't stood. The readout showed a respectable 85 pounds of nitrogen in place. On the end where water stood for four days, only 18 pounds remained.

Under anaerobic conditions, microbes that can live without air will actually decompose plant residues, taking oxygen out of the nitrate nitrogen for life support. Nitrogen gas remains briefly before it comes up through the water and escapes into the atmosphere.

Aerobic microorganisms require oxygen to live and work. These critters work in the top six and three quarter inches of soil. Anaerobic microorganisms do not require oxygen. They break down materials in the soil by harvesting oxygen from parent materials in the soil. This means anaerobes can work without direct oxygen availability; aerobes have to have oxygen. We want to have the aerobes work because they are the ones that go into action when we have 25% air space.

Measuring nitrogen is both difficult and rewarding. It is difficult because nitrates leach easily. Nitrogen from manure is basically in the ammonia form. It goes from ammonia to nitrite to nitrate. When it reaches the nitrate form, it goes out with the water. Nitrate nitrogen is volatile, yet this is the form the plant can use most easily. Nitrite nitrogen is an anion. Nitrogen has a negative charge and attracts a positive charge. In terms of soil physics, such a compound won't attach to the clay particle. The same thing is true of sulfates and boron.

In any discussion of nitrogen, the subject of the tissue test comes up. A tissue test will tell you whether your plant is getting enough nitrogen, and makes its suggestion as to

Hands-On Agronomy

whether an addition can be done in a timely manner. A lot depends on the numbers on the tissue test and the experience of the person making the test. Crop needs and stage of growth are determining factors. In my case, it is easier to evaluate the nitrogen requirement from soil analysis than it is from tissue testing.

Many other considerations figure in making the nitrogen connection. If soils require aeration, the right amount of nodulation will not materialize. If there is too little calcium, nodulation will falter.

At the same time I must report the case of a client near Mason City, Illinois. He was growing edible soybeans for the Japanese market, and he couldn't get good nodulation on his beans. He started to use one of the microbial inoculants on his soils. The plant nodules went from small to some as big as a thumbnail. The only change he made was to use the inoculant. Obviously, the other conditions were correct or it wouldn't have happened. This means he had his calcium level in place, and enough phosphorous. It means he had enough sulfur.

The title page in making the nitrogen connection might well be, nitrogen in the life of a corn plant. Nevertheless, this last is the time when plenty of nitrogen for the crop is indicated. This puts the ball in my court as a consultant. I have to be sure that the nitrogen is breaking down at the proper time or that nitrogen is released in a timely manner. At tasseling and silk, the corn plant really needs nitrogen. Then it starts to taper off. For that brief moment in time, it is important to get that nitrogen in fast. Using a source that gets into the corn plant quickly, or using a foliar type is important.

The soil has to have good levels; still, a quick release of nitrogen is required to take care of a deficiency. A rule of thumb is to make an application a week before tasseling if a commercial source is used. You can actually put that on when the corn silks and still get a response if you apply a fast releasing nitrogen such as 32% liquid using a high-boy with drops, or dry ammonia nitrate using a plane. If dry urea is used, absorption efficiency will falter, but small amounts of urea applied in water have been very effective as a foliar source of nitrogen in cotton. A small amount of foliar material at about the four leaf stage—especially slow acting material such as a microbial inoculant—can be chancy if the deficiency is considerable. Ammonia nitrate or urea in very small amounts, fed through the leaf at the six leaf stage with micronutrients, can be effective. Personally, I like a foliar best at silk, especially if micronutrients are a consideration, using nitrogen and potassium in combination with the trace elements.

The basic rule is to use a nitrate and ammonia analysis, or a tissue analysis, but don't count on a regular soil test to tell you whether or not you have enough nitrogen. Either invoke a special test, or rely on the art of getting it right by observation. Most people, when they rely on intuition, use

Nitrogen deficiency in corn and grain sorghum is characterized by the "yellow V" which shows in the tips of the oldest (lower) leaves first, designated as nitrogen starved here.

NITROGEN
STARVED

NORMAL
PLANT

Hands-On Agronomy

too much. The usual propensity is to rather use too much than not enough, the cost in terms of lost bushels weighing most in mind.

Deficiencies lend themselves to both laboratory and pragmatic analysis, especially in corn production. On the previous page is a drawing of a good healthy corn leaf, compared to what a leaf looks like at the same stage of growth when nitrogen deficiency reveals itself. I tell farmers that they are well ahead of the game to get pollen down the back of the neck by walking through corn fields. At tassel time the cornfield becomes a veritable encyclopedia. Better yet, walk the fields a week or two before corn tassels, and then walk them again when they tassel. Then walk those same fields two weeks later. Even when the corn is starting to dry down, walk the fields again. If time is a governing factor, at least walk the fields between tassel and silk. See what you look at. If you start seeing the leaves pictured here at tassel time, you are in trouble. If you want to know how short you are on nitrogen on corn, whether you use a biological program or a commercial program, count the leaves that exhibit a nitrogen deficiency. If you have four leaves that exhibit these signs and symptoms, or worse, just understand that for every leaf starting with the bottom one and coming up, each leaf with a V or that is dead, you are short ten pounds of nitrogen. Let's say we find three leaves. That translates into a 30 pound shortage of nitrogen. How much yield is that going to cost if nothing is done about it? If you have over 20% magnesium, divide by 1.5. For every pound and a half of nitrogen, it is going to cost you a bushel of corn. If you have three leaves showing the telltale V, it is going to cost you at least 20 bushels of corn per acre. And yet it is not too late at tassel time to do something about it. Every leaf below the ear builds the stalk, and the ear leaf and those above it build the grain for corn. If you can stop debilitation before it gets to the ear leaf, the projected yield will be maintained. If you see three leaves at tassel, that means you need 30 pounds of nitrogen to take care of the problem right now.

If you are growing corn short of nitrogen and if the magnesium percentage of soil saturation is under 20—say 18 or 19—the divisor is 1.45. If the reading is 15, 16 or 17, the divisor is 1.35. If magnesium is 12, that sum becomes its own dividend since the divisor is 1. If you have the 68/12 recommended level for calcium/magnesium and you have three leaves showing nitrogen deficiency, it will cost you 30 bushels of corn according to that three leaf index.

If you have one part of a field that is high magnesium, and another part where the magnesium is optimum, here's what will happen. Where the high magnesium shows three leaves, the 68/12 would only be showing two. So a high magnesium soil would show three leaves, whereas a good soil would only show two because we are going to be short 20 bushels.

If you are turning to a commercial source of nitrogen and you don't really have a lot of microbial activity—especially when you are below 2.5% organic matter—and if you do not accomplish that nitrate and ammonia analysis, you are not looking at the true picture. You are seeing three leaves. But by the time you take remedial action, you could have about five leaves. The cut off point seems to be 40 pounds of actual nitrogen. If you have a pivot system or access to an aerial applicator, you can still make a difference but testing is the best.

Once you see that V in the corn leaf, it is already too late for that particular leaf. If you analyze the leaves above it, a shortage of nitrogen will already be evident. Even though you put on the nitrogen required at that time, some yield will be lost. In fact, we do not want to see the visual effects of any nutrient on the plant leaves, not a trace element or whatever. Failure to see a nutrient deficiency in the leaves does not mean that crop is not short of a particular nutrient, because of what we call *hidden hunger*. It means that we do not have enough of a shortage to show up at visual inspection. Once you see that V it is too late to do anything for that specific leaf simply because it was short a long time before the V became evident. I have clients who fly on dry ammonia nitrate at tassel time. When applied to a part of the field, it takes only three days to see the difference. Even if it is put on dry, it will be taken up from the soil into the plant. This is one thing we can do when we have poor aeration and a microbial stimulating-type product is used to supply nitrogen, but for whatever reason has not done the job.

When the farmer has used biologicals in tandem with poor aeration, or he had an over-abundance of residues to break down, then if he does not get that nitrogen in place, he will lose the bushels.

That figure of ten pounds per leaf is not something I came up with. A lot of people have known this fact. Today it is simply a matter of delivering that information in usable form.

Normal (top) leaf compared to three with nitrogen deficiency's characteristic "yellow V."

A summary of sorts is now in order. If you know what your calcium-magnesium ratios are, you can compute the efficiency of the pounds of nitrogen involved. Here are the different stages.

In the illustrations on the previous page, the leaf starts to die back. Next the yellow V. Above that, a little bit of yellow. Finally, the solid green leaf.

If you take these three leaves off a stalk and the one indicated above is still green—counting from the bottom leaf—then you can be certain that you should have used 30 pounds of nitrogen. Whatever the source, 30 pounds of nitrogen not applied earlier in the season is now the governing factor.

Actually, if you had put on 30 pounds nitrogen to get it utilized in that stalk before tassel, the deficiency in the leaves would never have shown up. It doesn't have to be put on at planting time though. It can be put on as a top dressing, or if necessary, latter in the season.

I have seen fields at tassel with no yellow leaves. Yet on a long, full-season corn, there would still be three leaves showing up as deficient before ripening. You can have an excellent green looking stalk at tassel and still have a nitrogen deficiency later on. A nitrate and ammonia analysis before tassel can suggest the degree of deficiency that will show up. Such a readout will give the relationship between the nitrate and ammonia in the soil and make its suggestion as to whether that corn is going to properly make it or not.

If you use ammonium sulfate, the very best time to get the most response on corn is to put it on as close to the day you plant as possible. It takes 60 warm days to get a maximum nitrogen release. Some clients ask if they can put their ammonium sulfate on in fall for the next spring. If they do it, they waste money because they have to put on extra in order to have the proper availability in spring. If you put all that ammonium sulfate on in the fall and you get 60 warm days from the time you put it on, you are going to begin to get your major push on that 60th day. This could be in February, too early to plant in the cornbelt, and for best results, you want it 60 days after planting.

Anhydrous ammonia has to be mentioned. It releases faster than ammonium sulfate. Many commercial growers will not give it up, even though there are many problems with this product. The best time for anhydrous use is as a side dressing after the corn is up and growing. Even then, I advise clients that it will require 20% more nitrogen from anhydrous to get the same yield as a good broadcast nitrogen source.

I know some farmers who put a nitrogen inhibitor with it. That inhibitor actually kills the nitrogen fixers in the soil and stops them from breaking ammonia down to nitrate nitrogen. The idea is to repopulate the bacteria after they have been annihilated. I don't think this is a good idea. Anhydrous ammonia can be defended for post-emergence use. The corn plant can take the ammonia nitrogen from anhydrous or ammonia nitrate or from ammonium sulfate or from any ammonium source. As the crop inches its way toward maturity, the full-season corn taps this resource. Short-season corn may not adequately convert the ammonia nitrogen directly to amino acids, which translate back to yield; it needs a faster release of nitrogen than full-season corn.

Time the nitrogen application rather than use an inhibitor. The nitrate portion of any nitrogen form, generally, is immediately available. The ammonia portion is going to find use farther down the line, say, 30 to 60 days later, depending on the soils. If you use ammonia and have a pH of 7.5 or less, it is going to be more of a case of that slow 60-day breakdown I have been talking about. If you use ammonia on a high pH soil, say pH 8, ammonia will break down just as fast as urea in such soils.

The bottom line is simple in the extreme. More nitrogen at the right time doubles corn from the same amount of water. Nitrogen applied with other needed nutrients at the right time can actually double the corn yield.

pH / (')pē-'āch / *n* **1** the negative logarithm of the effective hydrogen ion concentration or hydrogen ion activity in terms of gram equivalents per liter to express acidity or alkalinity on a scale with values 0 to 14, 7 representing neutrality, less than 7 representing acidity, numbers greater than 7 representing alkalinity **2** in soils, acidity denotes deficiency—calcium, magnesium, sodium or potassium, or a combination **3** by bringing calcium, magnesium, sodium and potassium into equilibrium in terms of the Albrecht equation, pH becomes adjusted automatically in soil systems suitable for plant growth **4** in neutral medium (high pH), soil colloids tend to be stable (gel) **5** under conditions of acidity (low pH), a more mobile (sol) state is achieved **6** when molecules of clay and humus become mobile because of acidity, more nutrients are etched from parent soil materials

6

Concerning Commercial Nitrogen Sources

THE ORGANIC FOLKS OFTEN WINCE when I detail the many facets of nitrogen application, especially when I describe the metes and bounds of ammonium sulfate use. I have to remind them as gently as I can that microorganisms need "go" foods as well as "grow" foods. Every plant cell needs nitrogen in the right form.

Admittedly, ammonium sulfate is a synthetic nitrogen, usually containing 20.5% nitrogen. It loads over or adsorbs to the clay component of the soil colloid readily and is not subject to leaching. This nitrogen form gets on quite well with most soil microorganisms.

My purpose here is not to debate the nitrogen forms, or even to explain William A. Albrecht's concept of *Insoluble*

Yet Available. Readers are directed to *An Acres U.S.A. Primer* for exposition and analysis of the subject. I will agree with the *Primer* that plants need their nitrogen cafeteria style, not as a whole-hog feeding at the beginning of the season.

My clients recite their records with great aplomb, setting up goals and systems to achieve those goals. For instance, a 25 pound application through irrigation is both valid and feasible. In a Minnesota study, 100 pounds of nitrogen delivered as four 25 pound applications produced 154 bushels of corn per acre, or 1.11 bushels of corn for each pound of nitrogen used simply by spreading it out over a longer period of time. Two hundred pounds of nitrogen in one application at planting time provided the foundation for 158 bushels per acre, or .58 bushels of corn per pound of nitrogen. Eight 25 pound applications through the irrigation system made 192 bushels per acre, but the efficiency was not as good—three quarters of a bushel of corn per pound of nitrogen. These data are quoted to show that spread out applications of nitrogen, even on corn, account for much better efficiency. If total application is made before planting time, less efficiency per pound of nitrogen will be the norm, not more. It is going to take more nitrogen to do the same job, because of the way the conversion is accomplished.

I have mentioned ammonium sulfate. A lot of farmers in my area believe the ammonium sulfate people have paid me because I have so many farmers using the product to buffer their high magnesium levels. In fact there was a rumor that I received ten cents a ton for every bit of ammonium sulfate that was sold. After I was in the area for about two years, the sales rep who sold ammonium sulfate to fertilizer dealers caught up with me one day. He said, "I need to shake your hand. We weren't selling any ammonium sulfate at all in this area until you came here." About three years later he made the following comment in my presence, "The first year that Neal started working in this area, we sold maybe a semi-load of ammonium sulfate. The next year we sold 4,000 tons." (I would like to have received ten cents a ton for that, but I didn't receive a penny, and still don't.)

Many of my clients were growing a lot of wheat and corn in soils with high magnesium levels. Everything they had ever learned told them to use commercial nitrogen. This being the case, ammonium sulfate was the first recommendation. If you need sulfur and nitrogen, there is no source at a lower price. Second, ammonium sulfate takes 60 warm days before you get a major push. Ammonium sulfate put on a month before corn planting is still there after two to three rains. I never recommend its application a month before corn planting. But in one case the farmer intended to plant when it suddenly just got wet. It was a month before they could go back into the fields.

I analyzed the residence time. Virtually none of the nitrogen had been lost in that time frame—maybe five pounds per acre. Still, for corn and cotton, application should be made as close to planting as possible, otherwise the release will come before the crop most needs it.

I have clients who will wait until they get their corn planted, and then use a buggy to spread the ammonium sulfate over the top. This is not too late. Ammonium sulfate and ammonium thiosulfate belong in the same category, used late in the season on irrigated corn.

The above are the most stable forms of nitrogen in terms of application ease and lasting effect. On the other hand, if you are growing wheat and you are using ammonium sulfate, you've got to keep it in mind that it is a slow release material on soils below pH 7.5 (this is water pH). You have to get the nitrate nitrogen to that wheat at a specific time because there is a nitrate requiring enzyme that determines how many kernels are going to develop in a head of wheat. Unless there is nitrate nitrogen for that enzyme at all times, it can run short and cut the yield accordingly. If ammonium sulfate is used as a nitrogen source in wheat production, a rule of thumb calls for application four months before normal harvest date. This may seem to be a long time, but on cold soils it works out just right. In warmer climates, application two months before the normal harvest date is sufficient. Basically, in our area we want it there in March and April. The last date we can consider for application in southeastern Missouri is February 7. The normal early harvest date for the area is June 7. We can apply the material as early as the first of January. The soil will be cold at that time of the year, and loss to a warm soil is not a problem. I tell farmers near my home that any time between January 1 and February 7 is appropriate for ammonium sulfate application to the wheat field.

Ammonium nitrate is half nitrite nitrogen and half ammonium nitrogen. We use it when we need a quick push. If low spots start to yellow out, say, in April, and the wheat hasn't headed yet, you can expect the rest of the field to be a little behind. The low spots usually leach nitrogen out first. When wheat in the low spots starts to yellow, I recommend calling in an airplane, using the last 30 pounds of needed nitrogen in the equation as ammonium nitrate. Those 30 pounds applied on one part of the field and not on the other will produce an extra ten bushels of wheat to the acre. I have farmers who put four or more applications of nitrogen on wheat. If the soil is not dry enough to accommodate ground-level application, they will hire a plane.

In northeastern Arkansas, the average wheat yields run about 60 bushels or less per acre. One farmer who monitors his wheat, goes out and takes the leaf samples himself. He makes sure that the nitrogen is in it. When the nitrogen drops below the proper level, he makes another application. He had an 80 acre field. The north 40, the better of the two, made 108 bushels of wheat to the acre. The south 40 made 96 bushels. Not many farmers enjoy that kind of yield. Fertility use is the answer.

Hands-On Agronomy

Insoluble Yet Available

The soil's behaviors, like those of many other things in nature, do not conform completely to the "laws" we learn in laboratory chemistry and by which we have been explaining the natural nutrition of plants. In the laboratory, the solubility of a substance in water, in alcohol, or in certain reagents is commonly the foremost criterion for its description and classification. We are mentally disturbed, then, when we find that some natural substance or commercial product, commonly soluble in the laboratory, behaves as an insoluble one, or vice versa, when put into the soil.

We experience similar confusion when, for example, some insoluble substances on coming in contact with the mucous membrane of our body, like that of the lungs on inhalation, is soluble and harmless there. We are more disturbed when some so-called soluble substances are as disturbing (and fatal) to the lungs as the insoluble silicates of rock dusts are in the case of the disease known as "silicosis." Land plaster, consisting of the mineral gypsum, or of the chemical compound calcium sulphate, is considered soluble in the laboratory. Yet its inhalation brings a breakdown of the lung tissues which on X-ray examination suggests silicosis or even calcification by its accumulations there.

—*William A. Albrecht*
The Albrecht Papers, Volume I, 1975

That is one thing that I learned working with wheat growers in Germany. They have higher fertility levels than we find in almost any of the soils in the U.S. They have used manures on their soils for years, if not centuries. In terms of certain trace minerals and other basics, they simply leave American growers behind.

In terms of phosphate and potash, they actually have levels that are so high they forego manure application. Too much can inhibit yields instead of contributing to them. In fact, I had to get some clients to stop using phosphate and potash in order to get their yields up. Those farmers in Germany who are making 120 to 180 bushels of wheat per acre are putting their nitrogen on three, four or five times each year. Most of them put it on four or five times.

Ammonium nitrate is a source of nitrogen that will work in grass type crops in about three days. If an emergency situation develops and it comes down to the proposition that if you don't do something you are going to lose yield, you can apply ammonium nitrate on corn, and in three days that corn will show the effects. If urea is used, it becomes a case of "Can you work it in?"

I learned this from Dr. Roland Hauck, who does research at Tennessee Valley Authority in Muscle Shoals, Alabama. He pointed out that urea is the worst form of dry nitrogen if application is to be made on top of the soil. There are two reasons for this. Number one, there is a chemical reaction between pellets of urea that touch each other. They actually start to volatilize nitrogen immediately, which means you start to lose nitrogen immediately. If application is not followed by the half inch rain needed to carry it in, the result can be a dead loss. Urea converts from urea to ammonia to nitrite to nitrate. When it converts from urea to ammonia, it becomes a gas. If the material is deep enough in the soil, the gas will adsorb to the clay and humus. But without incorporation into the soil or adequate rain, you can lose an average of 25% of urea nitrogen in three days. In seven days,

138   *Hands-On Agronomy*

50% can be lost. Many fertilizer dealers will tell you that this is not true. Simply do a nitrate and ammonia analysis and see the situation as it is.

As for the nitrate portion of ammonium nitrate, the plant has to take it up or the soil solution will carry it away just as soon as water moves through the soil. Nitrate moves with the water. If you put on 100 pounds of ammonium nitrate, 34-0-0, then you have 17 pounds of nitrogen that either the plant has to use or it will leach away with the water. The other half is in the ammonia form. It has to go through the conversion from nitrite to nitrate. Basically, the process comes right back down to that 45 to 60 days.

Carrying nitrogen through a sprinkler system to the crops calls for 32-0-0 or 28-0-0 or else ammonium thiosulfate. The 32 form, generally, is half urea and half ammonia nitrate if it is less than 1% ammoniated, which most of it is. I tell farmers that when they order a semi-load, get up on the semi, lift the lid and smell. If it sort of knocks you back, you don't want it. There is a whole lot more than 1% ammonia in it. The part that gives the ammonia smell means it is getting away. At times suppliers inject anhydrous ammonia into the nitrogen to get the level up to 32-0-0. That is why you buy a 32% less than 1% ammoniated.

The consideration that brings this topic together is well stated in the saw—a pound of nitrogen is a pound of nitrogen is a pound of nitrogen and the source makes no difference. Admittedly, once you get commercial nitrogen into the plant, a pound of nitrogen is a pound of nitrogen in terms of how it affects the plant. For years and years, I have told farmers, don't topdress urea if you can use ammonium nitrate. Others said it made no difference. All at once, about five years ago, ag research came up with a nitrogen inhibitor that could be applied to urea that would cause it to break down more slowly. All of a sudden the universities made a new discovery. Researchers everywhere who worked with urea inhibitors discovered it. They set up plots of corn with the usual control. They used ammonium nitrate on one experimental plot, and paired it with the same number of pounds of nitrogen from urea with and without an inhibitor. The control was way down, of course. The next worst was urea. Next was urea with the inhibitor and ammonium nitrate. Urea with the inhibitor and ammonium nitrate yielded the same. The highest yield was with ammonium sulfate. They showed this via slides and wrote it up for the journals.

Here is the way they approached it. For urea to be as good as ammonium nitrate, you have to use the urea with inhibitors. By the time you put the inhibitor in it, it costs about the same as ammonia nitrate. That says that when they were previously telling us that urea works just as well as ammonium nitrate, the economics were not right. At one meeting they talked for 30 minutes about this corn experiment, and the last comment was that the highest yield was with ammonium sulfate, but that it was too expensive for the farmer. The reasoning, I suppose, was that it has sulfur in it, and "the farmer does not need sulfur." Universities are actually on record in several states saying that farmers don't need that much sulfur for corn. Our work shows that sulfur is one of the most under-rated nutrients in farming.

Once you establish that sulfur is needed, ammonium sulfate becomes the most inexpensive of all the forms of nitrogen to use. Instead of saying it is too expensive, they should let the farmer try it and find out how much effect it has on his yield. Again, the researchers did the same thing with cotton. They exhibited the same nitrogen sources and the same type of results at the National Cotton Council Meeting. They said the highest yield of cotton was with ammonium sulfate, but it was too expensive. The reason it was too expensive was not given. Could it be because sulfur is not needed for cotton either? Yet I wrote these lines to tell you that almost all soils that I check need sulfur. Most soils need so much sulfur, in fact, that a lot of farmers are not going to take care of the problem the first year.

I have farmers who put urea on after the corn is growing and plow it in. If you put an inhibitor with urea, then you can harvest more efficiency from this nitrogen form. I also have farmers who use anhydrous. More important, I have a lot of farmers who tell me if I can show them some other nitrogen source for the same amount of money, they will switch.

I often ask farmers who tell me this to run a 40-acre test, two 20s, and if they have the capability of using broadcast nitrogen, they can cut the amount of nitrogen they use by 20%. I've done it time and time again. A big difference is in dangers associated with overuse of nitrogen. When you overuse nitrogen or any other nutrient, consider that every time you put too much of something in a soil, something else suffers.

Let's talk about anhydrous. With anhydrous you have to use the nitrate and ammonia test differently from when you broadcast. On a medium to heavy soil, even on a clay loam or a silt loam soil, anhydrous down the middle will furnish valid information. In, say, two to four weeks, a soil probe can be used to get a 12-inch sample, three inches out from the row. Another 12-inch sample should be taken the next three inches out, and so forth, to the middle. Sampling design should call for one probe exactly where the anhydrous knife ran, other probes being taken three inches either way. All should be analyzed separately. A 36-inch row will call for 13 samples. Starting with the sample from the middle, tests will reveal that 96% of all the nitrogen that the anhydrous knife inserted generally remains in a six or seven inch band. Only 4% moves out of that band—and it hardly moves! In other words, the nitrogen moves only three inches either way from the knife. In a heavy soil, it does not move further. This suggests that when you apply anhydrous, the roots had better be able to move out and pick it up. You don't want to wait very late. If this weren't the case, you could actually put the anhydrous on very late and get a tremendous response for corn.

These data make their own suggestions. That is why it takes 20% more nitrogen to grow the same crop via anhydrous than when nitrogen is broadcast. The efficiency of the roots is increased by at least that much.

One of my clients, comparing anhydrous (82%) and ammonium sulfate (21-0-0-24), told me that by the time he figured the cost of the sulfur and the cost of the anhydrous, ammonium sulfate still saved him money. He said it saved him $5 an acre to use ammonium sulfate as compared to anhydrous ammonia and the purchase of sufficient sulfur to go with it.

What about that six-inch area in which the knife inserts the nitrogen? How much havoc do we create by putting that huge amount of nitrogen in one place? Certainly roots are going to bypass a lot more nitrogen than they do if the nutrient is spread out. This, indeed, is why it takes 20% more to do the same job. But consider what happens if nitrogen is over-supplied? First of all, too much nitrogen can induce a zinc deficiency. Zinc is instrumental in moisture absorption, therefore it takes more water to do the same job in, say, corn production. Also, excessive amounts of nitrogen tie up copper. Copper is what confers stalk strength to the plant. That is why the field that gets the nitrogen in the proper amount will exhibit quite a different scene from the one that gets too much nitrogen. In the last case, you can actually cut the stalk at tassel near the ground and see the inside starting to disintegrate. By the time this plant has matured, there will be hardly anything left at the bottom of the stalks. The stalk falls over. One of the things that causes this is a copper shortage. It is well documented that too much nitrogen stops copper uptake. All the manufactured nitrogen forms are guilty. But when we have to use one fifth more product in an anhydrous application, the worst effect

Hands-On Agronomy

The pH Equation

As each of the equations for each of the chief cation elements fall into place, a principle of eco-farming becomes transparently clear. pH becomes self-adjusting when calcium, magnesium, potassium and sodium are in proper equilibrium. To answer low pH with lime regardless of the character of that lime rates attention as frustration agronomy.

pH means acidity to some people, but to eco-farmers it means a shortage of fertility elements, the same fertility elements named in the paragraph above. Professor C.E. Marshall of the University of Missouri once designed electrodes and membranes to measure ionic activity of calcium and potassium in the same way hydrogen ions are measured to determine pH. Marshall's pK and pCa illustrated clearly that ionic activities of a mixture of elements were not independent of each other. Taking calcium and potassium in combination, he discovered that potassium gained ascendancy in relative activity as cations become narrower. Magnesium, pound for pound, could raise pH up to 1.4 times higher than calcium. A soil high in magnesium and low in calcium could test pH 6.5 and still be entirely inadequate for the growth of alfalfa. Any of the major cations—calcium, magnesium, potassium and sodium—in excess can push pH up, and any one of them in lower amounts can take pH down. They have to be in balance, or the pH reading is likely to be meaningless. An equilibrium of pH at 6.2 or 6.3 for farm crops (based on these four elements in balance) will prompt plants to grow well and produce bins and bushels in tune with both the pedigree of the seed and the character of the soil.

—Charles Walters & C.J. Fenzau
An Acres U.S.A. Primer, 1979

of all can be expected. And right in the area where the roots have to feed, anhydrous will be held in escrow, which means the least amount of copper and zinc will be released.

Furthermore, the higher the concentration of nitrogen, the more humus will be lost in the soil. If you have a soil with a magnesium level above 20%, and you want to raise that elusive 200 bushels of corn, it is going to take 300 pounds of total nitrogen to achieve that goal, based on the formula of a pound and a half per bushel of corn. A total of 5% organic matter will deliver 100 pounds of nitrogen. This computes out a remainder of 200 pounds of nitrogen. Application of exactly the amount of nitrogen the corn crop needs should comply with this rigorous computation, except that enough additional nitrogen to break down residues is still required. The old rule of thumb is that it takes one pound of nitrogen per 100 pounds of residue, and this rule will work very well for corn, wheat, and other row crops. Corn on corn will often mean 2,000 pounds or more of residue,

---

CAUSES OF INCREASED
SOIL ACIDITY (LOWER pH):

- **Development from acid parent materials.**
- **Plant removal of basic cations such as calcium and magnesium.**
- **Leaching of basic cations by rainfall.**
- **Nitrogen fixation by bacteria on legume roots.**
- **Bacterial conversion of nitrogen compounds in the soil, including some nitrogen fertilizers.**

---

therefore 20 pounds of nitrogen will be required for its breakdown in addition to the 200 pounds mandated by the commercial crop. Add all these figures together and the summation says 220 pounds. But it is not possible to put on 220 pounds of nitrogen with anhydrous ammonia and get the computed response. In fact, 20% more is now required. That is just a rule you have to know.

You may think this rule is way out of line, but based on the university experimental plots in DeKalb County, Illinois back in the 1980s, that is what farmers were told, namely that it takes 240 pounds of nitrogen to grow not 200 bushels of corn per acre, but 175 bushels. The reason it takes so much nitrogen is that those DeKalb County soils had 40%+ magnesium and 45% calcium on its soil colloids.

Now, if your calcium is 85 or 90% base saturation, and your magnesium is 7%, it is tempting to say that since magnesium is 7%, I won't need that pound and half of nitrogen. Magnesium still has the effect on the soil so that air and water space is not right. The magnesium may be tied up in terms of availability to the plant, but it still has an effect on the physical structure of the soil. At 85 or 90% between calcium and magnesium, there is too much effect from the magnesium, meaning you still have to use that pound and half of nitrogen. As a result, we get an over-concentration. Every pound of nitrogen used over what is needed to supply the crop and break down the residues gives false stimulation to the microbial populations. It is a lot like pushing down on the accelerator and giving your car more gas to take off and go faster.

This added source of energy on the protein side of the equation turns microbes into feeders rather than fixers. As long as the microbial workers have residues in the soil that require digestion, the residues remain their food source. When they run out of crop residues, they don't just fall over and say, "Well, too bad, we don't have any more to eat." Quite the contrary, they look for another alternative food source. The next available source of food is seated in the humus content of the soil. But the microbes will not turn to humus as long as crop residues remain on-scene. When crop residues are used up, they turn to the humus and start to break it down as a food source. Humus is thus incorporated in their bodies. Extra nitrogen causes this sequence to unfold and mask the effect of nitrogen. Plenty of nitrogen with a yellow color suggests that there is not quite enough sulfur, boron, or phosphate. When humus starts to break down, microbes start dying. Plants in turn start to pick up a portion of all the other elements that are released out of the humus. A lot of the time, nitrogen gets the credit. But this isn't nitrogen alone. It is the products microbes are breaking down out of the humus.

This is how many farmers mask their trace element deficiencies. Unfortunately, this mask can be worn only as long as there is a humus supply. The lower the humus gets, the shorter the time for this crutch's survival. That is why farmers with high organic matter have the buffering capacity we are talking about. They can have a micronutrient deficiency and get by with it, whereas the grower with a lower humus content is sandbagged.

These several observations unveil the big dangers associated with nitrogen overuse. Anhydrous in the strip suggests 20% more nitrogen, but the effects of the microbial breakdown of humus are enhanced dangerously. Any one of the synthetic nitrogen sources can be dangerous if overused.

Nitrogen drives out calcium. When the soil is open and nitrites leach out and go with the water, it is never a solo journey. It always takes along a passenger. If there is a cache of sodium, nitrogen can take sodium. Otherwise it takes calcium. Nitrogen never takes out magnesium, but as nitrogen leaches downward, the passenger status of calcium is assured. If calcium levels are excessive, this may be a solution of sorts. A corollary follows. For every percent calcium taken out by nitrogen, magnesium goes up 1%. Removal of

10% calcium by a nitrogen over-supply will increase the magnesium level by 10%. This is one reason nitrogen has a reputation for tightening soils.

In the area where I live, some of the soils are light sands. Many farmers still use anhydrous. Anhydrous was introduced in the southeast Missouri area by 1955. By 1965 farmers had quit using it on their heavy black soil. Farmers concluded that anhydrous use made the soils harder.

Some few farmers may question this statement. After all, research has determined that using anhydrous does not cause soil to be harder. This intelligence has been printed in almost all farm publications. It is nevertheless my observation that any form of nitrogen—when it drives out the calcium—contributes to making soil harder simply because it brings the magnesium level up.

Let us now consider the pH factor. Recall that pound for pound, magnesium influences pH more than calcium. Thus removal of calcium from the soil—with magnesium taking its place—will actually cause the pH to reflect less of a decrease than the actual amount of calcium removed. This means that the use of pH to calculate whether or not to lime should be questioned. If you lime back to the same pH you had before, this must be backgrounded by the fact that you no longer have the same soil you had before overusing nitrogen. What you actually have is a soil that is higher in magnesium and lower in calcium. It will be tighter than it was.

That is the situation with any corn farmer who limes according to pH. Over the years, soils worsen if pH is the sole criterion, and the ability to produce goes down.

In the panhandle of Texas, they use tremendous amounts of nitrogen on their grain sorghum and corn. pH is still high, but our tests often suggest a ton and a half or two tons of lime. The university says, "You don't need any calcium, you don't need any lime, because your pH is fine." And still those soils will not have enough calcium to support a good crop. The farmer who will pay attention to this advice and put on the needed calcium will actually get his yields back up to where they used to be. But growers who believe that pH is the only worthwhile index will continue to experience faltering yields and higher fertilizer requirements. Nitrogen, in fact, is driving out their calcium.

If you use 100 pounds of nitrogen from ammonium sulfate and 100 pounds of nitrogen from ammonium nitrate (or a similar source), the ammonium sulfate will take out the same number of pounds of calcium as the 34-0-0 or as urea or as 32% or any other nitrogen form. The only thing that the ammonium sulfate does—if the calcium is above 60% base saturation—is take out magnesium. When it takes out magnesium, it lowers pH. But when schoolmen see the pH go down, they discern no association with magnesium because the universities believe it is impossible to remove the magnesium from the soil. Based on this fiction, they count every bit of that as calcium. They rely on pH, and fail to measure what is leaving. They translate this into loss of calcium, which is not the fact. Use of ammonium sulfate means taking out magnesium at the same time, and better control. The farmer who uses ammonium sulfate—without measuring calcium and magnesium—when he limes to adjust pH is taking magnesium out with the calcium. Yet, if he has excess magnesium, he is better off than the fellow who uses straight nitrogen and no sulfur. Sulfur does not have to come from ammonium sulfate. Any sulfur source has a measure of merit. Using nitrogen and sulfur has far greater effect on keeping the soil where it used to be than using nitrogen by itself. This is true because sulfur takes out magnesium. If you have less than 60% calcium and use ammonium sulfate, the procedure is not going to take the magnesium out, and so you are in the same position as the grower who is using commercial nitrogen. Sulfur accumulates in the soil, builds up, and will be leached out, trucking along all kinds of things, but it won't take the magnesium because

pH and Availability

The labeling of calcium as fertilizer element of first importance was delayed because scientists, like other boys, enjoyed playing with their toys. The advent of electrical instruments for measuring the hydrogen ion concentration gave tools and slight provocations and causal significance widely ascribed to them, when as a matter of fact the degree of acidity like temperature is a condition and not a cause of many soil chemical reactions. Because this blind alley of soil acidity was accepted as a thoroughfare so long and because no simple instrument for measuring calcium ionization was available, it has taken extensive plant studies to demonstrate the hidden calcium hungers in plants responsible in turn for hidden but more extensive hungers in animals. Fortunately, a truce has recently been declared in the fight on soil acidity. What was once considered a malady is now considered a beneficial condition of the soil. Instead of a bane, soil acidity is a blessing in that many plant nutrients applied to such soil are made more serviceable by its presence, and soil acidity is an index of how seriously our attention must go to the declining soil fertility.

Now we face new concepts of the mechanisms of plant nutrition. By means of studies using only the colloidal, or finer, clay fraction of the soil, it was learned that this soil portion is really an acid. It is also highly buffered or takes on hydrogen, calcium, magnesium, and any other cations in relatively large quantities to put them out of solution, and out of extensive ionic activities. It demonstrated that because of its insolubility, it can hide away many plant nutrients so that pure water will not remove them, yet salt solutions will exchange with them. This absorption and exchange activity of clay is the basic principle that serves in plant nutrition. This concept comes as a by-product of the studies of calcium in relation to soil acidity.

—William A. Albrecht
The Albrecht Papers, Volume I, 1975

sulfur can't take magnesium until calcium is at least 60% saturated on the soil colloid. It will take out calcium. It will take out potassium. It will take out sodium or any one of the other cations, but it won't take out the magnesium.

If you take your calcium from 82% down to 70% base saturation, then you are going to raise an 8% magnesium level by that many percentage points (12). If you use enough sulfur to control the magnesium at the same time, then you are not going to get into that same problem.

It is fact that free ammonia is toxic to living organisms. When you knife anhydrous ammonia into the soil, you are injecting free ammonia, and you are going to burn out some of the organisms. If anhydrous is applied in only a six-inch band, the assumption is that it can populate back. This is true. Just the same, the more you spread free ammonia, the harder it is on microbes. Also, the reaction of ammonia with soil moisture produces ammonium hydroxide, which raises pH. A raised pH has an effect on microbes. The most beneficial soil fungi, for instance, do not like a high pH. In fact, many can't survive in such an environment, and so they die. Later, the conversion of ammonia to nitrate is accompanied by a production of acid, which lowers pH. Now bacteria have problems.

Anhydrous ammonia is NH_3. The ammonia that attaches to the soil colloid is NH_4. NH_3 is ammonia gas. NH_4 is ammonia that is already stabilized. When urea goes from urea to ammonia, it goes from urea to NH_3 ammonia gas and then to nitrite and then to nitrate. This becomes the observed result because microbes convert it into a gas, after which it goes from nitrite to nitrate. Urea will hold, of course, if there is at least a half inch of water—rain or irrigation. Otherwise, the material must be applied and incorporated in the soil.

Nitrate is an anion, NO_3, with a negative charge. Chloride has a negative charge. Sulfate, SO_4, has a double negative charge. That means it is stronger and more difficult to

150   *Hands-On Agronomy*

dislodge from the soil. Chloride leaves the soil easily. Nitrate also makes an easy exit. Sulfate stays around longer. That is good because we want it to stay put.

Sulfates move with soil water, but not as freely as nitrogen. If the sulfate didn't move out, it would never carry out the magnesium. Only the materials that move through are going to carry out those things we have in excess. That is why nitrogen can carry out calcium and why sulfur can carry out calcium, magnesium, potassium, or sodium—because they do move with the soil water. As a result, it is not good thinking to build up huge stores of these nutrients because they represent money thrown away.

The operating principle is to open the soil so that water can move through, else those things are never going to leave. When sulfur combines with magnesium, it forms epsom salts, and these salts are easily leached away in water.

Where does soil water go? Somewhere downstream you are going to get another deposit of epsom salt, or magnesium sulfate.

We'll get back to sulfate. But next to be considered is phosphate, P_2O_5, the subject of the next section.

Phos-pho-rus / 'fäs-f(e-)res / *n, often attrib* [NL, fr. Gk *phosphoros* light-bearing] **1** a solid nonmetallic element of the nitrogen family existing in at least two allotropic forms, one yellow (poisonous, inflammable, and luminous), the other red (less poisonous, and less inflammable) **2** chemical symbol:

3 release in soils depends on decomposition of organic compounds **4** contained in all tissues with concentrations most pronounced in young plants (seeds and flowers) **5** superphosphate, triple-superphosphate, rock phosphate, and organic fraction phosphates, proteins, phospholipids, etc. are labile—undergo chemical and physical change while not necessarily available **6** essential for building sound bones and teeth, and for assimilation of carbohydrates and fats **7** necessary for enzyme activation

7

The Reluctant Nutrient

THERE IS A PREGNANT PARAGRAPH in *An Acres U.S.A. Primer* that merits reproduction here, and an instant replay at least once a year. It says . . .

"When farmers talk about phosphorus, they usually talk about phosphorus deficiency. Indeed, phosphorus deficiency in humid soils has become legend. It is an anion, but it is united rapidly with divalent calcium, a cation, to become insoluble, and therein lies the whiff and whoof of phosphorus fertilization. The weak carbonic acid from a plant root can't seem to activate bound up phosphorus. Apatite is quite insoluble. Rock phosphate in any form becomes available reluctantly, and this is one of the reasons why soils should be at least slightly acid. But the fact is science still does not have a clear picture of what happens with phosphorus in the soil."

Phosphate has a triple negative charge, and that charge makes phosphate strong enough to stay put. It can attract itself to calcium—which has a positive charge—for which reason the two of them can be held in the soil. Phosphate has to be placed where it is needed. If placement is restricted to the top quarter-inch of soil, it will not feed the plant once the soil dries out.

Most plants contain .2 to .4% phosphorus. Even though it is considered a major nutrient along with nitrogen and potassium, the amount is small. Out of every applied pound, there is only .2 or .4 pound—or not even a half pound—of phosphorus in 100 pounds of plant material. Phosphorus is the workhorse of plant nutrition because it has to be there for cell division and growth, for photosynthesis and for energy transfer from ADP to ATP. It is absorbed into the plant as orthophosphate ions. In other words, H_2PO_4, with a single negative charge, or HPO_4, with a double negative charge. This means phosphorus has to be combined with hydrogen in order to get it into the plant, meaning enough hydrogen has to be on hand for phosphate to make the combinations necessary to get into the plant. The phosphorus and the hydrogen do not do it all by themselves. As my friend, Zoell Colburn, used to say when he taught agronomy courses, "The soil is the plant's stomach." That stomach, for eight tons of alfalfa, has to process 450 pounds of nitrogen as well as 95 pounds of phosphate. A 150 bushel corn harvest takes 85 pounds of phosphate. Soybeans require 55 pounds in terms of a 50 bushel crop. Wheat, at 60 bushels, takes up 55 pounds of phosphate.

Spring or fall application is governed by the crop you are going to grow. If the crop is winter wheat, then conditions change versus growing a spring crop, especially corn. If you are going to grow soybeans, then a different situation comes to the fore. If in doubt, and it is a crop to be planted in the spring, the suggestion is to apply phosphate in the spring.

It can be applied the day of planting, and if it is the right forms of phosphate, it will be picked up.

Fall applications are special cases as far as I am concerned —special cases having to do with the type of crop or type of phosphorus to be used. Type in turn differentiates between plant feeders and soil feeders. A plant feeder type of phosphorus must be applied close to planting time. Plant feeder phosphates are usually the cheapest; 0-46-0 triple superphosphate is a plant feeder. You can apply 500 pounds, or 1,000 pounds, and make a fall application. Next spring you won't have any more phosphate than you had the spring before. The product is a plant feeder, not a soil feeder. Within one to two months after it is applied, it reverts back to a form that the plant cannot pick up unless it is a legume.

Phosphate value depends on availability. The farm publications talk about phosphate tie up. They are talking about plant feeders. The other phosphate product that used to be talked about in the same category is superphosphate, 0-20-0. It is not used too much in production agriculture these days. Phosphates won't leach out of the soil. They only get tied up or else they stay put in an available form. The condition of the soil will help determine how available the phosphate will remain.

A reserve of phosphorus in the soil is always needed. In fact, it is always better to have more than the crop requires. When test figures reveal a phosphate deficiency at least the minimum desired value for crops must be provided. You can get by with a little less on soybeans, but if you are raising 150 bushels of corn or more, you can't get by on the minimum, shown as desired value on the test. You will actually limit your yield especially in years when you have cool, wet seasons.

Because phosphate is not easily moved, the only way to lose it is via wind or water erosion. If you need it on top, then put it on top. If you need it down under, then try to put it on so that you can get it worked and mixed into the top six or seven inches of soil. I am not suggesting that you work it down 12 inches. Work it in as deep as the fencepost rots because that is how deep the microbes are going to work on it and keep it available. If you put it down deeper, chemical reactions in the soil take place, none of them of necessary benefit to the crop.

Some crops need more just to make the kind of yields I am talking about. It used to be that 100 bushels of corn was considered a lot. For some areas it still is, but not in southeast Missouri or the cornbelt. On the other hand, if you have a soil with excellent phosphate readings, it is human nature to think you don't have to worry about phosphate "this year." That always depends. If you start working the field wet so that some mud holes survive, and you run through those, then it turns cool three or four days, you are going to see a phosphate deficiency in those areas. Whenever that soil gets packed and the roots can't move out, the plant will not get the phosphate unless you put it right there on the spot. If you already know that you have to plant corn and work that soil wet or else you will never get over all your acreage, you might just as well say, "When I do that I need some starter phosphorus!"

Down in my area, every so often we have such cool, wet weather. The farmers who put on no phosphate, or actually put too little on their corn, show a phosphate deficiency to the point that the corn turns brown. Many people in the area will say that you don't need that much phosphate, just a little triple-super for a starter. I have a reputation in the area for saying that farmers need more phosphorus than they really need! That is what the people who don't use me say about my recommendations. There are some labs that tell these same farmers they don't need any phosphate at all.

Well, a few years ago, a fertilizer dealer called me and said, "Neal, every farm you don't work with, the corn is turning brown." When that shows up in corn, you have already missed your top yield. When that purple color comes into the leaf of that corn, you have missed 15 bushels of corn. You don't ever want to get to that spot. As a consequence, I always look to see that there is some reserve phosphate. When you are growing 150 bushels of corn, I am going to tell you that on the type test we use, 240 pounds of phosphate is not enough. If you are above 300, then if you don't work it wet that is enough. If you tell me you are going to work it wet, you need to put a starter in there anyway,—not very much, but a little bit! Phosphate availability in the soil is affected by the amount and type of clay. Availability is also affected by application time and method. If you put it on top, it is going to stay there and it is not going to be available except when there is moisture at the top.

Phosphate availability is also increased or decreased with aeration, compaction and moisture. If you have plenty of moisture, the roots will feed right at the top and go on down as far as there is moisture. When you have compaction, the root can't move out. Roots have to move and come in contact with phosphate. If you don't have adequate aeration, microbes are not going to be able to do their work and you are not going to get the proper conversion and get the hydrogen added to the phosphorus in order to get it into a form the plant can use. Availability is also affected by the level of phosphate and other nutrients. If I have a soil that is borderline in phosphorus and has high zinc, the zinc can actually cause a problem—and you don't get enough phosphates. Actually, it works both ways.

I once worked with an Illinois farmer. He had one field with good soil. He raised good crops, but never made as much yield as he expected there. When he put this field in corn, yield was always short compared to his other fields. Soil samples were taken and sent to the lab, and the audit agreed that this farm had a tremendous soil. His calcium was right and his magnesium was right. All the micronutrients were there. Then I got to the last thing on the list—

zinc—6 ppm zinc being enough; 50 ppm zinc reportedly can kill a 50 year old grapefruit tree. He had 275 ppm zinc in that field. He had five times more than enough to kill an old tree, and he was still raising corn. That field was located near a glass factory. Smoke coming out of the stack was showering zinc on his field. The only thing I could tell that farmer to do was to put on some extra phosphorus. He applied extra phosphorus that year. Later I learned after harvest that this field—for the first time ever—was just as good as his other fields in terms of yield. The zinc was so high it was keeping the phosphorus from doing a good job.

Usually, soil out of kilter with high zinc will not produce corn. But balance in the top six inches—other than high zinc—will make it possible for the plant to tolerate that high zinc level. You can have an excellent phosphate level and have zinc levels so high that the phosphorus is not getting into the plant properly. When the weather gets cool, the plant can't pick phosphate up very well. When the soil temperature gets cool, the ADP conversion to ATP is slowed down or stopped.

Finally, phosphate availability is affected by soil pH. With a pH of 6.5, phosphate availability is generally going to be as good as it can be. The other thing that affects it is calcium availability. Most phosphate contained in crop plants is in the fruit or the seed. In a 180-bushel corn crop there are 78 pounds of phosphorus in the grain and 30 pounds in the stalks. In 60 bushels of soybeans there are 48 pounds of phosphorus in the grain and 16 pounds in the stalks. Every time you harvest a 180-bushel corn crop, you are taking off roughly 78 pounds of phosphorus. In and around Charleston, Missouri, our corn yields run 170 to 175 bushels per acre. The old rule of thumb for our corn soils calls for maintenance of phosphorus at 70 pounds per acre. If we don't put on a maintenance level of 70 pounds on our corn crop, we can't stay where we are. If we double crop soybeans and wheat, we will lose ground on 70 pounds of phosphate. If we have 500 pounds in the soil and we are going to take 70 out, then we are not in too bad a shape. If we have 300 pounds in the soil and take 70 out, that puts us down to 230, and there is not a soil I know of that is not going to go backwards on such a low phosphate level. Plants need phosphorus for photosynthesis, for respiration, for energy storage and transfer, and for cell division.

A case report now comes to mind. A research farm received 40 pounds of P_2O_5 per acre, and came out with two bushels less than where no such fertilizer had been applied. The second four years, he had 19 bushels more yield. The third four-year period he had 28 bushels per acre more yield. By the fourth four years, he had 43 bushels per acre more yield. How can you put on 40 pounds per year when I am telling you to put on 70 pounds? It depends on the crop to be produced. If you are talking about wheat or soybeans you can do that. You shouldn't do it, but you can. Eventually you will build up a phosphorus level. I tell each farmer to start watching numbers. If he is going backwards, he is not using enough fertilizer, or he is using the wrong kind.

Now, what materials can one use to get phosphate? There are super-phosphoric acid and phosphoric acid for liquid. Basically, I talk about concentrated superphosphate, or triple-superphosphate, or 0-46-0. That is the common, lowest, cheapest priced phosphorus material on the market. Under that is diammonium phosphate, 18-46-0, monoammonium phosphate which is 11-48-0 or 11-52-0, normal superphosphate which is 0-20-0, basic slag which has 6% phosphate in it as P_2O_5, and then rock phosphate which has roughly 35 total pounds P_2O_5. The rock phosphate is not broken down. It is sometimes called colloidal phosphate or soft rock phosphate. If you take concentrated superphosphate (0-46-0), and diammonium phosphate (18-46-0), and superphosphate (0-20-0), and run the test I use to show phosphate availability, this would be true. You don't have to use the 0-20-0. You could run it between the other two. You can run the test in

The Corrective Treatment

The most ideal situation, therefore, is for the farmer to work into his soil the total amount of rock phosphate recommended in his soil report, and then apply from 20 to 80 pounds per acre (according to his phosphorus values) of a water-soluble P_2O_5 fertilizer in the first season, and to continue applying from 10 to 40 pounds per acre of water soluble P_2O_5 yearly thereafter until the analysis of the soil shows that he has attained the desired level of active phosphorus in the soil. At this point he may live upon the interest only, not touching the principal itself.

On the other hand, there are some farmers who have the honest conviction that rock phosphate is not effective as a phosphorus supplement to soil. They insist on using only the water-soluble forms of phosphorus fertilizers available on the market.

Many do not realize that the phosphorus thus supplied them comes from rock phosphate in the first instance. For example, by treating 1,400 pounds of a 33% rock phosphate material with 1,200 pounds of sulfuric acid, a 20% superphosphate fertilizer is produced in which the tricalcium phosphate form of phosphorus in the rock phosphate is converted to the water-soluble monocalcium phosphate form. Such chemical reaction causes 20% superphosphate to be represented by approximately 45% of monocalcium phosphate and 55% of calcium sulfate (gypsum).

Thus, in 100 pounds of the usual 20% superphosphate (0-20-0) fertilizer, two separate materials are provided in the one package, representing approximately 45 pounds of water-soluble monocalcium phosphate, which is desired and approximately 55 pounds of calcium sulfate which may or may not be desired. In 100 pounds of the concentrated triple superphosphate (0-45-0) the acid treatment is made with phosphoric acid. This eliminates the calcium sulfate from the fertilizer material. Ammonium phosphate such as 8-32-0, 11-48-0, etc., involves the use of concentrated phosphoric acid in its processing.

However, the fact that such unstable monocalcium phosphate is subject to natural reversion to the stable tricalcium phosphate form must be given practical concern. This rate of reversion to the stable form differs greatly in soils, and is usually subject to the amount of organic matter, the pH, and the free calcium in the soil.

—*Rudolf Ozolins*
private papers, *Acres U.S.A.* collection

any kind of combination. The Tennessee Valley Authority, back in the 1950s, published a study that is of maximum interest. The fertilizer people have access to it as much as I do. Most people simply do not pay attention to the research. As a matter of fact, I had a fellow who spoke at one of my seminars in St. Louis on corn production, namely 200-bushel corn production. He was a researcher for one of the commercial fertilizer companies. He was from Germany, where he earned his doctorate. I had him address our group because he understood base saturation and exchange capacity. He made the comment at a meeting I attended that if you balance out your soils by using the proper amounts of all the nutrients and get your base saturation percentage right, it will take less fertilizer to do the same job and you can raise much higher yields. At lunch one of the farmers said, "You are researching all this, but I never hear any of this from your company." He said, "You know, it is an amazing thing to me. They pay us this money to do all this research and the marketing arm never pays any attention to any of the research that we are doing. The people in marketing, even though it is written up and printed and shown, never say anything about this because the executives are too busy avoiding a loss to be concerned about helping the farmer. I don't mean they are trying to make a profit, I mean they are too busy avoiding a loss. In the fertilizer industry today it is a matter that the prices are such that they are just trying to stay where they are and keep from losing money."

Facts about fertility are not highly rated in importance for most fertilizer companies. If you attend a two-day fertilizer seminar, you will hear maybe two lectures on fertility. They will have one day on getting new accounts, holding and keeping the accounts you have, and keeping up with the accounting.

Anyway, TVA did this study. They ran a soil test—and this is something you need to do if you are going to do a study. You take triple-super (0-46-0) and 18-46-0 and you go out in a field and take one part of that field and run a soil test. You don't put on any phosphate. This enables you to see where your phosphate levels are. Then, whatever source of phosphate you normally want to use—this is talking about a fall application—put that source of phosphorus on the other half of the field. Try to get a field that is relatively even in terms of phosphate availability. If you use 18-46-0 and you put on 70 pounds of phosphate in the fall, and you come back next spring and run a test on the side that didn't get any phosphate and on the side that did, you will have right at 70 pounds more phosphorus available on the test we use for that crop than on the side where you didn't put any. If you use 0-46-0 and you put on 250 pounds of phosphate and you come back in the spring, the side that didn't get anything will have just as much phosphorus available for the plant as the side that got the 250 pounds or the 500 pounds or whatever it was, because 0-46-0 (superphosphate) ties up in the soil within one to two months after it is applied. That is what TVA studies revealed.

They determined this by taking those materials and treating them with a radioactive substance before application was made. Tissue analysis measured the uptake of phosphorus. Because it was tagged with a radioactive substance, they could measure how much of the phosphorus came from the commercial source and how much of the phosphorus came from the soil. With 0-46-0, in a year that had excellent growing conditions, 20% of the phosphorus came from applied phosphate, and 80% came from the soil. Incidentally, the year with good growing conditions, that phosphate kept on being taken up by the plant for two months. In the years when they had poor growing conditions, the phosphate that was tagged would only be taken up for about four weeks. Fully 90% of the phosphorus in that plant came from a source that was already in the soil and 10% came from the factory fertilizer.

With poor growing conditions, it stayed available for four weeks. Under good growing conditions, it stayed available for eight weeks. At best, only 20% had its tag mark. The rest came from sources already in the soil.

If you are going to apply phosphorus in the fall, use an ammoniated phosphate. Use diammonium phosphate (18-46-0), monoammonium phosphate (11-48-0), or polyphosphates, if using liquids. If you use enough, polyphosphates will build just like the ammoniated phosphate. You have to put on enough polyphosphate to get 70 pounds of phosphorus if you are going to build 70 pounds for that next crop. Normally, by the time you compare diammonium phosphate or monoammonium phosphate with polyphosphate, the liquid is so much more expensive that it is not going to be used to build your phosphate levels.

When a "plant feeder" source is used, the key to increased springtime soil phosphates is residue. Phosphate levels will go up if microbes have enough residues to break down. The increase is from breakdown of the residues, and not from phosphate that is applied. That is why a check is important.

Why does a soil system tie up an 0-46-0, and why doesn't it tie up an 11-48-0? Triple-superphosphate has a pH of 4.4. When you put something that has a pH of 4.4 on a soil that has a pH of 5.5 or 6 or 6.5 or 7 or 7.5, how long do you think it is going to stay in the form it is in? The answer is, "Not very long!" In a year with adverse conditions, it is not going to stay more than a month. In a very good year, it could last as long as two months. When you put on that pH 4.4 material, it will start to combine with calcium because phosphorus loves calcium and is drawn to it the way a southerner is drawn to black-eyed peas. What you wind up with in four to eight weeks is tricalcium phosphate. Tricalcium phosphate is the parent material in hard rock phosphate. To make triple-super, 0-46-0, they take hard rock phosphate and process it with sulfuric acid, the resultant product being styled 0-20-0. To get sulfur and calcium out, and a higher concentration of phosphorus in, they process the parent material with phosphoric acid. This yields a straight phosphate material, but the pH is 4.4. Unless your soil will breakdown and use rock phosphate, or unless the crop you are growing there will breakdown and use rock phosphate, then you are not going to get any more good out of that phosphorus after four to eight weeks. That is bad for wheat, corn, and grass-type crops. It is not so bad for legumes because even the old literature will tell you that when you put on hard rock phosphate, legumes will take the phosphate they need for the first year. So if you have places where you have used triple super phosphate, the legumes can actually start to process some nutrient out and make it available. Once the legume processes it out and gets it in the right form, it is not going to revert back to the unavailable form again. Once the plant picks it up, that will be the first source the next set of plants will tap.

In Florida, I ran some samples on soils that had pHs as low as 5.5. If you are going to get triple super phosphate availability, you are going to get it on 5.5 pH soils. Area farmers grew cabbage, and their customary practice for cabbage was to put on 600 pounds of 0-46-0 per acre per year. The soils where they had grown cabbage 20 years ago had finally come to the point that the superphosphate was breaking down and making the phosphorus more available.

When you put on phosphorus, use an ammoniated source. I grew up on a farm, some of it rented, with 500 to 1,200 acres. When I started to learn about soils from William A. Albrecht, I actually didn't remember whether P stood for phosphorus or potassium.

Farmers order by product. They tend to call up and say, "I want 120-50-90," or whatever, and the fertilizer dealer sends it out. There are still a lot of farmers who do it this way. It is the easy way. Sometimes the fertilizer dealer knows no more about fertilizers, other than costs, pricing and where to get it, than most farmers do. Too many dealers don't generally know how it works in the soil. When you go to the fertilizer dealer, don't say 18-46-0, say diammonium phosphate or ammoniated phosphate.

What he may do—if you don't specify—is take 0-46-0 already on hand and mix it with some urea so that the analysis won't be exactly 18-46-0. All you have to do is have 18% nitrogen in it. So he mixes the urea and the concentrated superphosphate and spreads it on your soil and says, "You've got 150 pounds of 18-46-0," but you don't. That superphosphate still has a pH of 4.4. For diammonium and the monoammonium phosphates, the pHs run in the middle sixes. When you put those phosphate prills down, you are instilling pH 4.4 and it is going to tie up quickly. If you apply 18-46-0, it will stay available because it is already matched into the pH and is not grabbing for calcium to balance itself out.

In my meetings with farmers, I always make the comment that if you put on 150 pounds of 18-46-0, you are applying 69 pounds of available phosphorus for the next crop. When we put that on and do a soil test the next year—if we have grown a 150-bushel corn crop—the phosphate will be back to where we started. So we really have gained nothing. On the other hand, if we put on 250 pounds of 18-46-0, which is 115 pounds of phosphate, rather than 69, when we come back next year and take the same 150 bushels of corn off, instead of being where we were before, we will actually have gone up by 100 pounds of available phosphorus. This represents an increase of 100 pounds when I put on only 115.

I once said I didn't know why this happened. One of the men in the crowd, who used to teach horticulture at Purdue University, sent me a paper by a Dr. Fox from Columbia University, who went around the world studying phosphates. What he found was that when you put phosphorus on a soil, a certain amount is actually absorbed by the soil and then after you saturate the soil with phosphorus, the rest will stay there and be used by the plants. That partially answered it, but could the real answer be that when you put that much on, the microbial population in that soil uses the nitrogen. In effect, you are enabling the microbes to breakdown some extra phosphorus. Otherwise, how are you going to be able to apply 115 pounds and still have 100 pounds left, suggesting that you took out only 15 pounds to grow that 150-bushel corn crop? It will happen year after year after year. A maintenance level in general for diammonium phosphate or monoammonium phosphate is about 70 pounds per acre.

If you are using 30 pounds every year and you already have a good phosphate level, that means you have a good microbial activity or you have a good phosphate release in that soil. If your levels aren't going down, then you don't have to change those 30 pounds. Just monitor it along, but if you see that you are using over 30 pounds and you keep on steadily declining, it's time to do something.

I have a good friend who used to be a consultant in the area of Marion, Ohio. I made a connection with him because that is where a lot of liquid fertilizer materials come from. At a seminar in Texas he came up to me literally with tears in his eyes. He was 64 or 65, and he said, "You are the first man to say what I have understood about soils and used all these years."

He had no love affair with some of the liquids that people used in place of basic fertilizers. He said, "If you have never used them before and you don't know what your soil situation is, you can use them for one year and be pretty safe if you have been putting on fertilizer regularly. If you don't know what your soil situation is and you use them two years in a row, you are pressing it. The fellow with poor soil who doesn't know his soil situation and uses them five years, by the third year will start saying, "Well, the weather is not the same or this condition is not the same." It will generally take six or seven years before they realize what is happening." This is talking about where a product like this is marketed and they tell you that you don't need anything else and you have low fertility levels. If you have medium fertility levels and you start out that way, then it depends on how fast you are taking it out. In theory, you can last for several years. If levels are excellent, nothing would be required for several years longer.

I am not saying that people selling these materials are hurting soils on purpose because they have farms that show their findings, and they deeply believe in their hearts that it works. But do they take a soil test that shows the whole story? A soil test that revealed exchange capacity and base saturation percentages would be more to the point. You can have tremendous levels of phosphate and potash that will stay for years. Yet some will see high levels gone in three years. Some may last five years or longer.

There are farms that I work with right now on which it has been seven, eight or nine years since phosphate or potash have been applied, all without manures or biologicals, and levels are still there. I had a good client up near Gibson, Illinois. He called me during a drought year. He said, "I have rented 160 acres next door to me, $125 an acre. I want you to analyze the soils." His neighbor had been farming it for years and he didn't have any idea what the fertility levels were. I analyzed that soil. It was extremely deficient. In fact there was a 150+ phosphate deficiency. He had 200 to 300 pounds potash deficiency. Percentage wise, the potash was below 2%. His dilemma was self-evident. "I have already rented it," he said, "and next year the owner's son-in-law hopes to farm it. I probably won't get it again. How can I build these levels up without spending a huge amount of money that I am not going to be able to get back?" I asked him to find out if the landlord had ever used a product such as 9-18-9 or 10-20-10. The answer came back: he never had. I told the farmer, "You can grow a fine crop as long as

Hands-On Agronomy

you put either product two inches beside and below the seed, and put on plenty of nitrogen as far as the corn is concerned. He bought the material and he put it on all of his corn. He applied the nitrogen that was required. He made an application on the beans until he got to his last tank. He saw he wasn't going to finish the field. So he stopped and went to the far side of the field to finish up. Therefore he had a little area in the middle of the field that didn't get any treatment. He told me later that this was his check.

My wife comes to many of my meetings and helps with registration and the like. She seldom pays attention to the fine points of fertilization. She lets me handle that and she concentrates on doing all the things a good wife and mother does. We were visiting with this farmer and his wife and in time we went out the back door for something. Here were his soybeans out on the ridge. She looked out at them and said, "Jim, what did you do to those soybeans in the middle? Why are they so yellow?"

Later, Jim said, "Neal, where I came in and applied that small amount of liquid fertilizer like you said, I made 16 bushels more soybeans to the acre over where I didn't." That was a situation where I was trying to get him by for one year.

Now let's conclude on phosphate, specifically rock phosphate. I put rock phosphate into two classifications—hard rock and soft rock. Hard rock is not generally available in the market these days. If you do have access to hard rock phosphate, keep in mind that while it can raise the phosphate level in the soil, the only crop that can easily benefit during the first year is a legume. It takes the second year to release enough for wheat. And it takes a third year to bring the release sequence up to where you want to be. Once pH gets above 6.5, hard rock phosphate gets harder and harder to make available. Microbes and acids in the soil literally face a meltdown-proof stone wall. For this reason and for these several reasons, hard rock phosphate has gotten a bad reputation.

Commercial fertilizer people say to avoid soft rock phosphate because it has so much aluminum. In 1973, when the fuel crisis came along, we also developed a phosphate crisis. Farmers had to find some new answers. One consultant took a sample of soft rock phosphate and sent it in. There was nothing in it that was toxic. Growers started using it by the carload in Iowa, where I originally learned about it. I had some of my clients start using it. Accordingly, several lessons emerged. If we had a slight phosphate deficiency and a corn crop coming up, we could put on 300 pounds of soft rock or colloidal phosphate in the spring and get the phosphate available for the corn. There would be no deficiency that year. The minimum amount indicated is 300 pounds, and that is much like putting on 150 pounds of diammonium phosphate. You just maintain where you are and the next year you will have to do it again. When you put on 250 pounds of diammonium phosphate, which is 115 pounds of phosphorus, you raise your levels by 100 pounds. If you put on 500 pounds of soft rock phosphate, you can also raise those phosphate levels by 100 pounds per acre. The levels will actually go up from one year to the next if you use 500 pounds. If you have 200 pounds of available phosphorus and you put on 500 pounds of soft rock phosphate, next year you will have 300 pounds of available phosphate. If you have a high calcium soil, soft rock has to be ruled out. This is because 500 pounds of soft rock phosphate will also supply 100 pounds of available calcium. So with the soft rock, we put on 100 pounds of available calcium and you increase the phosphate store by 100 pounds per acre. If you already have too much calcium, application of more is not an option. If you need calcium and phosphorus, this is a terrific source. There is a drawback. A mere 500 pounds of that material is not "commercial" as far as many handlers are concerned. They have to

Hands-On Agronomy

Protection by Proteins

Plants also protect themselves by means of proteins. Experimental trials have demonstrated that by increasing those fertility elements in the soil which were serving for increasing proteins in the young plants, there was provided increasing protection against the attack by a fungus, suggesting one connected with the "damping off" disease. In another experiment, more nitrogen and more calcium offered to vegetable plants for higher concentrations of proteins in these food crops, gave more protection against attack on the plants by leaf-eating insects. Here was suggested the possible converse of this demonstration, namely, that the increasing fungus diseases of our crops and the increasing insect attacks on them seem to be premised on deficiencies of protective proteins in the plants, and these in turn on the deficiencies of the fertility in the soil.

Shall we not, then, open our minds to the possibility that the shortages of proteins and shortages of all that is associated with them in their synthesis by microbes, by plants, and by animals, are prohibiting us through a kind of malnutrition from collecting and creating the necessary list of proteins by which our bodies can protect themselves, or build their own immunity?

—*William A. Albrecht*
private papers, *Acres U.S.A.* collection

order it by the carload. The dealers do not want to get stuck with unsalable product. This puts sourcing into the farmer's corner. The product rated 18-46-0 doesn't last as long as the soft rock phosphate. Soft rock has a lot of goodies that breakdown over a longer period of time. I have clients who use soft rock. They simply figure that once they attain the proper level on a good soil, it is going to be five, eight or maybe even ten years before they have to make an application again. Crops need phosphate for rapid seedling development. If you want to get a crop started, you have to have plenty of phosphorus, not only for winter heartiness, but also for disease resistance, efficient water use, early maturity and maximum yields.

You can't skimp on phosphorus. I learned this from a good friend of mine in Virginia who has a master's degree in animal nutrition, but also works with soils. He used the same soil test I do. He said, "We had a new clover that was introduced in Virginia for pasture and livestock. Some farmers loved that clover. Others cursed it because they said it caused terrible bloat in their cattle. I started looking at my client's pastures. Most farmers check all their fields, but if the pastures ever get checked at all, they come last. Anyway, what he found was this, any farmer who had 300+ in phosphates, his cattle didn't bloat on the clover. When there were phosphate deficiencies, they were certain to bloat. With adequate phosphorus in the soil, there was no bloat problem.

What am I talking about when I say 300 pounds? There are at least a half dozen ways to run a phosphate test. There are different ways to report the results. Low numbers on a phosphate test, say, 50 to 70 pounds, is adequate, and 80 pounds mean excellent in terms of the P_1 water-soluble phosphate test. The P_1 or water-soluble phosphate test tells you what you have right now, this minute. It does not measure the amount of phosphorus that is going to be released over an entire growing season. Moreover, this test is

Hands-On Agronomy

Calcium and Phosphorus

Calcium and phosphorus are deposited in the bones and teeth in chemical combination with each other. If one is lacking, there is nothing for the other to combine with, therefore one without the other is of little value. Phosphorus is found in meats, dairy products, foods made from grain, and vegetables. Of the eight major soil minerals, phosphorus is by far the least abundant. A deficiency of calcium, the most abundant mineral element in the animal body, is associated with the lack of phosphorus. The importance of having an abundant supply of these minerals in the soil is at once apparent when we consider that 95% of the inorganic bone material in animals is composed of calcium phosphate. Sea water contains 0.1 ppm, and although much less than its calcium content, it serves a very important function.

—*Charles B. Ahlson*
Health from the Sea & Soil, 1962

not accurate after a 74% calcium tabulation has been reached. Once you get to 74% calcium, phosphate will actually show lower than it is.

The test that I use for phosphate is a water-soluble, acid-soluble test. The reason for the test is to see what the phosphate availability is for the entire growing season. This is a P_2 test. Since it is a water-soluble, acid-soluble phosphate test, it does calculate the acid solubles that are going to be released over a growing season. If pH is above 7.5, then this test is not always accurate either.

Automatically, when you send a soil test to me, I tell the lab that I will pay the extra expense. If it is above 7.5, I want a second phosphate test, namely the Olsen test. Relying on the Olsen test, if your calcium is correct and your other levels are there, 80 pounds per acre is enough. If you have 120 pounds, it is enough no matter what. When I say 300 pounds per acre is the minimum you need, the subject is water-solubles plus acid-solubles. And this is the minimum. I like to see phosphate levels in the 500 to 750 range. At 500 pounds per acre, I say *excellent*. When I see 750 or more, problems are coming down the pike on the other side. When phosphorus gets too high, it starts tying up copper and zinc. Above 1,000 pounds per acre, problems come in platoons. I have seen trees in citrus orchards die because phosphate levels were above 1,000 pounds per acre on the test we use. The conventional wisdom says nobody ever gets there. There are a lot of people who use manures and get there.

The P_1 water-soluble test will drop when the calcium goes over 7.4. It gives a false reading. That is why the Olsen test is used above a pH 7.5. And that is why in my recommendation we tell whether the calcium level is excessive or excellent or good or deficient. I will do the same with the magnesium, potassium, phosphorus, sulfur and the trace minerals. We always hear about getting phosphorus on and keeping it there early, except for corn. With corn we don't

174   *Hands-On Agronomy*

just want it there early. After about 30 days on growing corn there is a good, even uptake of phosphate until almost the 100th day. Corn uses phosphate from start to finish, and it takes more between the 30th or 40th day to about day 100. A phosphate shortage will be revealed by a reddish-purple color. Younger plants tend to exhibit more pronounced signs and symptoms. Most of the time the roots can compensate, still it is possible to have phosphate deficiencies and never see purple in the leaf. Phosphate shortage interferes with pollination and kernel fill. It causes the ears to be small and twisted. The key to getting ear development is phosphorus in seed production. I have clients who show 400 and 500 pounds of phosphorus per acre. Still they will say they need more phosphorus because the last half inch didn't fill out. For the particular analysis we use, a reading of 300 pounds per acre is enough for 150+ bushels of corn.

When you have 400 or 500 pounds of phosphorus, you are well past having enough. When you fail to get fill on the end of the cob, the first order of business is to look for a phosphate deficiency. If phosphate reads 300 plus, the problem may be borate as from boron. The first fellow I ever heard about who used boron on corn was a man up in Illinois. According to the University of Illinois, two pounds of boron will kill corn. This fellow used four pounds of actual boron to the acre, and if he couldn't get it on any other way, he would hire an airplane to fly it on. He said it made him more corn. When I asked exactly what four pounds of boron did for him, I was told, "Well, it makes the cobs longer." It looked like the ears actually got longer because it filled them all the way out to the end and put a kernel on the tip. Consider phosphate first, but do not let the lack of borate fool you into buying more phosphate when enough is already present.

Po-tas-si-um / pe-'tas-ē-em / *n, often attrib* [NL, fr. *potassa* potash, fr. E *potash,* sometimes fr. *kalium*] **1** a silver-white soft light low-melting univalent metallic element of the alkali metal group, abundant in nature esp. combined in minerals (see Mendeleyeff Periodic Table of Elements) **2** chemical symbol:

3 a catalyst and a prime requirement in chlorophyll construction **4** a governor for taking free nutrients from the air—carbon, hydrogen, oxygen **5** needed so plants can make starches, sugars, proteins, vitamins, enzymes or cellulose **6** dangerous to microorganisms when embodied in muriate of potash **7** in animal life, promotes normal growth and muscle function, also a cell regulating element **8** regulates osmotic pressure in cellular tissue and fluids

8

The Free-Lancer in Plants

IT SAYS ON PAGE 97 OF *The Fertilizer Handbook* that potassium will leach in certain soils. Yet ads in agricultural publications tell you to apply potash in the fall so that you don't have to do it next spring. Some will tell you that potash doesn't leach. But when you put potassium on, if you don't have the right conditions in the soil, you are always going to lose it.

The Fertilizer Handbook does state that potassium will leach under certain conditions. "Conditions" here translates into sandy soils.

Considering medium to heavy soils, you can build potassium only when there is enough room in the soil for it to be held on the clay colloid. How do you know there is enough room in the soil? pH is the key. If pH (speaking of water pH) is above 6.5, don't put potassium on your soil in the fall to grow a crop in the spring. As a matter of fact, I tell my clients not to put potassium on in the fall unless they have a severe deficiency, even if they are going to plant winter wheat. Wait until you make your winter application of nitrogen and then apply potassium. One reason we do it that way in southeast Missouri is because we are going to raise a second crop. If you are going to double crop behind your wheat and you put the potassium on in the fall, the wheat will pick up some of it, but by the time you get to the double crop, that potassium is not there and is not available under conditions of pH higher than 6.5.

Fertilizer researchers know that if they pull a soil test in the fall—while all the residues are still on the ground—phosphate and potash will exhibit a tremendous increase between fall and spring, once decomposition takes place. You always see your soils at their worst in the fall. If you want to see your soils at their best, pull the samples after all stover and organic matter have decomposed. May and June are prime periods in this regard.

If you haven't taken a soil test in three or four years, the best time to do it is *now*! If you are going to set up a program and already know the soil audit figures well, then you can make your choice. Do you want to see it at its best so that you know the minimum amount to put on, or do you want to see it at its worst so that you will know what you are going to face in terms of building up percentages? I tell clients to look at soils at their best. In this way it is possible to know exactly what to put on to reach the minimum requirement.

The biggest phosphate and potassium deficiencies will always test out in the fall. A soil sample taken in spring will reveal a better level than in the fall. If you pull a full soil test in the fall and again in the spring and apply no fertilizers in between, phosphate and potash levels will still be better in spring as a consequence of phosphate and potassium release from stalk breakdown. If you put potassium on that

Potassium-Bearing Minerals
as Soil Treatments

The acidity in the soil, created by the plant roots (and by the soil microbes), is nature's chemical reagent for processing the rock and mineral fragments there much as we process rock phosphate with sulfuric acid. This root acid converts their contents of unavailable nutrient elements into forms more readily available for plant and microbial nutrition. While the clay separate of the soil is the intermediary between the roots and the silt-sized mineral fragments; and while it is the clay that carries the stock of nutrients we measure when testing soils for their "available" supplies of these; it is the finely ground mineral and rock particles serving as the reserve fertility from which the clay is restocked. The clay is the means of passing the acid from the roots to the minerals and, in turn, the nutrients in the reverse direction, or from the mineral fragments to the plant roots. The nutrients held on the clay are the "starter" fertilizer for a single crop. It is these reserve minerals—mixed with the clay—as the soil skeleton that are the sustaining fertility for many crops over many years.

. . . there were pronounced differences in the amounts of potassium delivered to the crop by the different minerals applying equal amounts of potassium to the soil. Also it is evident that in many cases these minerals were undergoing transformation as a result of incorporation into the soil, resulting in the additional amounts of potassium going to the crop. It is evident that in this soil with a degree of acidity no more severe than that represented by a pH of 6.6, the reaction rate between this soil growing the crop and the various minerals was rapid enough to provide significant amounts of potassium in the cases of some of the samples used.

—*E.R. Graham & William A. Albrecht*
private papers, *Acres U.S.A.* collection

entire field, take a soil test beforehand, come back next spring and take another soil test, the uninformed guess will be that you applied potassium, so consequently you have more potash. Therefore the potassium is bound to be working. But it isn't true when the pH is above 6.5.

Muriated potash and potassium chloride are the same thing, regardless of whether it is the red 0-0-60 or the white 0-0-62. If pH is 6.5, it is possible to build the potassium level a little. If pH is 6.6, this product won't build the potassium level very much. At pH 6.7, there is not much chance to build the level at all. At pH 6.8, there will be no buildup even though 2,000 pounds are applied to each acre over a five year period. There simply is no place for that potassium to attach to the soil colloid. If you have pH above 6.5, few negative sites remain. Rarely can potassium find the hydrogen site, push it out of the way, and attach itself to the soil colloid. Only rarely can you get a little bit of an increase, generally because something has changed the other cation levels.

On the other hand, at pH 6.8, there are very few sites left. Calcium and magnesium and potassium are always evident in soil water. The textbooks call this the soil solution, but we are really talking about water in the soil, and that water carries various nutrients. Potassium floats along. It finds the hydrogen and pushes it out of the way, taking its place. Hydrogen has a single plus charge. Potassium is stronger. Along comes a calcium ion, and it has double plus charge. It is stronger than the potash. It can actually push the potassium out of the way and take its place on the colloid. At a high pH, few negatives occupied by hydrogen remain, hence potash can't find a parking place. At pH above 6.5, don't spend a lot of money trying to build up potassium levels with salt fertilizers; consider only maintenance if potassium is needed, and you must buy it as commercial fertilizer.

If you have sandy soils, you don't have to spend a lot of money. In general, the potassium levels are going to build anyway. On the average, if we are targeting a 200-bushel corn crop, or 60 bushels of beans, or 80 bushels of wheat, and potassium is needed, the farmer should put on a maintenance level of 90 pounds of potash. Those 90 pounds will take care of the crop for one year. Building the potassium level should be held in escrow until pH is maneuvered below 6.5, or until something is available other than a commercial source.

Compost and manures will not fit this rule. Only so-called commercial materials comply. If you have a pH of 6.8 and start using manures, you can build your potash levels because manures work on a completely different principle. If potassium levels are above 6.5% of base saturation and you have an exchange capacity in the 7, 8 or 9+ range, trouble is waiting in the wings. This means there is no need to throw money away trying to build potassium, without manure, compost, etc.

Two brothers who were clients were having problems with their soils, and they thought the common denominator was potassium. I didn't know they thought it was potassium. They farmed north and east of St. Louis. Without knowledge of the histories of those farms, one of my friends sent in two of their tests along with his. We met to deliver the results. The last thing I considered was potassium. They had something like a 300-pound potassium deficiency. I told them to apply 90 pounds of potash. The one guy looked at me and said, "What do you mean? We have been putting on 500 pounds of 0-0-60 each year. We can't get our potash levels up, and you are telling me to cut back to 150 pounds. There is no way that is going to take care of our corn." I explained how much potassium corn took up, and detailed why pH was too high, and that if he had some other land that had a pH that was below 6.5 the potassium level would build. The problem was not potassium. It was sulfur and boron. They had about three farms and they pulled samples on each field and sent them in. Every place pH was below 6.5, potash levels were building way up.

The average midwestern soil—if you measure every bit of potassium in it—will have 30,000 to 50,000 pounds of potassium in the top seven inches. This potassium will generally be in the wrong form for the plant to use. If the soil can be managed to turn loose this mother lode of nutrients in very small amounts over a period of time, it is possible to go a long time without potassium inputs. We can take off crop after crop without running out of potassium. The key is to get microbial activity going in the soil. That is why the man who uses manures on his soils can actually raise the phosphate and potash levels by more than can be accounted for by the manure content alone.

Earlier, we looked at nitrogen and said that nitrogen ran from 2 to 6% of plant content. Phosphate was a fraction of a percent, 0.4% at most. Potassium was designated at 2 to 10%. This means a lot of material goes into plants as potassium. The intake can be higher than the amount of nitrogen percentage-wise.

Potassium is called a free-lancer in plants because it doesn't actually form any compounds. It helps with photosynthesis and the transport and storage of carbohydrates. That means it helps get reserves into the roots, presides over winter hardiness, and foundation cell development, wall construction, and therefore reduces stalk lodging. In the case of cell development and strong wall construction, we have to look at potassium in relation to sodium. We can actually cause problems in the soil because we don't have enough potassium in relation to sodium.

When you see white, glistening spots in your field, you always want to make sure your soil tests measure the amount of sodium. It is possible to get into trouble by having too much sodium in relation to potassium because of cell wall development. Crops take up large quantities of

K_2O. In an eight-ton alfalfa crop, the nitrogen numbers are 445, potash 440. A 150-bushel corn crop takes 200 pounds, the same as nitrogen. A 50-bushel soybean crop takes 120 pounds; 60 bushels of wheat takes 80 pounds. Again, I am not suggesting that we make that much of an application. The reason we don't have to apply that much is the one that often puts us in a corner with organic producers. Almost any soil has a nutrient content that is unavailable. Microbes and plant root secretions convert these nutrients into available forms as long as the biology and chemistry and physics are in place.

There is a soil audit called a total nutrient test. Usually, we talk about an available nutrient test. This last details what plants can pick up and use immediately. If a farmer is interested in how much potassium there is in every form, the total nutrient test has the answer. In a light, sandy soil with anywhere from five to six feet of sand, we still find 14,000 pounds of potassium in the top seven inches. It is unusual to find more than 1,000 pounds of phosphate, however. Nevertheless, it is not unusual to find 500 pounds. It is possible to do a total analysis and scrutinize what there is to be released. Most of the time it is much more than what you have. I tell clients to run a total analysis only if consumed by curiosity, because it can get expensive. A standard tab for a total analysis is often $100. Once the total analysis has been determined, it becomes a matter of knowing whether it is there to be released. Some understanding of the exchange capacity and how the exchange capacity works is necessary before a determination can be made as to why potassium is needed in large amounts and why it can't be built in the soil and recovered. Here is the dilemma. We put on only 90 pounds, yet an eight-ton alfalfa crop takes out 440 pounds.

Some of the universities have farmers put on as much as 350 or 400 pounds of potash in a given year. Yet the growers who listen to academia are only gaining when the pH is below 6.5 (using a water pH test).

Potassium has important roles in crop production. It is vital to photosynthesis, essential in protein synthesis, and improves water use efficiency. There is a saying that potassium is the poor man's irrigation. It is the key nutrient to improving water use efficiency. It also increases yields, improves crop quality, and reduces disease. Potassium is sourced from solid rock or soil rocks and minerals.

This is a Midwest theory: potassium gets around in water and finally gets trapped between the colloids, and it can't get loose until something is done to change the soil chemistry. In that form, it is unavailable because the soil colloid has trapped the potassium. That is why whenever magnesium gets higher and higher and the soil gets tighter and tighter, potassium availability gets lower and lower. As you bring the magnesium level down and the soil loosens up, you actually turn loose potassium that is trapped between soil particles, but as you bring magnesium down, you make more sites available on the clay for potassium to attach. Potassium moves out into the soil water and then up to the soil colloid. This potassium is available in soil water and in the colloid to feed the plant.

Below pH 6.5, potassium attaches to the soil colloid. A certain amount moves with the water. Factors that affect potassium requirements may not always be identified by soil tests. Soil temperature does affect it, but dry soil means it takes more to do the same job, and the plant has to feed from deeper down. Wet soil, if it is saturated, will annihilate aeration. High cation exchange capacity (CEC) affects the potassium requirements. The higher the CEC, the more potassium is required to get the minimum percentage available. When you have pH 6.5 or better, there will be a greater tie up of potassium. It will be tied up in calcareous soils because it does not have room to attach to the colloid.

Subsoil potassium does have an effect, especially if top-soil is completely dry. Under this condition, moisture in the subsoil will be the only source of potassium mobility because soluble potassium that moves with the water is all a plant can get. In the presence of ammonium nitrogen, there will be a problem with microbial fixation and attachment to the soil colloid. The higher the nitrogen, the more potassium it will take to do the same job.

Crop rotation, high yields, forage use, any of these can have an effect on potassium. But the key to potassium availability is the CEC and pH levels. I used to think a high CEC was between 20 and 30, but when I started working with swamp soils in Arkansas and the Red River Valley soils of North Dakota, I found a high CEC to be 40 to 50. I know farmers who say they farm sand and heavy land, but their "heavy land" is lighter than many sandy soils as far as the exchange capacity is concerned. I also have clients in Iowa who say that they have sandy soils with exchange capacities in the high teens. They are so used to working with heavy black soils that they call upland forest soils sand. The latter really aren't sand at all. For me, anything from CEC 7 up is medium to heavy soil. The point here is that you have to have a pH below 6.5 before potassium will build in soils with a CEC above 7 or so. There are exceptions, especially when manures and composts have been used.

But then, some soils are just naturally high in potassium. This potassium influences pH the way lime does. That is one of the reasons why I say you can't tell by looking at pH whether or not you need lime. In a high potash area, potassium can influence pH more than calcium or magnesium.

Potassium means less dockage for moldy beans. I have in mind an Ohio case in which no potassium was used. A 38-bushel yield was achieved. This translated into 31% mold and a 58 cent dock. So, 120 pounds of potassium for a 47-bushel per acre yield became an official tally, but 12% of the beans were moldy and the dock was 23 cents a bushel.

On soybeans, I first look at the percentage of potassium to tell you whether any more is needed. It takes a lot of potash to grow beans. If you have more than 100 pounds per acre deficiency and you put on 90 pounds per acre, that application will make seven bushels more beans. If there is ever a 125 pound deficiency, in general, the 90 pounds per acre application will make you ten bushels more beans to the acre. If you are above 2% and have less than 100 pound potash deficiency, you don't really have to worry about it if you plan to raise beans that year. You could skip a year. But if you get above 100 pounds deficiency, it will make a difference.

The most common fertilizer source for potassium is muriate of potash or potassium chloride, and it is the cheapest of all sources. Potassium sulfate is 50% potassium and 18% sulfur. Sul-Po-Mag or K-Mag are 22% potassium, 11% magnesium and 22% sulfur. Sul-Po-Mag is effective when all three are needed. Potassium nitrate is 44% potash and 13% nitrogen. Many farmers want to know about using potassium chloride versus potassium sulfate. I don't have much to back up the idea that potassium chloride hurts the soil. I do have one comment that makes me cautious. I know that on soybeans and cotton, high rates of potassium chloride, 0-0-60 or 0-0-62, can kill the germinating seed. If it is possible to get a level that is high enough to kill germinating seeds, then what does it do to the microbial activity in that soil? It is bound to affect it.

The potassium side won't burn anything. You will never kill a germinating seed with potassium sulfate. I know a farmer in southeast Missouri—a fertilizer dealer—who has studied the potassium chloride versus potassium sulfate issue for years. Several years ago, on his entire 3,000 acres, he used potassium sulfate. After two years, he said he couldn't really tell the difference where one was used versus the other. If you are raising soybeans and you have a 100 pound deficiency, and you don't want to use 0-0-60 and

Hands-On Agronomy

wonder about whether potassium makes much difference or not, then at least try some potassium sulfate. Use 200 pounds or so of potassium sulfate versus 150 pounds of potassium chloride to get basically the same analysis. That is going to be 90 pounds from the KCL and 100 pounds from the K_2SO_4. K_2SO_4 is potassium sulfate. If the farmer says this is too expensive then I tell him that he has three choices to make. If he'll put on 90 pounds of potash even as 0-0-60, he is going to make another seven to ten bushels of beans. If he skips the potassium, it will mean losing that yield. On the other hand, if he believes what I'm saying, he could use the more expensive 0-0-50 and make enough extra soybeans to more than pay the difference.

Potassium reduces sorghum lodging and harvest stress. Experiments on sorghum have proved that without application or a proper level of potassium, 88% of the plants lodge for a 95-bushel yield. Application of 40 pounds of potassium result in a 105-bushel yield and 71% lodging. With 80 pounds, there is 45% lodging, and with 160 pounds there is 16% lodging, all according to experiments. It is not necessary to go that high in order to get some good effects. More important, you can put on the whole 320 pounds, and if you have a manganese or copper deficiency, you will still get lodging.

Potassium is the first key, but the crop also has to have enough copper and manganese. Also, mineral interrelationships can underwrite problems because of the complex ways nutrients work in a soil system.

There are interrelationships between all the different elements in the soil, as illustrated on the following page. Follow each line to see the interrelationship. Look at sodium and potassium. The only line that goes to sodium is potassium. It doesn't go to any other mineral. The only relationship to be concerned about in terms of sodium is the sodium-potassium relationship. When the potassium and sodium base saturation percentages total above 10%, the plant

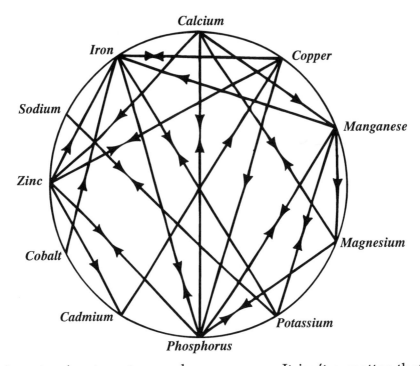

Calcium

Iron

Copper

Sodium

Manganese

Zinc

Cobalt

Magnesium

Cadmium

Potassium

Phosphorus

is not going to get enough manganese. It isn't a matter that the manganese is tied up. You can have excellent manganese levels. It is simply a matter of 10% saturation of potassium and sodium squeezing out manganese uptake from the roots. If you have 6 or 7% potassium, at that point you must become concerned about the potassium-sodium line. When you put on enough so that the combination totals above 10%, at that point the manganese stops getting in. Manganese, of course, is essential to grain formation. Two types of crops that exhibit a terrific response to manganese are legumes and small grains. If you are in wheat production or growing soybeans, you can affect either one faster with manganese than on corn. If manganese is missing, corn yield will suffer, albeit not as much as soybeans, dry beans and wheat.

There is another relationship between potassium and sodium that those white spots in a field put into focus. Any

Hands-On Agronomy

time you have sodium in a field and the percentage saturation of sodium is higher than the percentage saturation of
potassium, you are already in trouble. When sodium exceeds potassium in the soil, the plant will take the sodium
instead of the potassium. A plant cannot tell the difference.
As long as the plant is getting potassium, it incorporates
potassium into the cell wall. The day the percentage of sodium exceeds the percentage of potassium, potassium won't
get in and sodium is incorporated into the cell walls instead. As long as it stays nice and cool, everything works.
So in parts of southern California, they hardly ever see this
problem. When it gets hot and humid though, the sodium
will expand in the cell walls, and when the sodium expands
it starts to break the walls of the cells. This slowly kills the
plant. This phenomenon shows up easily in peas and beans.
It sets the stage for a problem that looks like nematodes, but
isn't. The lighter the soil, the worse the problem.

Certain university researchers determined that if you had
nematodes and you put on potassium, you could eliminate
the nematode problem in your soil. I have clients who have
problems with nematodes and believe me they put on the
potassium. Where we have nematodes, we never eliminate
nematode by putting on potassium. We can make the plant
stand it a little better and do a little better, but the nematode
stays on. You have to use other materials for nematode control. Where we have sodium that is higher than potassium,
it looks like a nematode problem—but you may not have
the nematode problem there. By building the potassium
level higher than sodium, the problem disappears.

What does it look like when sodium is giving you a problem? Let's take a typical scenario. Say you have base saturations 33.07% calcium, 40.38% magnesium, 1.51% potassium,
and 1.82% sodium. If that sodium was merely 1.52% we'd
already have a problem. All we have to do is put on 90
pounds of potash, and we'll solve that problem, meaning
the potassium-sodium problem. We have to do a whole

bunch of other things to solve the soil problem. Any time the magnesium is higher than the calcium you can't raise a crop. Even Iowa and Wisconsin researchers—who say magnesium is not a problem in their soils—actually admit that when magnesium is higher than calcium, nothing grows.

In any case, any time you see sodium higher than potassium, you're going to have a problem. The sodium will be causing a problem with cell wall expansion. Apply enough potassium to raise the level above sodium, and the problem melts away. Again, it's a matter of following through on the formulas.

Any time the base saturation of potassium gets above 7.5%, weed pressures increase. Where pasture grass grows versus where weeds take over, especially sticker weed (red root pigweed with stickers), or where stinging nettle thrive, potassium generally will test extremely high. If you're interested in how nutrients govern the parameters of weed control or proliferation, read *Weeds, Control Without Poisons*, by Charles Walters.

One fellow told me that if you want to find out what a soil program is like, taste the clover and the legumes that cows have to eat. He says, if you get a bitter taste then you know you're not doing the right thing. If it's sweet then you know that's how the cow is going to taste it, too. That also applies to vegetable gardens. A lot of organic gardeners believe that you can't overdo manure. I am an organic gardener and I am not making fun of that. At home we don't use anything on our garden that we feel is not 100% natural. To me that's important. You may not feel that it is, but that's a matter of choice. But a lot of organic gardeners say you can't use too much manure. Yes, you can, and the way you can tell is when you start to taste radishes that are bitter or squash that is bitter or cucumbers that are bitter and turnips that have that bitter off taste when you cook them.

The pH points to the real problem. It is getting too low because there is not enough calcium in the soil. The calcium is not controlling the phosphate and the potassium. Timely application of high calcium lime will take care of the problem. Bitterness in the plant means phosphorous and potassium are getting unusually high. I have known people who have lived for years out of their garden only to learn that their plot needs lime. They will tell you that after two or three years they feel a lot better because they are getting some imbalance out of their systems. When potassium and sodium in the bloodstream starts to increase, the doctor will tell us that we have an electrolyte imbalance. But livestock can't tell us that. We can safely extrapolate from plant to animal in this case. When the potassium-sodium level gets higher than the calcium-magnesium level, a cow dies.

We have all heard about the fellow with a small enclosure, about 40 acres, and all of his dairy cows on those acres. He buys his feed. The only green grass his cows get is what grows on those 40 acres where the manure is falling. If that man analyzed that pasture and kept calcium up, what I am about to tell you next would never happen. But because he doesn't keep the calcium up, potassium gets out of control. The potassium levels go up and the cows eat that grass. It is bitter, but it is the only green grass they have. Over a period of time, the potassium levels get too high. A lot of dairymen feed salt. As a consequence the sodium and potassium go up. The day the potassium-sodium level exceeds the calcium-magnesium level, that animal dies.

I have had dairymen tell me that their cows simply started dying, and the veterinarian couldn't find an answer. Unless there is a blood analysis, there will be no answer.

I told this to a Huron, South Dakota group one winter. One of the men came up and said, "I got out of the dairy business. I have had all my row crop soils checked for years, but I have never checked a pasture." About three years earlier, he lost some of his best heifers, then his cows began to die, but no one knew why. This was the first he had ever heard about the calcium and potassium connection. Hogs can die, cows can die, horses can die because of this. We would also die if the sodium and potassium exceeded the calcium and magnesium in our blood.

Take a corn plant. Does anybody know why that leaf looks the way it does?

The leaf illustrated in the picture below represents a potassium deficiency. Remember, the potassium deficiency starts on the side of the leaf and moves in. The leaf dies from the outside in. That represents a potassium deficiency. When you see it, you will know a buildup in those nodes (that black color) is on the way.

A lot of people look at that, but they don't see it. On soybeans, old crinkly leaves and coloration are dominant features, much as with corn. The damage starts at the edges and moves in. When you start to see edges die, start thinking of potassium.

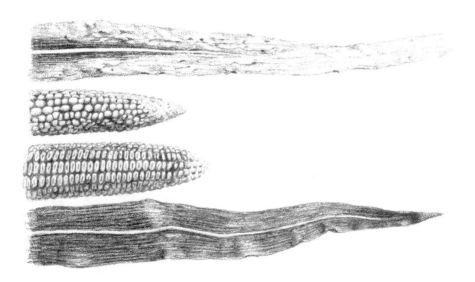

As with nitrogen, potassium deficiency (top leaf) begins in the oldest (lower) leaves first. But unlike nitrogen, which moves downward from the tip in a "yellow V" shape, potassium shortage shows up along the outer edges of the entire leaf.

Hands-On Agronomy

Every field has something limiting its yield. It may be the seed, but generally the field is limited by fertility long before anything else surfaces.

Getting the minimums in place right now is most important. I am not talking about doing everything possible. I have a client in Iowa. He set the highest corn yield ever made in the state one year. He had come to a meeting two years before that. He sat through it and took a lot of notes. When I got to trace elements, I recited what the minimum levels of the trace elements were, and I suggested the ideal levels for corn. He and his dad farm 4,000 acres on the Mississippi River between Fort Madison and Burlington, Iowa. Before he left he told me he was going to pull samples and send them to me to see if I could help him.

I said, "When you send the samples, don't just send the problem spots. Send at least one good soil, perhaps even a couple." This farmer had a big hog operation. Hog manure was put on every acre of the farm, albeit not every year. He and his dad raised 2,000 acres of corn and 2,000 acres of beans in rotation, except on irrigated land. On the irrigated land they produced continuous corn.

From the soils he sent, I told him why problem areas were problems and why the good ones were good. When we got to the last soil, I said, "Well, I am glad I met you because otherwise I wouldn't know what to say to you, or how to make it believable. If you ran a pH, phosphate and potassium test, anyone looking at it would say this field is the worst of all the fields you sent in." Because they used the hog manure on their fields, they didn't show any place where they had a phosphate or a potassium deficiency, except in the last field. It exhibited a 100+ pound phosphate deficiency and a 120-, 130-, or 150-pound potash deficiency. All the rest of the acres had excellent numbers. I said, "If you just looked at pH, phosphate and potash, you would identify this as the worst field of all we looked at, but viewed in terms of the aggregate, this one suggests itself as the best field I have ever seen in Iowa." I said, "I have never seen a field with as good a fertility level as this field." I didn't know the history and didn't know whether they had farmed it for years or not.

He was quiet for a minute, and then he said, "It is our best field. We made 215 bushels of corn per acre on this 90-acre field. We have only farmed it for two years. The guy we bought it from never really farmed it. I can tell you that last year on our other irrigated corn, the best we did was 198 bushels. On our non-irrigated corn, the best we did was 98 bushels. I would like to take that field and see what we can do in terms of corn yield."

That field had 68% calcium, but it also had 24% magnesium—a not unusual profile in Iowa. It had a phosphate and potassium deficiency, and in the trace elements department there was a boron deficiency. In Iowa some say that if you have more than 200 ppm iron, it will be toxic to corn. In this field, test results identified 1,224 ppm iron. High iron is not a problem, at least in terms of yield. Manganese registered in at 125 ppm—excellent. Zinc was about 11 or 12; 10 to 20 is excellent. Copper was exactly 5 ppm, also excellent. The next year, the son and father team again raised corn. Several other clients joined me for a trip to see the farm. They planted Pioneer and Garst corn. The Garst people had been out. They said, "You have 275 bushels of corn in this field." Every stalk had two big ears on it. That fall they harvested the corn, taking care not to run over the bean field in-between. In fact, they harvested the beans so they could get into the corn.

It started raining, and it was after Thanksgiving before they could harvest the corn. They had a lot of lodging by then, but they still made 225 bushels of corn per acre. Here is what we did to change that field. I had them switch to ammonium sulfate as a nitrogen source, and recommended boron as well as 70 pounds of phosphate and 90 pounds of potash per acre. In other words, I did not suggest big

Hands-On Agronomy

amounts of phosphate and potash. This really didn't take care of the potash deficiency, but it was enough for the season. Limiting factors were sulfur and boron. These farmers were putting on enough nitrogen.

Cutting back on fertility won't lower your land taxes, or interest rates, or seed and chemical costs. But cutting back on soil fertility will lower yields, potential income, and crop resistance to drought, disease and insects. Potassium plays a big role in this regard.

Ma-nure / me-'n(y)ü(e)r / *n* [ME *ma-nouren*, fr. MF *manouvrer*, lit, to do work by hand, fr. L. *manu operare*] **1** material that fertilizes land; esp. refuse of stables and barnyards consisting of livestock excreta with or without litter **2** material suitable for fermentation, with Actinomycetes and Streptomycetes first digesting sugars, with other organisms creating a mesophilic condition that raises temperatures sufficient to destroy pathogens **3** raw materials capable of breaking down, then building up for the production of humus for plant nourishment and nutrient release from soil stores

9

Considering the Use of Manures

ORGANIC MATTER, MANURE, COMPOST—these three are the most recited and the most misunderstood words in agriculture's lexicon. The late Ehrenfried Pfeiffer handled at least one of these mystery words in one of his talks which became an article, then a reprint, finally a fixture in the literature.

"Some old folks," he wrote, "remember that the odor of potatoes, when boiling in the pot, indicated very specifically the kind of manure—cow, hog, horse or poultry—which had been applied when preparing the soil for the growth of potatoes. Today we still notice that cabbage, cauliflower, broccoli and kale can give off very intensive aromas while cooking. This, too, depends on the fertilization of the soil.

"The reason is that breakdown products contained in the manure, such as skatole, indole and other phenolic compounds are not further decomposed. They enter the soil, are absorbed by plant roots and migrate into the plant tissue. These breakdown products have been excreted by the animal or human organisms, are toxic wastes of their metabolism and imprint their history on the soil and the growing plant.

"Night soil is particularly undesirable in this regard, but even sewage sludge contains many toxic compounds, unless properly decomposed by an aerobic composting process. The difficulty is that these byproducts are rather stable and can survive for a long time. Returned in food to the human upper digestive tract where they do not belong, they can cause many symptoms of indigestion, flatulence and maybe even allergic reactions.

"Biuret is a contaminant or byproduct of urea and urine. It is extremely stable. In greenhouses and field experiments at Purdue University it was demonstrated that it was toxic to growing corn plants. It caused leaf chlorosis, hyponasty and it severely stunted, twisted and deformed plants with their leaf tips rolled together. All fertilizer salts, when placed with the seed, resulted in decreased length of primary roots. The ability to survive germination damage was severely reduced by increasing the biuret content. The rate of growth and the yield were reduced."

For the past several decades, many of the intellectual advisers to the farmer have sought to shut down the use of manures on farm acres. Some have characterized this raw material as a low value fertilizer—a liability rather than an asset. Others, enchanted with the upgraded values inherent in well digested compost, have declared raw manure nearly worthless. One fellow, speaking at an eastern seminar, even recommended one day of jail time for each ton of raw manure spread on farm acres.

As usual, the best assessment rests somewhere between the extremes. In fact, manure has value far greater than a test of nitrogen, phosphorus and potassium numbers might exhibit. Even so, application based on the cost of such nutrients represents a bargain if phosphate and potassium needs are great. Indeed, when calcium and magnesium levels are correct, levels of phosphates and potassium will be enhanced by more than the amounts revealed by manure analysis.

Moreover, manures have character not always apparent according to species of birds and animals. Use of manures requires analysis, and it is best to get such an analysis both in fall and spring.

Manures help release nutrients already in the soil. This is where too many farmers miss out on computing how much manure is really worth. It is not appropriate to use an average of the nutrient content, or tons per acre applied, because this leaves too much to chance. First measure the amount of nitrogen, phosphorus and potassium in manure. With a good handle on the quality and character of the product, it is possible to spread manure on the field for sheet composting. Using broiler litter and rice hulls—with proper handling—can account for 50 pounds of potash and 70 pounds of phosphate per ton of material.

Let's say you could spread three tons of litter per acre and work it into the top few inches of soil at spreading. If you come back next year and analyze the soil—after taking off a good crop—you would expect the crop to have taken out more nutrient values than applied. Instead, levels of both nutrients would be up.

I saw that happen in east Texas with the use of feedlot manure. The operators would bring in old sawdust. Manure would be mixed in with the sawdust by the cattle stomping on it. About every three months the lot was cleaned out, the manure being spread on a field scheduled for silage production. First the field was analyzed, then the farm manager

The Restoration of Fertility

The night soil and urine of the population is at present almost completely lost to the land. In urban areas the concentration of the population is the main reason why water-borne sewage systems have developed. The greatest difficulty in the path of the reformer is the absence of sufficient land for dealing with these wastes. In country districts, however, there are no insurmountable obstacles to the utilization of human wastes.

It will be evident that in almost every case the vegetable and animal residues of Western agriculture are either being completely wasted or else imperfectly utilized. A wide gap between the humus used up in crop production and the humus added as manure has naturally developed. This has been filled by chemical manures. The principle followed, based on the von Liebig tradition, is that any deficiencies in the soil solution can be made up by the addition of suitable chemicals. This is based on a complete misconception of plant nutrition. It is superficial and fundamentally unsound. It takes no account of the life of the soil, including the mycorrhizal association—the living fungous (sic) bridge which connects soil and sap. Artificial manures lead inevitably to artificial nutrition, artificial food, artificial animals, and finally to artificial men and women.

The ease with which crops can be grown with chemicals has made the correct utilization of wastes much more difficult. If a cheap substitute for humus exists why not use it? The answer is twofold. In the first place, chemicals can never be a substitute for humus because nature has ordained that the soil must live and the mycorrhizal association must be an essential link in plant nutrition. In the second place, the use of such a substitute cannot be cheap because soil fertility—one of the most important assets of any country—is lost; because artificial plants, artificial animals and artificial men are unhealthy and can only be protected from the parasites, whose duty it is to remove them, by means of poison sprays, vaccines and serums and an expensive system of patent medicines, panel doctors, hospitals, and so forth. When the finance of crop production is considered together with that of the various social services which are needed to repair the consequences of an unsound agriculture, and when it is borne in mind that our greatest possession is a healthy, virile population, the cheapness of artificial manures disappears altogether. In the years to come chemical manures will be considered as one of the greatest follies of the industrial epoch. The teachings of the agricultural economists of this period will be dismissed as superficial.

> —*Sir Albert Howard*
> *An Agricultural Testament*, 1943

put down the indicated amount of manure. Next year the phosphate and potash levels were up by more than the numbers represented by the applied amount of manure, and he had taken off a crop. No other source of phosphate or potash had been used. The year after that, the same thing happened. I didn't understand about total nutrients versus available nutrients at the time.

This concept is constantly overlooked when evaluating the need for manure and its value in terms of purchase price, and in determining both its capacity to benefit or cause harm to the soil. William A. Albrecht explained this one. He said that when you put on manures, you stimulate microbial activity and also create mild organic acids that free up nutrients considered unavailable. That is how extra phosphates, potassium and trace minerals are released.

Now consider the different types of tests available. Tests generally used are concerned with measuring plant nutrient availability for crops to be grown. A standard soil test such as the one we commonly use measures nutrients according to categories characterized as major (nitrogen, phosphorus, potassium, sulfur); secondary (calcium, magnesium); and trace elements (boron, iron, manganese, copper, zinc, and sometimes molybdenum or chlorides).

Another test is called a total nutrient analysis. It shows that soils vary widely in their make up of nutrients. This test measures all nutrients in a soil, including those available for plant use, and those present in forms which cannot be utilized by growing crops. The amount of nutrients *present* in a soil can be many times greater than those in *available* form. For example, an average topsoil from the cornbelt can have 30,000 to 50,000 pounds per acre of potassium, yet all except 200 to perhaps 600 pounds per acre will be present in forms plants cannot utilize. Unavailable forms of phosphate, calcium, magnesium, sodium and certain trace elements are also found in higher amounts when total nutrient analysis is involved.

A caution must be inserted here. Manures will seldom increase available calcium in the soil. The only condition under which you can expect to see an increase in available calcium levels is when calcium is added to the feed ration, under which condition some of it comes out with the manure. Manure from laying hens is a good example.

The total amount of calcium in a soil is usually very close to the amount of *available calcium*. There can be thousands of pounds more magnesium in a soil than are *available*. There can be thousands of pounds more potassium in a soil than are *available*, and also there can be thousands of pounds more sodium than the amount characterized as *available*. Usually calcium will have less than the equivalent of two extra tons of fine-grind (1,200 pounds) limestone to the acre tied up, or in an unavailable form. This is true unless a calcareous soil is involved, one that has rocks containing calcium carbonate. Such rocks slowly break down. Obviously, we don't include the rocks when we check a soil. All we consider is calcium that will break down in a reasonable period of years. To measure the available soil calcium—what is shown on our normal soil test—we report only what can be picked up by the crops being grown.

When manure is applied to a soil, it certainly adds the nutrients contained in the raw product. But while stimulating microbial activity in that soil, mild organic acids are formed in the process which work on and breakdown the nutrients plants need. These can be converted in this way from the unavailable forms into forms needed by the crop. In soils that contain reasonable calcium and magnesium levels, this is a process that can be observed via soil analysis to add to the soil's nutrient level over a period of time.

When you apply manure, compost, or even some type of protein meal, always keep in mind both available and total nutrient levels in the soil. Remember that calcium, due to its general availability, cannot be expected to increase. But it can be expected to decrease when any material except manure from laying hens is used. Phosphates will increase, on the other hand, and if used to excess, it can tie up other nutrients. And potassium can do the same if increased to the point of excess.

The application of manure can increase the availability of phosphates and potassium well beyond the amounts removed by crop production if the soil is otherwise in good shape. Compost can do the same thing.

When it comes to applying manure or compost, don't overdo a good thing. Too much can be detrimental to crop yields, but not using enough can hurt production. As a rule of thumb, fields that already test high in phosphates and/or potassium should not receive indiscriminate applications of manure or compost. Only when a soil test shows the soil to be ready for more manure or compost should an application of either be considered. Finally, keep in mind that when manure or compost have been used repeatedly, and must be stopped, the amount of nitrogen usually supplied by manure or compost must be accounted for from other sources, especially for crops with high nitrogen requirements.

If a farmer continues to apply manure or compost and increases unneeded phosphate availability, and copper or zinc levels are barely adequate in comparison, the phosphate level can interfere with the uptake of these two minor elements.

As potassium levels continue to rise, boron and manganese uptake can be restricted, and if excessive—especially in lighter soils—even a magnesium deficiency can be triggered by too much available potassium. On some soils manure or compost can unduly increase available zinc. When not too high, this is fine, but when zinc is already very high in a soil, greater availability can cause problems associated with zinc toxicity.

Farmers with livestock in confined areas should be especially concerned about the ability of manure to release or convert elements for plant uptake. Crops produced in such

Hands-On Agronomy

areas can cause health problems. For example, dairy cattle that are confined to a relatively small area will consume grass that grows there even though under normal conditions they would not consider such material palatable, and leave it alone.

Certain problems can be traced back to the cumulative amounts of manure allowed to decompose on the land. Soil pH drops as available calcium is leached out of the root zone by the manure. At the same time phosphate and potassium levels rise higher and higher as manure releases forms previously unavailable. Plants that grow in such areas become bitter, and this indicator worsens as soil acidity increases. The danger in such cases cannot be overemphasized.

Most farmers tend to neglect their pastureland when it comes to testing and fertilizing until the bitter end, if they test it at all. Keeping such areas properly limed can help as long as manure accumulations are not excessive. But in too many cases, circumstances have gone so far that even properly liming the soil will not always solve the problem. The situation can deteriorate to the point that farm animals actually die as a consequence of the long term effects of eating plants that grow in such areas.

What happens in the end is that potassium levels in plants become so excessive they harm livestock. As potassium levels accumulate, calcium levels decrease. Also, excessive potassium can cause magnesium deficiency in growing plants. As these levels drop and potassium levels rise, levels of each in the bloodstream are affected.

In the blood, calcium/magnesium must always be above potassium/sodium levels. The day potassium/sodium levels exceed calcium/magnesium levels, the animal dies. Unless a blood analysis is done, there will be no apparent reason for such a death. No outward sign will signal the problem.

Too much manure and/or compost, as with anything else, can cause problems. Those who have gardens need to espe-

Our Compost

Our compost is an earthy-like substance, which is the result of a controlled fermentation of feedlot manure by implanting certain aerobic organisms. As in the brewery or cheese industry, where selected organisms are used to cause specific action, we use an inoculation of over 40 different specific organisms which each have a specific function to perform in the compost, and later in the soil in which the compost is applied. This process has been used successfully throughout the world over many years. The organisms were selected from leading productive soil types of the world starting some 65 years ago and analyzed in the laboratory for their function in the soil and compost matrix before inclusion in this inoculum culture. These organisms, under favorable moisture, temperature and other environmental conditions created and maintained in our compost piles, go through a whole series of actions and reactions, some of which are mentioned below.

Actinomycetes and streptomycetes first work on the easily digested sugars present. These are the same family of organisms used in making the antibiotics so widely used medically today on both man and animal.

These and other organisms create a mesophilic condition which carries the body temperature of the compost pile above 100° F. where thermophilic organisms then become active and generate temperatures up to 150° F. This action has proven so effective in the removal of pathogenic organisms that the poultry industry has turned to the practice of composting the old litter and manure for use as litter under baby chicks, with resultant decrease in death loss over where new litter is used. This fermentation destroys weed and undigested grain seed, hence eliminating that objection of the raw manure. There are cellulose digester organisms which work on decomposition of high carbon plant fibers. These work in conjunction with nitrogen fixers (normally recognized as in association with leguminous plants, but in our inoculum are ones independent of this symbiotic association) to produce humus of high plant nourishment because of the resultant good carbon nitrogen ratio attained. This organic material, unlike the inorganic form, in addition to its value as a soil conditioner, is stable and remains in the soil until needed, as opposed to the rapid leaching away and/or locking down as occurs with the N, P, and K fertilizers commonly used.

The benefit comes from the processes of the living humus. We do not recommend the occasional application of large quantities of feedlot manure (observed applications have been ten tons or more) which often causes distressing conditions in the soil during the first year.

We recommend the addition of a small application of compost which is stable living humus of balanced value to the plants and serves as an effective inoculum to the soil of these beneficial soil organisms. In this compost are organisms that consume organic chemical residue, (such as DDT and other insect poisons having a residual effect) and other contaminants of the manure and soil.

  —Fletcher Sims
   private papers, *Acres U.S.A.* collection

cially heed the lessons of too much manure. Not only can excessive use of manure increase phosphate and potassium levels and hinder the uptake of micronutrients, it can also contribute to health problems for people who rely heavily on garden food production. An indication that the problem has reached an advanced state is a bitter taste in cucumbers, squash and even turnips. The bottom line is the one William A. Albrecht repeated so often. A test is required, one that indicates the saturation of each soil in terms of calcium, magnesium, potassium and sodium.

Withal, the shortfalls mentioned above have a natural add-on. There is a tendency to apply manure on dry areas closest to the barn, to "pile it on" the garden every year, and to disregard small confined areas where livestock live out their lives. The degree of problems created depends on the shape of the soil to start with, and what it requires for equilibrium status.

Still, there is no need to shy away from the use of needed compost and manure in the garden or on the field. Always keep in mind, you can get more than you pay for when you buy manure, but if you keep putting it on and putting it on, you can actually cause certain toxic conditions to develop. Different manures will call for different application rates, according to the soil's needs.

Manure, of course, can contribute considerably to the soil's organic matter content. For example, a ton of beef manure containing 80% moisture will hold almost 400 pounds of organic material. Organic matter in manure helps control the slow release of nitrogen bound up in that organic matter. This nitrogen must be converted to ammonium before it can be used. Only about 50% of the nitrogen in manure is available for crop use the first year. Soils receiving manure with naturally high organic matter levels, will not deliver much of an increase in crop yields at the outset. But in shallow or leached soils, the initial response to manure is generally very good.

For effectiveness and availability, manure should be incorporated quickly. Its relative value in increasing crop yields is reduced by about 50% after four days exposure under field conditions.

Hog manure makes it possible to build phosphate levels much more easily than potassium levels. I have observed Iowa farmers using hog manure, with resultant improvement in phosphate levels. But they couldn't get their potassium levels up accordingly, and they couldn't understand why. In the case of soil with low phosphates and high potassium, hog manure makes it possible to build phosphorous without building potassium levels quite as much.

When crop residues are involved in soil management, the objective being to build humus, the carbon-nitrogen ratio must come into focus. Roughly, when you have corn stalks or bean plants or wheat stubble on a field, the carbon-nitrogen ratio will be 30 to 1, or greater. This complex has to be reduced to between 10 and 20 to 1 before you can build humus. Microbes attempt to do that, but the carbon to nitrogen ratio is different from the ratio in manures.

Dairy manure mixed with straw will deliver a carbon to nitrogen ratio of about 28 to 1. Provided phosphate and potassium are not overdone, I urge farmers to use their dairy manure almost anywhere they can get a good spread, albeit not in large amounts on legumes such as alfalfa. I have clients who say they get a good spread. Yet in too many cases too much is piled out right behind the spreader. A heavy spread is certain to give weeds a signal to increase and multiply. Why do weeds come through? Is it because weed seeds are transported with the manure? Not necessarily! Number 1, farmers have the weed problem because they get their potassium levels up above 7.5% of base saturation, an open sesame for weed pressure. Number 2, nitrogen is present in excess, and it enables weeds to out-compete alfalfa.

Some farmers hire custom operators to spread manure. I have seen an even spread of one ton per acre, the appropriate equipment being the key. Spread evenly at such low rates, manure does not generate weed problems, even in alfalfa fields that need extra phosphorus and potassium. The key is an even spread and control over how much is used.

Horse manure is called a "hot" manure because it breaks down fast. The carbon-nitrogen ratio is around 32 to 1. Nitrogen in horse manure is generally estimated at about 1.6% times the dry matter. Sulfur, on the other hand, is about .2%; phosphorous, .7%; potassium, 1.2%. Calcium is not quite as high, but it is not too far off the potassium level at 1.1%. You get quite a bit of calcium via horse manure, but not enough to overcome any serious shortage. Generally, the carbon-nitrogen ratio of feedlot manures is a lot lower than 32 to 1. This means that you are much closer to humus formation with feedlot manure *as is* than would be the case if you composted horse manure. You get more nitrogen out of it—something like 2.3%—but the highest source of potassium, other than from sheep and poultry, is from feedlot manure. Expect it to run between 2 and 2.5% potassium. Sheep manure runs even higher.

Poultry manure, in turn, must be considered as turkey or layer manure or broiler litter. Layer manure has a high calcium content if oyster shells are fed or some other form of extra calcium is used in the feed ration. Overuse of such manure is never suggested, otherwise the calcium can tie up other needed nutrients. Broiler manure is much like turkey litter. On soils needing the phosphorus and potassium, either can be used without ill effect. As far as poultry litter is concerned, where six or eight tons of other manures would be applied, you only need three to four tons. Both poultry litter and cage droppings incorporate urine, for which reason the saying has it, *poultry means hotter manure.*

Sheep manure is rich manure, right behind poultry manure. Other than nitrogen, sheep manure runs neck to neck with poultry manure. And even the nitrogen is pretty high in it.

What Compost Does in the Soil

The soil, having been inoculated with the desirable soil organisms, then becomes a compost medium itself. There are very few crops grown on the high plains which don't leave a sizable residue. Some, as wheat and milo, often leave many tons per acre of stubble, roots and crowns. In barren soils, as most of the high plains region soil series have become, this residue is often considered a liability rather than an asset. The cellulose digesters in our compost change this condition. They consume this material converting the carbon and banking it for later use in growth. The nitrogen fixers securing their nourishment from the atmosphere, or where inorganic nitrates are in excess in the soil, stabilize it with the carbon for use by the plant as organic nitrogen when needed. It appears that more free ion nitrogen has been applied to the soils locally than the crops have been able to utilize and it has leached to lower levels of the soil, now causing trouble to deep rooted crops, such as sugar beets. With the soil organisms of our compost this excess nitrate would be stabilized for later crop use, thus avoiding this particular problem and possible contamination of underground water.

Another group of organisms, the phosphate and potassium releasers, serve a very essential function. Since our soils are high in these elements it would be ludicrous if not so serious to observe that they are being purchased in such great quantities. Likely a large portion of those purchased join the ones present in this highly mineralized soil in becoming "lock up" or plant unavailable. Our compost organisms implanted in a similar soil under a controlled demonstration, increased the availability of phosphates 6,500% in 12 weeks. Their presence in our local soils will supply all the available phosphates any locally grown crop needs.

—*Fletcher Sims*
private papers, *Acres U.S.A.* collection

When manure is to be used, consider its properties carefully. Nitrogen conversion in the soil produces acidity. If you apply compost, soybean meal, alfalfa meal, cotton seed meal, or any kind of manure, without also adding the required limestone or other cations, increased acidity will result. The same thing is true for ammonium nitrogen fertilizers. Consider the chemistry. Two ammonia and three oxygen ions convert to two nitrate nitrogen and six hydrogen ions. The six hydrogen ions contribute to acidity. In other words, more hydrogen ions mean more soil acidity because hydrogen is the basis for all acids. Nitrogen conversion in the soil produces acidity. When you use nitrogen—whatever the source, manures included—pH is lowered because of hydrogen atom production. When nitrogen is applied and the nitrate leaves, it doesn't depart by itself. It takes along calcium or sodium or potassium or other cations present, magnesium being excepted. Taking away these cations and their replacement with hydrogen is a recipe for increased acidity in the soil.

Secondary nutrients in manures should receive far more attention than is usually the case. I have already mentioned calcium and magnesium, but I want to cover a few more points. Crops require considerable amounts of secondary nutrients. Eight tons of alfalfa with 445 pounds of nitrogen and 440 pounds of potassium, also has 175 pounds of calcium, 40 pounds of magnesium and 40 pounds of sulfur. Look at corn. Corn contains 42 pounds of calcium, 44 pounds of magnesium per 150 bushels—and 25 pounds of sulfur. Forget manure's undeserved reputation for sulfur content. I find that farmers who use manure still tend to have too little sulfur in their soils.

Most manures used today are not good sulfur sources simply because it is not possible to get anything out of manure except what is put into it. Since sulfur is not being put into rations, and since it is not present in the soil, we do not increase sulfur levels very much by applying manure.

Comparisons of Manures

At my lectures I am frequently asked to make comparisons in manurial values. One question that some of my listeners often ask is, "What is the difference between the manurial value of fresh farmyard manure and compost?"

Farmyard manure generally is made up of a solid and liquid excrement of farm animals, together with straw or litter. Animals cannot manufacture phosphoric acid, potash and nitrogen. The value of the manure, therefore, must depend to some extent upon the character of the food the animals consume. Indeed, the character of the food is easily the most important factor in determining the constituent value of *fresh* manure. When food is digested and assimilated by an animal, its manurial constituents are separated. In animals living on vegetation, the phosphoric acid and the undigested nitrogen of the food appear usually in the solid excrements, while the digested nitrogen and most of the potash are excreted in the urine. Fresh farmyard manure takes much of its chemical value from the nitrogen which it contains. If the food is difficult to digest, the chief value will be in solid excrement; on the other hand, if the food is easily digested the urine will have the greater value.

When cows are in pasture, or fed on concentrated food, the urine will contain about three times the value of solid manure so far as chemical fertilizing constituents are concerned; that is why it is important to make a liberal use of litter so as to absorb the liquid portion and avoid losing this valuable part of the manure. The values of manure obtained from the consumption of one kind of food can easily be calculated, and there are many authorities which have established figures.

—*Friend Sykes*
Humus & The Farmer, 1949

As suggested early in this chapter, there are several philosophies regarding the use of manure on the land. In a class on agriculture during my college days, we heard that manure in the barn wasn't worth cleaning out and hauling to the field. Commercial nitrogen, phosphorus and potassium was just as good and cost less. On the other hand, Earnest M. Halbleib, while operating Halbleib Orchards, McNabb, Illinois, would have manure applied on the land to be out of production for that year, this to give it more time to breakdown before being tapped for food crop production. Since animals refuse to eat where they leave their fresh droppings, should human beings pay less attention?

Even in the Bible, the word *dunghill* is often used, but closer study with particular sources of commentary will show that the translation would better be rendered *compost*. The term does not refer to a fresh manure pile. In this regard, I never noted the order of use mentioned in the parable of the fig tree in *Luke 13:6-9* until after an opportunity to discuss his program of natural orchard production with the late Dr. Paul Kritchkovich of Zagreb, Yugoslavia. The successes of those using his program over decades of production from the same set of fruit trees provided the proof of its effectiveness. He advocated that any use of fresh manure on fruit and nut trees be from cattle, and always applied on top of mulch, never worked into the soil. Working in the fresh manure causes excessive growth and results in a weakening of tree limbs, according to his work experience. In the parable of *Luke 13*, the dung is mentioned after the digging. Whether composted or not, could it be that even in the time of Christ it was actually left on top as Kritchkovich discovered in his work?

Regardless of the system invoked, agriculture and the environment will benefit far more from the use of manure—even in its crudest form—when it is worked into the soil, rather than left unused. Some will object that manure has to be treated before use, but again, perhaps an example from the Bible should be considered. Moses directed that even fresh human wastes be covered by soil, *Deuteronomy 23:12-13.* This is not meant to advocate the use of human waste for crop production, rather to illustrate that even in those ancient times they understood the importance of quickly handling a large volume of waste manure with adequate amounts of soil.

Manure handling is an ancient art. Still available in libraries throughout the United States is the 1938 USDA Yearbook of Agriculture entitled, *Soils and Men.* One entire section is devoted to manure handling.

The work is intensely practical. It seems to square with what I have observed in every area of the country. It seems far more important to have manure used presently, rather than to insist that it should only be considered for use after it is digested in a certain way, even though several improvements may be accomplished by doing so. I tell farmers to use it where it is needed, and then progress from there.

Sul-fur or **Sul-phur** / 'sel-fer / *n* [ME *sulphur* brimstone, fr L. *sulpur, sulphur, sulfur*] **1** a nonmetallic anion element that occurs either free or combined esp. in sulfides and sulfates **2** chemical symbol:

3 is a constituent of proteins and exists in allotropic forms, including yellow orthorhombic crystals **4** resembles oxygen, yet less active and more acidic **5** its release in soils is governed by the size of the organic matter bank account **6** its transformation is under the auspices of the decomposers of the biotic pyramid which take proteins and organic combinations—of which hydrogen and sulfur are simple forms—and turns them into sulfates and sulfites **7** essential to formation of sulfur containing proteins, a constituent in thiamine, biotin, glutathione

10

The Sulfur Connection

WHEN I FIRST STARTED TO WORK AS A CONSULTANT in 1973, the lab and my mentor, Dr. William A. Albrecht, taught about the importance of sulfur. As a consequence, I ran sulfur right along with phosphorus, potassium, calcium and magnesium. It was always checked by Albrecht, and had been for years before I even got started, the point being that there was already a good track record on sulfur testing. Perhaps other laboratories "aren't sure" about the accuracy of the sulfur tests they can run, but even in 1973 we could be sure because of instruction by the few who knew from experience. Perhaps if the authorities had spent more time in the field working with sulfur instead of quoting other authorities, production would not be hindered by dissemination of improper information.

The fact is, sulfate is needed just as badly and in much the same amounts as phosphate. Yet we put on far more phosphate than sulfate. Furthermore, phosphate is stronger than sulfate in the soil, and when the two compete for absorption, sulfate is the loser, especially when phosphate levels are very high. Consequently soils either high in phosphorus or on the receiving end of high rates of phosphate fertilizer will need more sulfur to produce as they should—otherwise, farmers won't get their money's worth for all the phosphate they put on.

Another fact—based on all these years of cumulative experience with sulfur testing—is that almost every soil I tested does not have enough sulfur to produce the top yields our crops are capable of today. Even soils that have been receiving manure, even heavy clay and loam soils, and soils with a high humus content, rarely have enough sulfur unless the farmer is specifically adding it into his fertility program.

When all the confusion about sulfur tests is settled, there still remains the question of how much to apply. Some fertilizer dealers tell their clients that 20 pounds per acre will kill the crop. Yet the fact is that if you could justify the cost and the soil exhibited a need for it, even 200 pounds per acre would not harm corn if applied at planting time, and 300 pounds per acre could be applied on growing alfalfa without harmful consequences. This is not to say anyone should do this. But any farmer can be assured that 20, 30, 50 or even 100 pounds per acre will cause no ill effects if circumstances determined by a reliable test suggest a need for the nutrient.

Just what does sulfur do for crops anyway? For one thing, when present in adequate amounts, it helps seedlings survive in cool, moist soils. Consider this for early planted crops such as cotton and corn, and for conservation tillage fields. Adequate sulfur presides over more rapid root development during early periods of growth. I've seen 50% more root development in the same fields with and without sulfate on wheat. Sulfur is also important for increasing the protein content of crops, signs of which can readily be shown. If there isn't enough sulfur, alfalfa will not contain the best level of protein possible.

One thing you can be certain of—more certain than the conceit ten years ago that midwest soils needed no sulfur, according to most agronomists. Sandy soils need sulfur. Before too many years it will be recognized that farmers should use far more sulfur in order to harness the crop's ability to produce at a maximum.

Some farmers know that it takes equally as many pounds of sulfur—in the sulfate form—as phosphate to grow 150 bushels of corn. Some will say that this is not right because it takes three times more phosphate than sulfur to raise a crop. In terms of pure elemental sulfur, perhaps it does. But I am not talking about phosphate as phosphorus.

If you reduce phosphate down to phosphorus, then we are talking the same terms again. Otherwise you have to convert sulfur to sulfate to get it up to the phosphate denominator. The big difference is that when some agronomists talk about phosphate, they talk about P_2O_5, and when they talk about sulfur—instead of talking about SO_4—sulfate, they talk about S-sulfur. To get the equivalent, it becomes necessary to multiply sulfur by three, which yields 75 pounds of sulfate for a 150-bushel per acre corn crop. Phosphate runs something like 85. Unit for unit, it takes one pound of sulfate and one pound of phosphate to grow the same amount of corn. According to some, the big difference is the time frame in which either nutrient is used. Some 90% of the phosphate is used by the time the corn completes tasseling, 10% afterwards. With sulfur, 10% is used before the corn tassels, 90% afterwards. The objective is to have the phosphate on-scene early, and the sulfur in place in the sulfate form later on.

At times the yellow striping designating a lack of sulfur is visually confused with magnesium deficiency in corn. Magnesium deficiency causes whitish strips along the veins and a purplish color on the underside of the lower leaves. When you see that striping, you are a long way past hurting your yield. It is the same situation I was talking about with potassium on corn earlier. A lot of trace element deficiencies look very similar. I have seen zinc deficiencies that look almost exactly like a textbook description for magnesium deficiency. If in doubt, a leaf analysis to identify the problem is indicated. But never discount the possibility of a lack of sulfur in your crop.

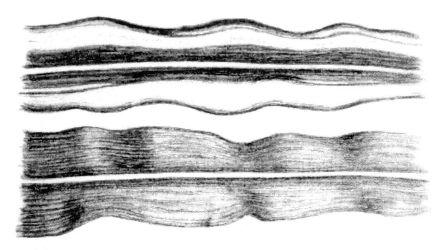

A magnesium deficiency in corn shows yellow stripes of varying widths on the tops of corn leaves (above). Though similar to certain other nutrient deficiencies, it may be differentiated by a purplish tinge on the bottom side of the leaves.

In fact, there is no substitute for sulfur. If you need it, you will have to supply it, or the crop will suffer. It is the fourth major nutrient in terms of the amount required for most crops. In terms of numbers, please note that it is required in amounts higher than calcium and magnesium. It compares with nitrogen, phosphate and potassium as a major requirement. Plants need sulfur to make protein, to craft chlorophyll, to fabricate enzymes and vitamins. The first consideration for building protein in alfalfa is calcium. The second consideration is sulfur, next phosphorus. Any one of these nutrients can be a problem, and *the problem*. Just keep in mind that plant content for phosphate phosphorus is close to the same as for sulfate sulfur for many crops. Sulfur, in turn, is a component of several amino acids. Deficiencies are increasing because yields are being pushed higher.

In fact, varieties in use today can give much higher yields than they used to, but less sulfur is incidentally included in the fertilizer program. Fabricators process it out. Thus, what we grow has less potential for acquiring sulfate sulfur from the soil.

Sulfur is worth more as such these days. Fabricators can process it out of raw materials and sell it. Also, they process it out of some fertilizers because of transportation charge considerations. Another sulfur source is being diminished as a consequence of public policy. Sulfur emissions are lowered by pollution control measures. Finally, we don't use nearly the amount of sulfur-containing manures that we used to spread, and this was once a good source of sulfur.

Farmers who use manures still need to apply sulfur. Today we do not have a high humus level in most soils. Humus is what holds sulfur in. If you get down to 6 ppm sulfur, you have to remember that there is no plant that will not respond to a proper application. If you are below 20 ppm, begin to think about doing something to get the sulfur level up. At that level you don't have the moderate amount of sulfur required—which is 40 pounds of actual sulfur in the sulfate form—to assure that sulfur-requiring crops are sufficiently supplied.

Sulfate sulfur leaches. By way of contrast, phosphate does not leach. It stays put until roots pick it up. Sulfate will move right out, albeit not as easily as nitrate. Yet in agriculture today so many worry about adding phosphate, which

Chelation, a Unique Union of
Metals and Organic Molecules

In the form of salts and ions, the larger amounts of trace elements may be hindering, rather than helping, life processes. They may be poisons, but when there are gross dangers, there are often gross advantages if and when the conditions responsible are understood. Emphasis on trace elements as poisons inclines us to close our minds to their large service when so little of them is present. But only trace amounts may also be anti-catalysts. They may be displacing the helpful metals. When "enzymes are carriers of vitamins, minerals, and amino acids," [written by John J. Miller, "Minerals in Nutrition, Present, Past and Future," in *Journal of Applied Nutrition*, 1962] the failure of the mineral part as only a trace may pervert the enzyme.

"The essence of this situation is that the minerals are tied into the enzyme by special bonds—called coordinate bonds—and when so bound the entire molecule takes on new properties. Soluble forms of minerals may become insoluble, and vice versa; color changes may follow; speeds of action of a mineral salt may be multiplied a thousand fold, and mineral elements, which otherwise cannot enter a cell, may participate readily in the intracellular activities when the metal becomes partly or completely surrounded by the organic portion of the enzyme. A partial surrounding of the mineral with the organic part of the enzyme is called a 'complex,' whereas a completely surrounded mineral is said to be 'chelated.'

"In view, then, of the discovery that strategic metals may be trapped (complexed or chelated) by certain organic substances and of the fact that all biological activity depends on enzymes that use the minerals in 'complexed' or 'chelated' arrangements, it is vital to ask 'whether the body can absorb and utilize the complexed and chelated forms of minerals more readily than the inorganic forms.' Logically the answer is that the complexing and chelating remove the positive charge from the metals as they become dissociated in the stomach or intestine—through combining with the chelating materials (organic)—thus permitting the neutral or slightly negative complexed molecule to slide through the pores of the intestinal wall. These pores are negatively charged; hence cause some degree of fixation of positive minerals at the pore entrance whereas the negative complexed or chelated mineral is induced to enter and then to pass into the blood stream."

—*William A. Albrecht*
private papers, *Acres U.S.A.* collection

does not leach easily, and overlook sulfates—which should be on the same par for corn and certain other crops—which will leach away. Until this approach is corrected, both quality and quantity of production is adversely affected.

The response from an appropriate level of sulfur can be tremendous. Considering the various nutrients discerned by tests to be missing from fertile soils today, sulfur gives the best response of anything, albeit only when the big three—nitrogen, phosphate and potassium—and calcium and magnesium are present in the proper amounts. When I talk about having the minimum amount of sulfur, I like to see 20 to 25 ppm, meaning 40 to 50 pounds of sulfur per acre. Once this level is achieved—if there is no excess magnesium to be leached out, and no excessive phosphate to cause a problem, or some other factor that can drive sulfur out of the soil—no more sulfur is required. In short, the indication is to use sulfur when it drops below the level mentioned above. That situation will occur almost every year if 25 ppm is the normal reading: cropping will use up the sulfur that year. If a good high humus content is in place, the level will hold a little longer, but it will not be possible to keep sulfur for long because it is going to be used up or leached out when it is present in the sulfate form. So expect to need a maintenance level of sulfur on a regular basis.

If you don't get a lot of rain and you don't get leaching—it isn't just extra irrigation water that causes leaching—then you won't have to buy as much sulfur as the farmer who gets a lot of rainfall. If your soil is such that you want sulfate to leave so you can take out the magnesium with it, then it becomes a case of having to observe how much of an effect it has. In western Kansas, down around Sharon Springs and south near Leoti, they count on as little as eight inches of rainfall a year. They still have sulfur deficiency. Whether or not it is because the sulfur is leached out or used up by the crop or tied up somehow remains a question. They still need to use sulfur.

Farmers often wonder aloud whether pH affects the availability of sulfur. Actually, the calcium-magnesium balance is more of a pH governing factor. The closer the calcium-magnesium balance, the less fluctuation in the sulfur level. Once an equilibrium is achieved, it is not as easy for sulfur to grab hold of something in excess and leave. So what we actually see is a leveling out of the sulfate in a soil once we get a balance of the cations. But as long as we have something in excess, we can apply higher amounts of sulfur and it will continue to disappear. At a point where there are no more excesses to drive out, we have only to apply small amounts to keep the sulfur nutrient load in the 25 ppm range.

It should be emphasized here that the sulfate reading on our test would not necessarily apply to what it should be on tests from other labs using other systems. There are perhaps a dozen ways or more to analyze and report sulfur levels. Therefore to try to apply one formula to another lab's test report would usually translate into one big mistake.

Although sulfur occurs in the soil as a sulfate ion, the major soil source for sulfur is humus. The higher the humus content, the less likely a need for sulfur. Therefore, the humus level and the rate of its increase or destruction is an index to sulfur availability. The bottom line remains the same: overuse of nitrogen will burn out the humus supply, and equally destroy the sulfur storage system. Heavy use of nitrogen to cover for sulfur will translate into less humus, ergo less sulfur to sustain future crop production. At 7% humus content, it is possible to get by with a lower sulfur level than if the humus content is 5%, or only 2.5%.

On the basis of soil analysis results, I generally have to recommend at least 10 to 20 pounds of sulfur a year for most soils. A few numbers are of interest. Grain sorghum takes 34 pounds of sulfur for a 180-bushel yield. In turn, 60 bushels of soybeans require 27 pounds. And a 75-bushel wheat harvest takes only 17 pounds of sulfur. That is why wheat may not respond to sulfur as well as do certain other crops.

The university people at one of the state experiment stations in the midwest made this last inventory of information official. Not too long ago they ran three years of replicated tests and concluded that sulfur had absolutely no significant effect on wheat yields. Officially, they got no response between the control and where they used sulfur.

Since this had not been the case in neighboring states, another agronomist visited the site to learn more details. During his visit, the farm manager observed: "When they tell me to use triple superphosphate, I always use 0-20-0, superphosphate." Now, 0-20-0, superphosphate has sulfur in it. Therefore his control had as much sulfur as the rest of the field used for wheat production tests. So here was a situation in which people doing the experiments didn't realize their farm manager was applying sulfur all the time. They didn't see any response to sulfur on wheat because adequate sulfur was used on the control as well as on the test plot. A reliable sulfur test would have helped here.

Most soils that I measure have less than 15 pounds sulfur per acre. Levels do not usually increase with soil depth. I have taken a number of subsoil samples for analysis. In most cases, less sulfur is detected in the subsoil. Either it survives in the topsoil, or it vanishes. If you could keep it in the subsoil, roots would pick it up.

Sulfur, in times past, was replenished primarily from atmospheric sulfur dioxide gas, from fertilizers and certain insecticides. As a practical matter, we can forget about sulfur dioxide gas because we are not getting as much of that these days. We can also forget about fertilizers because, as pointed out earlier, sulfur is not much of a component in trade products. Certain insecticides contain some sulfur, many do not. All things considered, this leaves only manure as a prime sulfur source. And we have previously outlined

Hands-On Agronomy

what has happened in that regard. Until the soil is adequately replenished to the point that our crops can pick up adequate amounts of sulfur, sulfur will continue to be a problem.

Adequate sulfur improves the palatability of any crop. Clients who use sulfur on watermelons report a terrific taste improvement. All fruits are vastly improved in taste and keeping quality when sulfur is supplied, and the nutrient also improves palatability of grasses and animal feeds. Sulfur increases protein content and cancels nitrate content to a marked extent. If you have problems with nitrate in the feeds, one of the very first things to consider is increasing the sulfur supply.

Sulfur deficiency impairs both yield and quality. Inside the plant sulfur forms proteins, helps with enzyme and vitamin development, promotes nodule formation on legumes, aids in seed production and, not least, is necessary in chlorophyll formation. Elemental sulfur is indicated at times. Ammonium sulfate also works well, depending on the area. Other sources include copper sulfate, which has 12.8% sulfur. It's an excellent copper source, but at only 10 pounds to the acre, such an application will not supply much sulfur. Iron sulfate has 19 pounds sulfur, but at 50 pounds per acre, this computes to only eight or nine pounds of sulfur. Gypsum is 12% sulfur, which makes it a good source when calcium and sulfur are both needed. Magnesium sulfate finds little application ditto for manganese sulfate. Sul-Po-Mag is 22% sulfur and can be of use where sulfur, potassium and magnesium are all needed. Normal superphosphate has almost 12% sulfur in it. Concentrated superphosphate hardly has any sulfur—actually 1.4 pounds per 100 pounds of the material styled 0-46-0.

The last line here is that whether you put sulfur on with superphosphate or anything else, more must be provided than just the amount the plant can pull up. Most agronomists will tell you that 10 to 20 pounds of sulfur per acre is enough. If it were possible to get every bit of it in the soil into the plant, this assessment might possibly be right. The problem is, the root is not going to cover the entire area. Therefore it is not always possible for the plant to pick up all it needs. Withal, it is now enough to say that we don't have to have 80 pounds of sulfur in the sulfate form to get it into the plant the same as we do with phosphate. Phosphate is not mobile. Sulfur is. Since sulfur moves around in the water, we can get by with 40 to 50 pounds of sulfur in the sulfate form. But we require phosphorus—based on a water soluble P_1 test—to the tune of 70 to 80 pounds.

If a sulfate sulfur test reveals 200 pounds per acre, considered by some as an excess, that is not necessarily a problem. It depends on what other strengths and weaknesses a particular soil might reveal. Sulfur deficiency symptoms in general are exhibited as a light green or yellow color appearing first on younger leaves. Almost everyone who walks a corn field can identify this symptom. If you don't see it, that means you have an unusual amount of sulfur in your soil. Sulphur can be deficient even in a leaf that is deep, dark green. An ear leaf too low in sulfur held to the sun will exhibit thin yellow lines. A good tissue analysis will confirm sulfur deficiency. With furrow irrigated corn, use of 250 pounds of ammonium sulfate per acre—that is 24% sulfur—means an input of 60 pounds of sulfur.

On the best soils I see in southeast Missouri, sulfur is one of, if not the limiting factor on corn, even though 60 pounds of it have been applied in the sulfate form at planting. In terms of dryland corn or corn grown under pivot irrigation, we may get by with less. With furrow irrigated corn, we still have to apply ten pounds of elemental sulfur in addition to 60 pounds of sulfate in order to keep sulfur from becoming the limiting factor on yields. Sulfur levels depend on how much water each soil receives. Experience with both soil and leaf analysis tells us there is no need to guess.

Two hundred bushels of corn contain 40 pounds of sulfur. If you are going to raise 200 bushels of corn and you have 2.5% organic matter, there is no way you are going to get 40 pounds of sulfur out of most soils. Two hundred-fifty bushels of corn contain 50 pounds of sulfur. On the other hand, if you go backward, 150 bushels of corn take only 30 pounds of sulfur. If we only have 20 ppm sulfur in a soil, that is just 40 pounds. Technically we would have 10 pounds to spare. But again, the roots can't reach every gram of soil where sulfur might be positioned.

Ten tons of alfalfa contain 55 pounds of sulfur. Soybeans also have their requirement. I routinely ask my clients to start using 10 pounds of sulfur broadcast with fertilizer on soybeans. Most of the time the fertilizer for soybeans, other than lime, is potassium. Because many farmers have heavy clay soils, they also have potassium deficiencies. If farmers use 10 pounds of sulfur with their potassium input, beans flourish. Yellowing in a soybean plant can denote a sulfur deficiency. If the sulfur inventory falls below 20 ppm, there isn't a chance of making 60 bushels of beans on most soils. Sulfur can cause toxicity. However, when applied to the soil before planting, this happens at such high rates most people can never afford to do it. There is a danger of burning plants if too much sulfur is applied to the leaves while growing, however.

Sulfur dust has always been used for insect control. Various companies still make a liquid sulfur. These products are not sold as an insecticide, of course, because Washington bureau people do not approve. Nevertheless, it can be sprayed on leaves in the proper amounts for disease and insect control. Old timers are quick to remind that a prime remedy for taking care of many problems is sulfur dust. On the other hand, I have clients who use elemental sulfur, some who use ammonium sulfate, and yet they have problems with insects. I can't honestly say that sulfur will do such and such, but I will tell you that if you balance out your soils, sulfur—in combination with right equilibrium of the other nutrients—is going to make it easier to handle many problems.

One of the proofs I use for this is something I learned from an entomologist named Everett Dietrick. He was one of the first to teach, and then put into practice, integrated pest management. His objective was to watch for problem areas and control them with insects. Dietrick once told an *Acres U.S.A.* Conference that he did not wait for an infestation to take command of the entire field. He always went to the weak spots immediately. "The insects always come to the weak spots first," he said. If there is a place in the field that doesn't do well and has the worst fertility record, that is where the problem will appear. If you don't have a weak spot, then they are going to come to the edges. If Dietrick couldn't control insects with other insects, he sprayed, but most of the time he didn't have to. This observation has been confirmed time after time. A shortfall or imbalance in fertility draws the insects first. If the fertility of a field is already right, and the weak spots can be corrected, the problem with insects will be even more likely to disappear. Even so, there are steps which farmers can take in the meantime.

A good friend of mine tells about his experience with an older farmer who lived pretty close to a fish processing plant on the east coast. This was back when nobody wanted all the entrails and waste products of fish processing because of the offensive odors. He spread these materials on his farm and disced them in. All of a sudden an infestation of Japanese beetles appeared. These insects invaded farms like vandals from the north. Yet none camped out on this fellows's farm. His crop was excellent, even though adjacent fields were ruined. There are reasons for such occurrences, and nutrient levels in the soil play a big part.

Earlier in this chapter the use of a leaf analysis was mentioned for determining sulfur needs for corn. Just as with soil testing, many farmers do not trust the use of a plant or leaf analysis, not always without justification. For determining what has been done, or what should be done, some tests aren't worth the paper they are written on.

But for a starter, consider putting the particular analysis you choose to use to the test. Just select leaves from a poor-growing area of a field for one sample and leaves from a good-growing area for a second sample. Mark the samples so as not to give a hint about which is which, but keep a record so that you will know. Send them in and ask the lab to identify which sample has the problem, and why, and what specifically should be done to the problem area to bring it into line with the better one. If you want to try this with me, read the rest of this chapter first, because I require more of you than just two leaf samples to actually determine any problem and issue suggestions as to what to do about it.

There are several ways to determine problems in plant nutrition, specifically for sulfur or the other needed nutrients. You can look at the leaves and try to differentiate between the various patterns. But generally it is too late for such a remedy. It is also possible to conduct a measured response test. This is accomplished by using the nutrient in question on a part of the cropping area to see if there is an actual improvement in yield. So often such tests are begun with good intentions, but the pressures during harvest season push the determination of the end results out of the picture. Or as another choice, you can take a plant or leaf test in combination with an accurate soil analysis.

This is extremely important. Don't look at a plant analysis to determine long-term fertilizer needs. Look at the levels in the soil first, and then consider a plant analysis for verification purposes.

Southeast Missouri produces several thousand acres of potatoes for the chip trade. One grower hired me to help him with his 1,200 acres of potatoes. I took soil tests on all the different farms he had in potato production. One of those farms exhibited calcium levels in the 65 to 68% range. He raised great potatoes on that farm. All his other potato farms proved to be deficient in calcium. If you are deficient in calcium and you want to grow potatoes, and it is February and you are going to plant in March, you had better not apply large amounts of limestone even if you expect it to break down in time.

Such a procedure can create a scab problem in the potatoes before the year is over. To be safe, you should put lime on potato ground at least 12 months before planting the potatoes. On the potato program, the next observation on the soil audits following the calcium deficiencies revealed copper deficiencies almost everywhere. Every soil also exhibited a boron deficiency based on analysis of this light, sandy type soil. This grower asked me to send leaf samples to a lab known for its competence in potato acreage analysis. The lab that I was using had not done many potato plant analyses. I once met an agronomist out of Texas who told me earlier about another lab that did a great job on leaf analysis for potatoes. The month before, there had been an article in a potato grower magazine about this laboratory and how well it did with potatoes. I didn't even know about the article. This client was overjoyed when told that I was going to send the leaf samples to the featured laboratory. Over time the fellow in the lab to which I sent the leaf samples and petioles became a good friend as well as a very close advisor. So after I got the soil readouts back and all the fertilizers down, and about the time the potatoes were blooming, I went out to every field and sent a leaf and petiole sample in to see where we were.

Now the very first field planted was right at the seed potato house. The day they started, a potato company fieldman from Florida came up. Something was said about putting on ten pounds of copper. What he really meant was ten pounds of copper sulfate. The agent from Florida said it would kill the potatoes. The grower tried to call me and I was out. They started planting and he left a message for me to call him. By the time I called, he had the first field planted. He explained, "They said it was going to kill the potatoes, so we didn't use any copper. Are you sure the copper won't hurt anything?" Now, I wouldn't tell him how to grow potatoes without checking with another grower who had extensive experience with growing potatoes in sand. It just happened to be one of the consultants who lived in Florida and who used the very same analysis I was using for potato production. Though I had called him already, I called again and he said they used ten pounds of copper sulfate every year on potatoes that needed the copper, and "it won't kill them." I called my client back and told him that, and he said he would compromise on the next field and just apply five pounds. By the time he got to the next farm he decided he would go ahead and apply the proper amount of copper. When leaf analysis reports came back, the results spoke in loud overtones. In the first field where planting was started without adding the needed copper, that was the limiting element. Right behind it was calcium. On the other field, where they had applied five pounds of copper sulfate, calcium was the limiting factor, copper trailing close behind it. On the next farms where the right amount of copper sulfate had been applied, there was no deficiency of copper at all. It was certainly not a limiting factor. But calcium continued to show most deficient. We finally came to the samples from the farm where the calcium levels were in the right order, where base saturation was 65 to 68% calcium. Every field had exhibited calcium as a limiting factor on yield until we got to this farm. Calcium didn't show up here as a limiting factor at all. Neither did boron, which had been applied as directed because deficiencies had been evident in the potatoes in prior years.

If the soil test calls for a nutrient, and you fail to put it on, the shortfall will be exhibited by tissue analysis. I have continued to use tissue analysis to verify various soil read-outs, and the procedure has always worked well.

Still, soil nutrients can be present in excess and yet show up as a deficiency in the leaves. You can have too much magnesium in the soil and actually show a deficiency in the corn plant, even though you can measure three times more available magnesium in the soil than you need. If you get it down where it should be between that 10 and 20% level, it won't show up deficient, but if you get it up above 20% you still can have deficiencies in the corn.

Manganese can present the same situation. Eyeball appraisal can often detect dramatic deficiencies, yet sometimes the situation escapes notice and requires confirmation via some other testing method. Leaf analysis is an excellent tool to consider.

Soil tests allow for application prior to planting. Plant analysis can be a good diagnostic tool for the current season. Neither method is foolproof. Both are better than guessing.

The following example will help illustrate how I use both. I have a client in California who received a call from a company in the process of completing a million-dollar landscape project for a home. Two and a half months after laying new sod, the grass was dying on a third of the lawn. The landscape architect called my client and asked for help. He looked at the problem and called me. We had the company pull soil samples and take leaf samples on the part of the lawn turning brown as well as from areas still okay by comparison. The company had leveled the surface and removed the topsoil from the problem area. No one bothered to put any of it back. In the area where they were down to subsoil, the grass died because of the imbalance in and lack of needed nutrients. This dying area of grass became a perfect indicator of what happens when calcium levels are lower than magnesium in the soil. A soil analysis promptly identified the problem and suggested the long term solu-

Hands-On Agronomy

tions. But we needed the analysis of the grass leaves to provide the program for what to do in the short term. I recommended, according to the tissue testing done, foliar calcium and trace elements that were deficient applied to the dying grass. In a week and a half, that brown grass was green again. Then instructions for the long term treatments were put into effect as indicated by soil tests. Six months later my wife and I visited the sites. There was no evidence of any problem area at all. It would have been impossible to save that grass by relying on either a soil or plant analysis alone. By determining what was immediately needed via leaf analysis, and then supplying each of the individual nutrients as a foliar, it was possible to accomplish a "green up," as it were. But only by use of the soil analysis were we able to eliminate continuously having to use the foliars in order to maintain the color in the grass. When you have specific problems, keep in mind that soil tests are the foundation on which plant analysis helps the grower build. Trying to skimp by with only a plant analysis can prove very costly. On the other hand, using plant analysis to detect a need or the correction of a need is extremely helpful, especially in a world confused about sulfur and micronutrient use.

So-di-um / ˈsōd-ē-em / *n* [NL, fr. E *soda*] **1** a silver white soft waxy ductile element of the alkali metal group **2** chemical symbol:

3 occurs abundantly in nature in compound form **4** very active as a cation **5** a cell regulating element that governs osmotic pressure in cellular tissues and fluids

Mo-lyb-de-num / me-ˈlib-de-nem / *n* [NL, fr. *molybdena*, a lead ore, molybdenite, molybdenum, fr. L *molybdaena* galena, fr. Gk *molybdaina*, fr. *molybdos* lead] **1** a metallic element that resembles chromium and tungsten in many properties **2** chemical symbol:

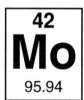

3 essential for plants in trace amounts, .01 to 10 ppm **4** governs microorganisms needed to set the stage for anion nutrient uptake, and is

interrelated as best illustrated in animal health, where an excess makes copper unavailable, depigments hair and accounts for severe scouring **5** deficiency in animals created by excess sulfur, which slows cellulose digestion **6** a deficiency of molybdenum slows conversion of nitrogen to protein

Zinc / 'zink / *n, often attrib* [G *zink*] **1** a bluish white crystalline bivalent metallic element **2** chemical symbol:

30
Zn
65.38

3 of low to intermediate hardness, ductile when pure **4** absolutely vital (along with molybdenum) to the life process of soil microorganisms, esp. *Azotobacter*, a non-symbiotic nitrogen-fixing microorganism **5** aids in the promotion of normal growth and tissue respiration in animal life; interrelated with insulin and vitamin B_1 deficiencies, important in the development of normal hair coat **6** now regarded as a dietary essential and constituent of carbonic anhydrase

Chlo-rine / ˈklō(e)r-ˌēn, ˈklö(e)r-, -en / *n* **1** a halogen element that is isolated as a heavy greenish yellow gas of pungent odor **2** chemical symbol:

3 especially a part of the compound sodium chloride **4** regard essential to the growth of some plants under some conditions **5** an excess of chlorine causes chlorotic spots on tobacco leaves and other plants

Hy-dro-gen / ˈhī-dre-jen / *n* [F *hydrogene*, fr. *hyde-* + *-gene* - *gen*; fr. the fact that water is generated by its combustion] **1** a nonmetallic element **2** chemical symbol:

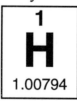

3 the simplest and lightest of elements, colorless, odorless, highly flammable diatomic gas **4** the base for acidity in soil systems

11

An Introduction to Micronutrient Needs

WHEN I FIRST BEGAN WORKING WITH SOIL FERTILITY, farmers were already being told that they should be concerned about only the major nutrients and lime. The trace elements, or micronutrients, were nothing to be worried about. Most of the consultants working with soil balancing techniques agreed with this. They had heard—or possibly even experienced—that when the proper amount of lime and fertilizer were applied, thus "balancing" the soil's nutrient requirements, the necessary micronutrients would be there in a form needed for plant utilization.

This explanation is only partially correct. It is true that micronutrients are most available for plant use when the major and secondary soil nutrients are properly supplied. A major assumption in such cases is that a sufficient amount of each trace element is present in the root feeding zone, albeit in the wrong form, to be released when conditions in the soil achieve equilibrium.

In many of the soils I have worked with, even those with proper cation balances, this has not proved to be the case. Therefore the "fertilize with major and secondary nutrients and the traces will come" assumption can cost farmers far more than most agronomists and fertilizer companies ever envision.

When a sign or symptom of a trace element deficiency is dramatic, it becomes visible. By then it is past the point where it has hurt you. The invisible deficiencies, the ones that can't even be seen, are still in the business of hurting yields. We call this "hidden hunger" in the crop. Several micronutrients can affect crop yields in this way. For example, the most common crop in which boron figures dramatically is alfalfa. A lot of vegetables also require additional boron. Peanuts and cotton do. The need in such crops is generally understood. But for corn, soybeans and wheat, farmers rarely consider the boron requirement. If it happens to be the weakest link in the chain, repair of its shortfall will furnish quite an increase, making boron an excellent example of the principle of hidden hunger for most field crops.

Most severe copper deficiencies are in high organic matter soils. Yet extremely low organic matter soils can have copper deficiencies that are just as bad. Deficiencies of iron are prevalent in calcareous soil—in other words, soils that are really high in calcium. But soil tests show that there are other soils that have iron problems, too. Generally, deficiencies of manganese are on soils where conditions of high humidity prevail, or high pH is a reality, but the problem is also extant in water-logged soils, and in extremely heavy clay soggy-type soils.

Zinc is probably the most universally helpful of all the micronutrients audited via soil test. If it is gone, it affects the crop. Pecans and other types of nuts are definitely zinc sensitive. But one crop it doesn't seem to affect as much is wheat. You can get by with a lower zinc level on wheat. However, zinc can make a real difference when the production crops are corn and soybeans. I have seen situations where every other nutrient level was virtually the same, and the farmer had the minimum recommended level of 6 ppm zinc versus too low on the rest, and the area with the adequate zinc made an extra ten bushels of soybeans to the acre.

If you take 999,999 bushels of wheat and mix one bushel of corn in it evenly, that is what we are talking about in terms of understanding parts per million, or ppm. Micronutrient needs are expressed as ppm. They are needed in small but essential quantities because they are the spark plugs or the catalysts for plant processes. They are what gets the other nutrients to the right place for maximum production.

SOME COMMON ZINC SOURCES:

SOURCE	ZN PERCENT
Zinc sulfates (hydrated)	23-35
Zinc oxide	78
Basic zinc sulfate	55
Zinc carbonate	52
Zinc sulfide	67
Zinc frits	Variable
Zinc phosphate	51
Zinc chelates	9-14
Other organics	5-10

Without micronutrients there would be no energy transfer or push to get everything going.

Most soils have from 20 pounds to 200 pounds of boron per acre. Most of them have from 2 to 400 pounds of copper. In terms of total iron, not the available form, the presence, can range anywhere from 10,000 to 200,000 pounds per acre. In other words, an acre of soil that weighs two million pounds will have a high component of iron. Manganese, in a typical soil system, will range anywhere from 100 to 10,000 pounds per acre. The molybdenum payload can range from one to seven pounds per acre. And zinc generally scales in at between 20 and 600 pounds per acre. When you produce 150 bushels of corn, it takes 0.6 pounds per acre of boron. To grow 150 bushels of corn, it takes half a pound per acre of copper, but it takes only a tenth of a pound of iron. It takes 0.08 of a pound of manganese to produce that crop; 0.03 of a pound of molybdenum; and

---

ZINC PLAYS A ROLE IN ENZYME SYSTEMS, GROWTH REGULATORS AND PROTEIN SYNTHESIS.
SOME SENSITIVE CROPS AND THEIR DEFICIENCY SYMPTOMS ARE:

SENSITIVE CROP(S)	DEFICIENCY SYMPTOMS
Corn, Sorghum	Interveinal chlorosis, shortened internodes, crinkled leaves
Soybeans, Dry beans	Interveinal chlorosis, severe stunting
Pecans	"Little leaf," die-back, rosetted leaves
Rice	Leaf lesions, leaf bronzing, shortened internodes
Citrus	Creamy, yellow chlorosis, die-back

Hands-On Agronomy

0.15 of a pound of zinc. When we consider the total pounds—and how little it takes for crop uptake—can you see that a person might tend not to worry about trace minerals and micronutrients? They are already there. However, this is talking about total nutrients and not nutrients available for plant use. A soil test usually measures the nutrient load in terms of "available form." This helps explain why soils should have 300 pounds of phosphate showing on a soil test, yet only 85 pounds are needed to raise 150 bushels of corn. Soils have to contain quite a bit more than the growth requirement so that roots can make contact and effect adequate uptake. Roots, after all, do not cover the entire ground-front.

Trace minerals are tiny keys to both crop and feed efficiency. There is increased interest in micronutrient fertilization nowadays because higher crop yields result in greater nutrient removal. Modern fertilizer use has tended to stress N, P and K as limiting factors. And newer fertilizer fabrication technology has resulted in higher analysis materials with fewer impurities, including micronutrients. In short, the trade has processed out the micronutrients and sulfur. As a result, earlier sources of micronutrients are no longer available. This problem is exacerbated by the fact that the humus content of most soils is lower than it used to be.

Soil pH is a factor in determining micronutrient availability in the soil. The range for maximum boron availability is between pH 5 and 7. Below pH 7, boron is more available. The maximum range for copper, as with boron, is pH 5 to 7. Once pH gets above that level, copper will be complexed. For iron, the equation says pH 4 to 6.5. Above that, iron starts tying up. For manganese, the proper pH range is 5 to 6.5. Molybdenum is most available between pH 7 to 8.5. When pH gets down into the range mentioned here, molybdenum is no longer most available. But molybdenum does make a difference in terms of yield, particularly in soybean production.

The last nutrient that merits attention here is zinc. Its maximum availability is pH 5 to 7, exactly as with boron and copper. As a matter of fact, between pH 6 and 6.5, there is maximum availability for boron, copper, iron, manganese and zinc.

But again, this can be true only if there is an adequate amount of each micronutrient to supply the need, and it will be of proper benefit only if—in addition to the ideal pH—the cations affecting the pH are within a proper range, and nitrogen, phosphate, potash and sulfate are adequate.

Molybdenum is the only micronutrient for which availability increases as the pH goes up. It is especially important to nitrogen fixing bacteria in legumes. In fact, it is important for nitrogen, no matter where. It is associated with nitrogen fixation. If availability falls below one ppm molybdenum, then this micronutrient becomes a limiting factor. On citrus trees, if you are below one ppm, the remedy is a 7.5 ounce per acre application of sodium molybdate if no other molybdenum application has been made during the last three years. And just that small amount can give an increase of 20 boxes per block of citrus trees.

Corn growers often conclude that molybdenum cannot be a limiting factor for their crop. I have a client in southeast Missouri who is a seed corn producer. He had me check his molybdenum in several fields. Some of the plots were low and some were not. Sodium molybdate can be used to repair a shortfall. The only thing you have to watch out for is the copper level. Molybdenum should not be applied when copper levels are deficient. In such cases, a proper application of both is necessary.

Few growers have done anything with molybdenum. In the entire United States, other than in the citrus groves— and one fellow with corn—I know few growers even interested in the possibility of a molybdenum problem. The main reason is that before molybdenum should be applied, every possible soil in the field must be checked. If certain

Only Small Quantities
of Minerals are Needed

In *The Diagnosis of Mineral Deficiencies in Plants*, by T. Wallace, that principle is stated in the following words,

"Since catalysts are not used up in the chemical reactions which they promote, we can understand how it comes about that quite small or even minute quantities of the 'trace elements' iron, manganese, boron, zinc and copper, may nevertheless be essential to the plant's health and growth."

Iron may be used as an example. As the most copiously required trace mineral, an iron level of 80 ppm is nevertheless considered fully adequate in the tissues of many plants. With such an iron content a big hay crop of 5,000 pounds of dry matter per acre would contain less than 8 ounces of iron. If the soil provides half of this, the farmer needs to find ways to provide 4 ounces in his fertilizing program.

In the case of a 120 bushel yield of corn per acre, we are still considering a need for less than one pound of iron. If the soil can provide half of it, the farmer needs to find ways of infusing the other 6 or 8 ounces into his crop; perhaps paying for it by the reduction of his veterinary bills.

—*Lee Fryer & Dick Simmons*
Food Power from the Sea, 1977

areas are above 2 ppm, and more molybdenum is applied, a toxic situation can be created. Feeding plants produced on toxic fields to livestock can result in molybdenum toxicity.

Some companies make a very weak liquid molybdenum for seed application. I have some at home. The instructions say, "When you plant your garden, just coat your seed with it." I haven't done it yet.

Molybdenum is essential for the nitrate reductase enzyme. Some sensitive crops and their deficiency symptoms are cauliflower and broccoli, alfalfa and clovers. If you are growing alfalfa, think about using an inoculant on the seed. Common molybdenum sources are molybdic acid and sodium molybdate. The last is 39 to 41% molybdenum. It is water soluble. It is the one I have used for applications on citrus and other crops.

Now I am going to mention the trace element called chlorine. It is the most recent addition to the list of essential micronutrients. Chlorine in the soil, in the form agronomists are talking about, is chloride. It plays a role in photosynthesis. Common deficiencies symptoms are leaf tip wilt, leaf chlorosis and necrosis. Some sensitive crops are tomatoes, lettuce, barley, alfalfa and sugar beets. There are no known field deficiencies. There is a fellow in Missouri who has a reputation for growing tremendous tomatoes. He told a neighbor that every year when he planted his tomatoes he took a pinch of salt and sprinkled it all around the plant at least six inches from the stem. Without doing a soil analysis, I don't know whether the chlorine or the chloride or the sodium side is the cause in this case. If you live in a light sandy soil and your sodium is below half a percent, that is going to make a difference. I tried it on my tomatoes and I can't tell the difference. According to soil tests, I have enough sodium in my soil but chlorides have not been checked. Some of the research on chlorine has been done in North Dakota and Minnesota. I don't know of any research that is being done in the south, but I can relate that from the soils I have seen in North Dakota and Minnesota, most of those heavy, black soils are deficient in potassium. If you look at the pounds, they don't show deficient, but if you look at the percentages, they are below 2% potassium. When farmers put potassium on those soils, they get a response. But I wonder about that conventional wisdom. Most of the potassium that is applied is potassium chloride, 0-0-60. When you apply potassium chloride to most of those soils, there will be a response because of the potassium. But North Dakota and Minnesota authorities say their soils don't need potassium, they "have enough" potassium already. Now, all of a sudden, research comes along saying that chlorides give a response to wheat production and various other crops. What I really wonder is this. Since many researchers do not understand about base saturation percentages, and they deal with soils that are below 2% potassium saturation, is it actually the potassium that is giving the response while the credit is being handed to chloride?

With the material here and the section under potassium sources, the chlorides discussion has gone far enough, except to say that high chloride problems can be expected to dissolve with the first movement of water through the soil. We just don't see high chlorides under normal circumstances without also having compacted soil, especially when the old standby—an adequate calcium level of above 60%—is present.

I have spent most of my lecture time and countless other presentations telling farmers about using the cation exchange capacity and base saturation percentage to determine how much fertilizer to use. *An Acres U.S.A. Primer* does an excellent job explaining the nuances of this Albrecht system, and the several volumes of *The Albrecht Papers* flesh out this most valid approach. That is why I was somewhat appalled by the formation of a committee headed by a professor from North Dakota State University. It is a part of an organization called Council for Agricultural Science and

A Pinch of Salt Will Do

By topdressing South Australia's "Ninety Mile Desert" with about 60 cents worth of bluestone salts an acre, they have increased productivity more than fourfold. Two healthy breeding ewes can now raise their lambs on an acre of this copper-deficient country which would not support a wether on an acre before it was treated with bluestone. A relatively small outlay has increased the area's income by millions of dollars a year. Similar treatment with bluestone could restore copper-deficient areas all over the world including parts of America.

Scientific evidence suggests strongly that copper deficiency might be a big factor in the steepest decline of sheep numbers in America's history. Experts have blamed economics for this fall, but there is little financial reason why owners should have sold their flocks so suddenly.

As bluestone is a solution of copper sulfate, the easier, more effective use of phenothiazine deprived millions of American sheep of their customary dose of copper. This is important because humans and animals need copper for complete nutrition and health. The amount is so small, however, that even the world's most delicate balances cannot measure it. Chemists report it as only a "trace" because their methods of analysis are not accurate enough to measure the true dose. Hence, metals such as copper, cobalt, molybdenum, manganese and zinc are usually called "trace" minerals in the soil or in humans, animals and plants.

Absence of copper can be detected most easily through the fleece. Black sheep are the best indicators of copper shortage because their wool turns grayish white when they do not get enough of this vital mineral. A smaller dose of copper than is needed to drench for worms will restore the typical black color. Another symptom of copper deficiency is the change in wool fibre from a regular crimp and soft, pleasant feel, to a staple which is almost as straight and harsh as fine steel wire. The trade calls such wool "steely."

"Steely" wool was traced to flocks on certain desert areas which had enough rain to grow good stock feed but failed to yield more than a low unattractive scrub.

After grazing on it for about six months, sheep developed "brittle bones" disease. This meant that their skeletons had deteriorated so much that the slightest knock with a stick or stone would break a rib, leg, or other bone. They recovered quickly when moved to districts with a similar rainfall but different soils.

Nutritionists prescribed calcium and phosphates to cure this obvious deficiency—but without success. Brilliant work by officers of Australia's Commonwealth Scientific and Industrial Research Organization diagnosed the trouble as lack of copper and cobalt.

Farmers should suspect their soils of being copper deficient if their sheep have become less thrifty since their bluestone drench has been replaced by phenothiazine. Cheap, easy application of bluestone is all that is needed to restore copper deficient soils to productivity. It is not too late to apply this new knowledge to help rehabilitate the nation's sheep raising industry. Nor is the task too large when only a part of a farm's soils need to be treated for a start and the amount of "trace" minerals needed is so small.

—*Colin Webb*
 private papers, *Acres U.S.A.* collection

Technology, acronym CAST. All the agricultural colleges in the United States belong to it. This professor told a good friend of mine that his job as chairman of this committee for CAST was "to do all I can to discredit the use of exchange capacity and base saturation percentage for determining how much fertilizer to put on a soil." My friend asked, "Why would you want to do that?" The schoolman answered, "Because we are on record that it won't work." My friend asked him if there was any other reason he could give. The professor said, "That is why we are doing it, because we say it won't work." The professor said that pH, phosphate and potash is enough.

I am not opposed to agricultural education and research at the university level. We need that. But the job should be to educate, teach and demonstrate to the farmers what should be done. Far too many have confused the need to educate with the urge to legislate. In too many states, farmers and those involved in building fertile soil are being denied the use of materials that in no way damage the environment. No matter how many other states accept or allow their use, that carries no weight. These products have to be "tested and approved" by the appropriate university researchers in that particular state first, all at considerably high costs. Supposedly this is in an effort to protect the farmer. Considering what has happened to farmers during the last few decades, it seems doubtful that they need more of this kind of help.

At one hearing I attended in California in the late 1970s, the chairman of the committee to approve new agriculture products provided an excellent example of the *legislate*, instead of educate philosophy. He told how there was a product that farmers had been buying to use on their land. They had it tested and "it didn't work." They did not say that it was considered harmful. They just couldn't get results. The product was barred from sale there. He went on to say, there were still farmers in California who believed it helped

Hands-On Agronomy

them and would buy that product if it hadn't been forced off the market. This is education? No, it is an excellent example of those who should educate choosing to legislate instead of doing their job.

When it comes to what is and isn't profitable in agriculture, the advantage goes to the farmer out in the field overseeing the work and his own profit picture over some "research" directed from behind a desk by someone who probably never in his adult life had to earn a living from what was produced and sold on a farm. Yet he "knows" what will and will not work on all the farms in the state.

This seems to have been the case with regard to micronutrients. Before they will work properly, the needed conditions for response must be met. When the soils meet the necessary levels mandated for major and secondary nutrients, trace elements or micronutrients of importance come into focus, but even then only if there is a deficiency and there is enough used to supply the minimum needed to provide a response. When the use of the cation balance system is ignored, micronutrient response is somewhat like trying to bet on the right number on a roulette wheel—but with far more at stake.

The soil test I use generally requires a readout for boron, iron, manganese, copper and zinc. Farmers who want molybdenum, chlorides and/or salt concentration tests can specifically request those results.

Any time more than 120 ppm chlorides show on our test, there is a salt problem. Some salt concentrations reach 1,500 to 2,000 ppm, when 500 is already considered a problem. But by far the biggest part of the problem, when such situations are found, is the sodium content. Whenever there is 5% to 10% base saturation of sodium, a problem should be expected. Such situations are among the worst in terms of affecting micronutrient availability.

On a good soil audit, down the sheet a bit, sodium comes into view with a slot for pounds per acre. Sodium in a soil can't get out unless water can pass through. Putting on sodium without good water penetration will result in an accumulation in the soil. Sodium can be delivered by the water used for irrigation, of course, or it can surface from sodium pockets. Often farmers in southeast Missouri will have the soil graded to level it out for, say, rice production, and in some fields huge white areas appear. These pockets represent various forms of sodium. The very first order of business to get such soils open is to correct the calcium profile to at least above 60% base saturation. I have never seen a soil with calcium above 60%—provided the water moves on through—that can't move out the sodium. Of all the classic cations, sodium will move out first. Anions such as nitrates and chlorates will also move out. If water moves through and there is not a 60% saturation of calcium, sodium does not depart willingly. A concentration of sodium and possibly sulfur will result.

Two brothers who became clients farmed a 750-acre rented farm. The south field of that farm was 125 acres. One bad area, some 25 acres in the southwest corner ran, about half way through the field, then all the way to the north end. They said that when they planted soybeans in that field they grew up so tall—somewhere between 6 inches and 10 inches—and died. On the outer edges the beans, as they grew, would turn a deep, dark green, then take on a blue green hue. The leaves would get crinkly and the beans would start dying. Their soil inventory told me in detail that they had a higher concentration of sodium than calcium. It also revealed the amount needed to properly correct the problem. In this case, four tons of fine-grind calcitic limestone were required to remedy the situation. After the liming was accomplished, yields improved during the next cropping season. By the end of the third year, the sodium was gone and you could not pick out the previous problem area. Crops have been excellent ever since.

If you have a high exchange capacity and it looks like a huge tonnage of lime is required, above 4 tons, you should always cut the "requirement" in half. Here is what happens. The added calcium actually causes a decrease in the soil's exchange capacity. I don't know for certain why it does this. I wonder if it has to do with the amount of free cations present. The soil lab determines a soil's exchange capacity, or TEC, by analyzing for the cations (potassium, calcium, magnesium, sodium, etc.) present and available, totaling them up to calculate the exchange capacity. This is sometimes referred to as the *sum of cations* procedure. But when these cations are in the extreme, the colloidal system becomes super saturated. On a high exchange soil, with a pH above 7.0, more cations can be present than can be held by the colloid. Under such circumstances, if the magnesium, potassium and/or sodium are in excess, liming can still be required to improve the soil. But after the lime is applied the unusually high saturation of the colloidal system is affected again, and consequently we get a downward adjustment in the TEC. Any time more than four tons of limestone are shown to be needed on a high TEC soil, my practice is to cut it in half and start from there.

Somebody once asked me about oil spills or "alkali soil" around oil rigs, or where the dike breaks. There are many such areas in southern Illinois, Kansas, Colorado and other areas of the west. Usually nothing will grow, and it is not unusual to measure 20,000 pounds of sodium in the top seven inches of soil. When you have 20,000 pounds of sodium, that overload will tie up a bunch of calcium. I have seen places where it appeared there would never be a response without 12 or 15 tons of high calcium lime. Needless to say, such an input will never pay for itself. Some few farmers have had me evaluate such situations, but I have never had anyone decide to spend the money necessary to correct the problem. But if the calcium ever got above 60% base saturation, the sodium would literally travel out with the transport of water. In short, it is virtually impossible to hold sodium in a soil with 60% plus calcium and adequate water penetration. Without water penetration, it becomes a case of "back to the soil conditioner." This will open up the soil. With more sodium than potassium, even if everything else is correct, there will be a problem with beans dying when it gets hot and humid. Anything that is a fast growing plant can die under such circumstances. Always keep the potassium saturation above the sodium saturation. For more information on this type of situation, review the material in the chapter on potassium.

With barley and sugar beets, if you have sodium higher than potassium, they can still survive and do well. According to base saturation percentages, sodium should be 0.5% to 3%. Below 0.5—if you want to raise sugar beets or barley—production will be less.

I received 200 soil samples from one farm in Germany. I tripped over there for an on-scene evaluation. One sampled area I came to had less than 0.5% sodium. I told the owner that he could grow all his other small grains there, but he shouldn't try to grow barley on that field. He asked, "Why?" I told him it was because he had less than 0.5% sodium. If you have less than 0.5% sodium, barley will not do well. He asked about several fields to check on my evaluation. There were two other fields that did not produce a satisfactory barley crop. Each had less than 0.5% sodium.

Broccoli, cabbage, cauliflower, sugar beets and barley all respond to sodium. None will thrive in soils with less than 0.5% sodium. Some of my farmer clients have less than 0.5% on some fields and more than that on others, and they tell me as long as other nutrients are adequate, they raise better corn where the sodium levels are up to normal.

One answer to inadequate sodium is manure and compost, both possibly rich sources. Lots of composts have tremendous amounts of sodium afloat in their digested mass, particularly in the west where the water used to compost is sodium rich. In fact, a watch has to be put on manures so that soils do not start getting above the 3% level. Still, this is not a worry if base saturation is above 60% calcium, and good water penetration is present.

But what can be done if you do not have manures and you have low sodium? A possible choice is to use a material called sodium nitrate or Bulldog Soda. Bulldog Soda is a mined product out of Chile. It is 16% nitrogen. The sodium content is very low. In most soils low in sodium you can use about 200 or 300 pounds of that material and build sodium up above 0.5%.

On the soils of southern California I find time and again extremely high sodium levels and a resulting high pH, but with deficient calcium levels. Gypsum is not the answer if the calcium saturation on the soil test is less than 60% or so. Whether field crops, lawns or landscaped areas, I first correct the calcium levels and use a soil conditioner to loosen it up and leach the sodium.

Sodium has a tremendous impact on pH. A high level makes pH look extremely high. If you are looking at pH as a guide, you are going to believe you don't need any lime unless you measure the calcium present as well. If you don't measure calcium according to base saturation, then you will never know where you are. You have to get at least 60% base saturation in order to get that soil open enough so that sodium can move through and out. And until this is accomplished, the micronutrients are not going to be properly available. In fact, some of the worst levels of trace elements are seen on soils that analyze high in sodium.

In southeast Missouri, a soil that is in the exchange capacities of the mid-20s and down—and we start to see sodium go up above 120 pounds per acre—then we know that water penetration is not operative. That is one of the tools I can use to tell a farmer he has hardpan. You can have 68% calcium and 12% magnesium and still have sodium accumulate in the soil if you have created a hardpan. That is another reason tillage and fertilization go hand in hand.

Another aspect of the soil analysis to consider in this chapter in regard to adequate trace element levels has to do with exchangeable hydrogen. Exchangeable hydrogen is always determined by using a water pH. Using salt pH will not provide a proper exchangeable hydrogen level reading. Using the water pH method, if the pH is 7 or higher, exchangeable hydrogen will be 0. Above pH 7, there will be no exchangeable hydrogen. At pH 7, a soil is neutral. The soil is saturated with something other than free hydrogen ions. At pH 6.9, exchangeable hydrogen is always 1.5%. At pH 6.8, exchangeable hydrogen is 3%. Every tenth of a point a reading drops below 7 will add 1.5% exchangeable hydrogen. This calibrates how much acidity there is. If you have 10 to 15% hydrogen, that means there is plenty of room for all the other nutrients to find the hydrogen, push it aside and attach to the soil colloids. At 10 to 15%, pH will be 6 or 6.5. The ideal pH is really 6 to 6.5, but it is only ideal when everything else is in the right equilibrium. Any nutrient required takes precedence over pH. This means you supply the deficient nutrients first, and when you finish balancing the nutrients, the pH will be right. If you have 10% magnesium and 80% calcium, the only indication is reduction of calcium by enough to permit potassium its proper base saturation, along with adequate micronutrient levels. If there is 80% calcium and 7% magnesium, I will tell you to start driving off calcium to a 77% level, with a resultant increase of magnesium to 10% base saturation. Once 10% magnesium is achieved, in, say, a medium to heavy soil, and if you have adequate potassium, it is no longer necessary to drive off calcium, provided you have enough iron, manganese, copper and zinc. Don't worry about putting on extra sulfur to buffer or drive out a miscellany of minor imbalances. It can cost more than what can be reaped back in benefits. Once all the other nutrients in the proper amounts are evident, and you have a high calcium reading, calcium merely enables entry of other nutrients faster. Basically, every other nutrient enters in on the back of calcium. So, if high calcium is measured and there is no deficiency of anything else, keep your high calcium. It always seems to make the uptake of other fertilizer nutrients more efficient when all are shown to be sufficiently present.

For example, if you have 80% base saturation calcium, it takes far less nitrogen to do the same job. At 80% calcium with everything else is in a proper relationship, a cut back in applied nitrogen is indicated. In any case, continued use of high rates of nitrogen will cause a weakness in plants. Lodging will result because nitrogen causes accelerated growth and ties up copper. And faulty fertilization, with either a shortfall or a marked imbalance of fertility, will invite bacterial, insect and fungal attack. Instead of a one-way ticket to a better crop, simplistic N, P and K fertility management merely becomes an insurance policy for the sale of lots of toxic rescue chemistry. To do the best job with regard to supplying plant nutrients requires more than pH, P and K as a soil test. Without the cation exchange capacity and the resulting measurements possible for determining fertilizer needs, the farmer will lose the most valuable tool available for the most profitable and environmentally safe use of fertilizers and soil amendments, including the keys to micronutrient availability and consequent needs.

Bo-ron / ′bō(e)r-‚än, bö(e)r- / *n* [*borax* + *-on* (as in *carbon*)] **1** a trivalent metaloid element found in nature only in combination **2** chemical symbol:

3 required for translocation of sugar **4** regulates flowering and fruiting, cell division, salt absorption, hormone movement, pollen germination, carbohydrate metabolism, water use and nitrogen assimilation in plants **5** functions in the synthesis of glycogen and the maintenance of body fat in animal life

Iron / ′ī(-e)rn / *n* [ME, fr. OE *isern*, *iren*; akin to OHG *isarn* iron] **1** a heavy malleable ductile magnetic silver-white metallic element **2** chemical symbol:

3 in biology, an indispensable carrier of oxygen required in the production of chlorophyll and as an aid in the prevention of chlorosis 4 a difficult nutrient to supply to plants in an available form 5 in human beings and animals, essential for hemoglobin formation because divalent iron occupies a central position in the hemoglobin structure 6 essential in oxygen transfer and cell respiration, and aids in blood cell development, and in the prevention of anemia

Man-ga-nese / ′man-ge-,nēz, -,nēs / *n* [F *manganèse*, fr. It *manganese* magnesia, manganese, fr. ML *magnesia*] **1** a grayish white usu. hard and brittle metallic element **2** chemical symbol:

3 resembles iron, albeit diamagnetic 4 aids the oxidase enzyme in carrying oxygen and enters into the oxidation and reduction reactions in plant life required for carbohydrate metabolism and seed formation 5 in animal life, is an essential biocatalyst in normal growth and bone development, maintenance

of body weight, and proper functioning of reproductive and mammary glands **6** activates
calcium, phosphorus, iron, etc., but may itself
undergo fixation by these elements **7** aids in
promotion of beneficial intestinal flora

Cop-per / 'käp-er / *n, often attrib* [ME *coper*,
fr. OE; akin to OHG *kupfar* copper; both fr. a
prehistoric WGmc-NGmc word borrowed fr.
LL *cuprum* copper, fr. L (*aes*) *Cyprium*, lit.,
Cyprian metal] **1** reddish ductile metal **2**
chemical symbol:

3 in agriculture, vitally important to root metabolism **4** helps form compounds and proteins, amino acids and many organic compounds **5** a catalyst or part of enzyme systems; helps produce dry matter via growth
stimulation, prevents development of chlorosis, rosetting and dieback **6** in animal life, essential for catalytic conversion of iron into
red blood cells, and an assist in tissue respiration

12

Applications
of Micronutrients

IT MAY BE THAT WE TAKE THE NUMBERS GAME too seriously at times. We see this when we leave the time honored plains of university agronomy and climb to the frontier uplands of biologicals. Using a biological such as Nitro/Max, Agrispon or Vitazyme calls for having basics in place, albeit with room enough for new parameters. In terms of phosphorus, for instance, if the numbers reach 236 or 238, I won't tell a farmer that he needs phosphorus when using a biological stimulant in his program. It now becomes the function of microbial activity to release enough phosphorus, which in any case is plentiful as warehoused in the soil. The perceived deficiency will not materialize. Yet if the so-called commercial fertilizer is to stand alone, the numbers should go up to 300. Our objective is to take care of major deficiencies, after which the microbes take care of the rest. We keep on monitoring the situation, of course. If it somehow starts to go backwards, there has to be a reason. I cannot think of a thing that will cause the phosphate level to go backwards, but there is one thing that can cause a biological stimulant not to work well, namely an over-supply of undigested residues. Without a proper decay system, there will not be an adequate release of phosphates held in escrow by those residues. But once a minimum desired value is achieved—as long as you use a reliable biological stimulant—maximum buildup is no longer indicated. In fact, a good microbial program can eliminate phosphate application for a matter of four or five years.

These few thoughts make their own suggestions when it comes to making applications of micronutrients.

Trace mineral or micronutrient deficiencies, for instance, can exhibit dramatic signs, or they can be invisible on the plant. Major nutrient deficiencies such as nitrogen, phosphorus, potassium or sulfur can generally be recognized and corrected, but trace mineral problems—considering the myths and lack of information extant—are not so easily solved.

So far the lessons are clear. If you have sufficient amounts of the major and secondary nutrients and a deficiency of a trace mineral, then start taking care of the latter. If you need phosphate or potassium and you have a boron deficiency, take care of the P and K first, because taking care of the boron is not going to work until your major and secondary nutrient levels are in place. Or if you have a zinc deficiency as well as a big phosphate deficiency, take care of the phosphate deficiency first. If you barely have enough phosphate and also have a zinc deficiency, and zinc is the next most limiting nutrient, deal with the zinc deficiency. Just don't overdo it. When you start considering trace elements, keep this in mind. If you put on "too little," you won't get up to what I call the first plateau. In other words, if you are deficient of a certain micronutrient and you make an application, but you fail to get above the minimum requirement in terms of payback for that crop for current yield purposes you might as well have done nothing. The yield will not adequately improve until you get above the deficiency level. If you need two pounds of boron and you put on one pound, you might think it will make up half the difference in yield, but it won't, even if all the major and secondary nutrients are adequate. If two pounds of boron are required and only one pound can be afforded, it is better to put two pounds on half the field and none on the other half.

How many field experiments have been used to say micronutrients are not needed simply because the research involved did not properly consider that the soil must have no limiting major or secondary nutrients? And even then potential results will not be achieved if the amounts applied fail to build levels sufficiently enough to reach that critical first plateau.

Micronutrients respond best when calcium is within 60 to 70% and magnesium is within the 10 to 20% saturation. If either one is deficient, a trace element response should not be expected. If calcium or magnesium is high and everything else is basically in line, and a deficiency of a particular micronutrient is detected, resolve the deficiency so long as it fits into the fertilizer budget. The important point is to first determine whether there are major or secondary element deficiencies. The information that follows in this chapter applies to only soils already well supplied with lime and primary fertilizer nutrients.

As noted in the previous chapter, the range for maximum boron availability is between pH 5 and 7. Below pH 7.0, boron is more available. This does not suggest that a reading above pH 7.0 is to be avoided in every case. If boron is low and calcium is required, and the calcium would cause the pH to go to 7.5, do not skip the calcium because it might hurt boron availability. Never deal with trace elements until major and secondary elements are properly in place. Always take care of the calcium and let the pH go where it will—and then, if you need to, purchase some extra boron or whatever micronutrient is indicated, and make the appropriate application. This does not suggest overdoing trace elements by applying amounts indicated for minimum availability even after pH drops back in later years. What some growers have failed to consider is that a boron application can be toxic to the immediate crop if the proper amount of limestone or another material is not used to supply adequate calcium.

You can lose at least two ways when applying soil micronutrients incorrectly. First, application at the wrong time can result in leaching in some few instances, whereas others will not become available rapidly if not applied at the correct time. Second, some forms of certain micronutrients will not raise the levels in the soil as effectively as other forms. In the long run, liquid forms are generally more expensive per acre than dry forms, yet do no better job. Of the dry forms, the more expensive ones are generally the best.

As with nitrate and sulfate nutrients, the micronutrients borate (boron in the form used by plants) and molybdate (molybdenum for plant use) can leach out of the soil. In the case of borate, the lighter the soil, the harder it is to hold in the soil. Because they will leach, borate and molybdate should be applied in late winter or early spring for crops in general. However, in the case of boron, if the crop is deep-rooted or the need is so great that a split application is essential, the largest amount should be spread nearest the period of greatest growth.

Whenever possible, spread zinc, manganese, copper and iron in the fall. *Always broadcast micronutrients.* Fall applications enable micronutrients to be more available for crop use the following year. When no application is made in the fall, spring-applied materials will still help the crop. Benefits may not be as great, but this is no reason to skip using the needed traces.

Boron is so low in many soils that the token amounts applied will not boost yields. This often causes the farmer who has made such application to decide he has all he needs. The problem is that for some crops two or three times more than was applied is needed to make the difference in yield. On the other hand, boron (used all by itself) can be effective as a weed killer. This means boron can kill a growing crop when used incorrectly. Legumes in the seedling stage are very sensitive to too much boron.

To begin a boron program, the amount present in the soil must be accurately measured, and then the levels—if insufficient—must be built up accordingly. Boron is the most unstable of the trace elements normally used and can be leached from the soil. The lighter the soil, the harder it is to maintain an adequate boron level.

Certain cautions must be kept in mind. On corn, for example, if there is not enough phosphate, the boron will be thwarted and a lack of grain-fill can result. Corn requires both adequate phosphate and boron for adequate ear fill. If nitrogen rates are high, the need for boron is always en-

NUTRIENT	RANGE IN SOILS (total lb/a)	ESTIMATED CROP REMOVAL (lb/a)	
		CORN (150 bu)	COTTON (1,000 lb lint)
Boron	20-200	0.06	0.05
Copper	2-400	0.05	0.03
Iron	10,000-200,000	0.10	0.07
Manganese	100-10,000	0.08	0.03
Molybdenum	1-7	0.03	0.02
Zinc	20.600	0.15	0.06

Applications of Micronutrients 265

hanced. Excessive amounts of calcium also increases the need for boron.

Boron increases nitrogen availability to the plant. It has several other functions in the plant as well, including a role in cell division, pollination, fruit set and seed development. Boron carries the starch from the leaf to the grain or fruit. So when available boron runs out, production suffers. Boron also helps in the nodulation of legumes.

Crops require a continuous supply of boron, because once boron is utilized by a plant, it has served its purpose, and cannot be used again. Several applications through the season would be ideal where possible. Conditions in the soil that contribute to boron deficiency are excessive potassium levels, excessive calcium levels, high soil pH, low organic matter, low moisture and highly leached soils.

I like to see at least 0.80 ppm boron for general cropping purposes. According to the testing procedures used to determine boron levels, most soils run between 0.40 and 0.60 ppm. I like to leave some room between what I call *excellent* and what I call *maximum* levels. Considering boron for most crops, the minimum is 0.80. There are some qualifications. If I have a reading of 0.80, then I look at everything else before I try to do anything about changing the boron supply. If anything else is low in that soil and boron isn't short, I strive to take care of the other matter before I work on boron because I already have the minimum amount. What I call *excellent* in terms of boron is anything above 1.0. Excessive boron is considered anything above 2.0 ppm. This is determined by looking at what is already present in the soil, and it suggests watching any increase in the concentration to that point. The material used to get to the appropriate level is much the same as with other nutrients. Too much nitrogen burns things up. Too much potassium also can burn the crop. Too much boron causes boron burn or boron toxicity in the soil. The maximum amount of boron that I ever recommend putting on at any one time is four pounds per acre, actual boron. Some crops can't stand four pounds per acre. If you put four pounds per acre on dry beans, alfalfa or soybeans at planting time, these crops will probably never grow. Once a legume arrives at the seedling stage, it will take all the boron it can get even to the point of "committing suicide." So two pounds of boron on legumes represent the maximum. Four pounds on most other crops must be considered maximum. What if you apply four pounds on corn this year and grow soybeans next year? You will not have a problem like that. Once the legume gets out of the seedling stage, you can apply as much as you put on corn, if needed and added in small doses. Alfalfa responds even better to boron than corn. If you have 0.7 ppm on our test and want to get to 0.8 ppm, how much boron does it take? Answer: one pound. If you are at 0.5, then three pounds of boron are required to get to a 0.8 reading. Two pounds will take the reading to 0.7. That is enough for soybeans, but not for corn or most other crops. This is an example of failing to reach the first plateau for those crops. Not all legumes respond to lower levels of boron. In alfalfa production, 0.8 is not the target, 1.2+ is actually needed.

It takes one pound of boron to raise ppm by one-tenth in the soil. The most we ever want to raise it at one time is four-tenths. This translates into not using more than four pounds. But if an option is available, I try to limit everything to two pounds. Therefore, the first application is usually two pounds, and then I recommend a second application of two pounds or less to meet the need. There is a valid reason for this. If the person who is spreading boron gets an overlap using four pounds of actual boron per acre, meaning a double spread where it overlaps, that area gets eight pounds of boron. This can create havoc, especially if calcium is low. With low calcium, boron toxicity is more than just a possibility. So if you need calcium, don't think that you can put on four pounds of boron. The first time you get three days of cool, moist weather—the same kind of weather that calls attention to a phosphate deficiency in corn—an over-application will have smaller corn plants turning white. Even a smaller concentration of too much in a field can be seen as a salt and pepper effect. I recall a recommendation made in the fall. The farmer told me that he had not put on lime and was going to follow through the next spring. He forgot that without calcium, he couldn't apply all that boron. The next spring, he didn't get the liming done and instead of putting on four pounds of actual boron, he applied 4.5 pounds. Three to four days of cool, moist, damp weather followed. There were places in the field where the corn actually died.

I have clients who use boron on acres and acres and acres of corn, cotton, rice, wheat and soybeans, and seldom run into a problem. With adequate calcium, boron works the best. If there is not enough calcium, the boron rate has to be cut in half.

Most growers use the terms *borate* and *boron* interchangeably. This causes a lot of confusion. How much Borate 44G translates into two pounds of actual boron? Fifteen pounds of 44% borate means about two pounds of actual boron. The 44 means 44% borate, no oxygen removed. That translates to about 14% boron, oxygen removed. When I make a recommendation, and I say *15 pounds of Borate 44G*, that means about two pounds of actual boron. When recommending ten pounds of Solubor, which is 21% boron and a material for use in a liquid program, that means two pounds of actual boron. Borate 44G is 14% boron, and Solubor is 21% boron.

Borax is 11% boron. It is a good source of boron, but harder to spread evenly when blended with other materials. It is a naturally mined product. Organic growers can use Borax or Solubor. They should not use Borate 44G, or Borate 48.

I had a client who used four pounds of boron for two or three years on his corn crop. The operator at a fertilizer

Essential Elements in Animal Nutrition with Special Reference to Dairy Cattle

In deficiency diseases caused by the soil, we have to consider factors affecting the chemical nature of our soil, its cultivation, climate, direct conditions such as supplying to our soils chemical fertilizers and so-called "minerals," which should properly be called inorganic nutrients; the extent to which they are absent, or depleted due to cropping and other causes. We should know not only the consequences of their absence, but also the consequences of their optimum presence. The type of crop, the intensity of cropping, and the state of plant growth at which cropping takes place are other factors with which the scientific farmer must be concerned if he wants to correlate animal nutrition with soil conditions.

It is safe to state at the present time that fertile soils should contain at least the following 20 elements: nitrogen, phosphorus, potassium, calcium, magnesium, sulfur, hydrogen, carbon, oxygen, iron, sodium, chlorine, aluminum, silicon, manganese, copper, zinc, boron, iodine, fluorine.

Until quite recently many scientists believed that only the first ten elements were necessary for growth and the maturing of crops; that only the first three should be considered as fertilizer ingredients; and that the others were supplied by soil, air and water, or were present as natural fillers in manures and fertilizer raw materials.

The modern agronomist, however, takes all these 20 essential elements into consideration, and many so-called "complete" fertilizers contain at least 16 to 18, if not all of the elements mentioned above. Cobalt, essential to animal nutrition, can also most economically be supplied through the soil, even though crops grow without. The same can be said of iodine.

> —J.F. Wischhusen
> *History of Randleigh Farm*, 1947

plant will generally start blending with the major nutrients and then add enough boron to get the proper numbers. In this case, the amount needed was four pounds of boron per acre, and all the fertilizer people had to do was pour a sack of Borate 44G into the mixture. The fellow who mixed the product told the customer, "I am sorry, but I have to tell you this. I made a mistake. I put a sack of Borate 44G in at the first of the mix, and I put another sack in at the end of the mix. You have spread eight pounds of boron per acre on that last load, rather than four." The grower marked the spot where the extra boron had been applied. I should add that these fellows had worked on my program for ten years. When they needed a nutrient, they put it on. So they had excellent calcium levels. We didn't have a spring with cool, moist conditions for several days in a row. If we had, they might have been in trouble on the corn that received double the boron recommended. As it was, you couldn't pick out where the eight pounds of actual boron had been applied in that field. One other thing happened on their farm the same year. One of the workers who was driving the fertilizer spreader either forgot to check, or wasn't paying attention, and the chain broke. Everything was kicked out right behind the machine. He didn't find this out until he got to the other end of the field. Then he surveyed the situation. The thing we were most concerned about was the amount of boron. We had calculated 100 pounds of Borate 44G per acre between two rows of corn. Of course, they had nitrogen and the other things with it. This meant about 14 pounds of actual boron between two rows. The father had been skeptical about using all these trace elements anyway. He was out there that day and he said, "Well, I'll watch those two rows and tell you what happens."

Sure enough, when I came back later that year, I said, "Well, have you ever been down to see how that boron is doing?"

He said, "I drive by there every day. I will tell you right now that the only thing that has happened is that those two rows of corn are greener and taller than all the rest of the field."

In this case, we didn't have the conditions for boron to kill the corn. Excellent growing conditions prevailed. We didn't get that cool, moist weather. If we had, this story probably would have had a far worse ending. The point is, just because you happen to get away with a mistake in a certain year, don't think you can continue that way and not have to pay for it when conditions dictate.

The next year the same farmer had a guy running the fertilizer spreader, and he wasn't careful enough. They were applying four pounds of boron per acre. This particular field had been in cotton for years. Cotton growers don't always pay as much attention to lime as they should. They hadn't added calcium recently to answer base saturation numbers. That put the readout down to 58% or 59% base saturation. This level still allows for an adequate cotton or corn crop if everything else is in place. In any case, the calcium was low. If the farmer had applied four pounds of boron and gotten an even spread, it would have been fine. In fact he got a two-row overlap. In those two rows, the corn turned white because we got several cool, moist days in a row.

When I talk about one and two pounds of boron, I am not talking about a problem, except in the case of soybeans or dry beans, where a two-pound application represents the maximum rate. For legumes, one pound the first time out and then another pound later on is better so that an overlap is prevented.

Boron can be tied up by overliming or by extra high potassium levels. If you have extra high potassium levels in a soil, then you are not going to get the same boron efficiency. Boron can leach from the soil the same as sulfate and nitrate. The sandier the soil, the lighter the soil, the lower the organic matter, the more boron it takes to keep a level where it should be.

In terms of leaf deficiencies, boron never shows up in anything I have seen, except alfalfa and cabbage, so it is hard to say what a visual leaf deficiency looks like.

Iron is something to be especially concerned about in high calcium soils. It is necessary for chlorophyll formation and electron transport in enzyme systems. Some sensitive crops and their deficiencies are grain sorghum and soybeans. The soybean crop is among the most likely to exhibit iron chlorosis. Still, it is possible to see a crop suffering from iron chlorosis without the familiar yellow showing up in the plant. Soybeans, however, represent an easy crop to evaluate, with the nearness of an iron problem at once apparent. Go out in your bean field where you suspect iron chlorosis or where your calcium is high. Take some soybean plants when they are about 12 inches tall and pluck all the leaves off, leaving the stems. Do that on two or three plants and watch how those leaves grow back. If there is a borderline iron deficiency, they will grow back yellow. If the leaves come back green, there is no iron problem.

Common sources of iron include the iron sulfates, available as 19 to 23% iron. If an iron sulfate is to be used, it becomes necessary to know which one should be used. There is one product called ferric sulfate. It can be used to correct iron problems, albeit only as a soil product, never on the plant. In fact, ferric sulfate can kill growing plants.

There is another iron sulfate called ferrous. Consider what color you buy when it comes to the use of ferrous sulfate. Most fertilizer dealers feel it makes no difference, but the black or yellow colored product should be avoided. The blue or white colored product is the recommended one. You can put ferrous sulfate on where plants are growing without a problem. If ferric sulfate is used on grass, it can kill the grass. Ferrous sulfate, on the other hand, at normal rates will do no harm. A cosmetic caution is now in order.

Iron sulfates can stain terribly in terms of concrete sidewalks around the pool or on the driveway. Sweep these areas immediately after application and before it gets wet.

Iron chelates can be used as soil amendments or in a foliar application, but they take care of the problem only for the one year. They also cost more than ferrous sulfate, which is roughly 20% iron. There are naturally chelated irons that are extracts of the corn plant and thus acceptable for organic programs. They can be applied as a foliar or to the soil. It generally costs more than the other iron chelates. Except in severe cases, I don't concentrate on adding iron sulfate unless the pH and the calcium both are down, and an iron deficiency still exists. In order to build iron in the soil, basically, all you have to do is apply enough sulfur to bring down the calcium level as well as the pH. Most soils have from 20,000 to 200,000 pounds of iron in the top seven inches. A base of 200+ ppm on our test is adequate. Excessive iron seems never to be a problem. Some fields have 3,000 ppm iron and still produce crops as well as fields that have only 300 ppm iron.

As for deficiencies, it will depend on more than just where your iron level is, because iron and manganese work together. Personally, I like to see 200+. Once you get below 100 ppm, there is reason for concern. If manganese is 75 and iron is 70, that is not good. For best results, iron should always be higher than manganese. If manganese is 125, we don't want iron to be 100. We want iron to be higher than the manganese. Most of the time chlorosis will not reveal symptoms until iron gets down to 75 ppm, or perhaps even 50 ppm, except in grain sorghum. Once the iron level dips below 100 in grain sorghum, the possibility of this as a yield limiting factor begins to reveal itself. The 100 ppm I speak of is based on the way our lab runs iron samples. Trace element readouts from laboratory to laboratory provide the widest variety of numbers on a soil test. Evaluations really run the gamut. Some lab numbers run high and some run low. One lab may say 3 ppm is good. Some other lab may say 300 ppm is good. It depends on how they run and interpret the tests. The results seem to be governed by the methods used to make the extraction. The usual procedure for our testing is to put the extracting solution into a test tube with the soil sample. The mixture is succussed for about 30 minutes. Most labs don't shake the tube that long. Accordingly, they develop lower numbers even if they use the same extracts. Is that why one lab talks about 100 ppm for milo, and another lab may suggest 10? The farmer has to stay with a lab he can trust and get used to its numbers.

In terms of the lab test I use for clients, once you start getting below 100 ppm, watch for a possible problem. If you are below 100 and you are growing soybeans, that is a good time to go out and pull off some leaves as described earlier.

The reducing action of manures decomposing in the soil aids in making available iron and manganese. These are present in all soils, but are sometimes unavailable under excessive oxidizing conditions. When you have an extra high calcium level and therefore an extra high pH, manure can help make iron and manganese more available. Manure in effect supplies nitrogen and drives out calcium, thereby lowering pH.

Now let's consider manganese needs more closely. Manganese helps crops in several ways. It accelerates germination and hastens fruiting and ripening of crops. It is important in the assimilation of nitrates, and is essential for the assimilation of carbon dioxide in photosynthesis. In combination with potassium and copper, it provides stalk strength to the crop. Manganese is an essential part of the enzyme system in plants and, in particular, activates fat forming enzymes. It is also directly involved in the uptake of iron, carotene and ascorbic acid by plants. Furthermore, it is directly related to the uptake of glutathione in plants. Stressed plants produce more of this substance than those doing

Hands-On Agronomy

well, and therefore attract insects. Insects eat the plants, gorging themselves in order to get the glutathione.

Soils most likely to show a manganese deficiency are light, sandy soils, water-logged soils and previously wet areas that have been drained, heavy cuts on graded fields, deeply eroded areas and alkaline soils.

The first plateau for manganese is 40 ppm. Excessive is 250+ ppm. The textbooks will tell you that 100 ppm manganese are good and that 200 ppm are toxic. I haven't been able to confirm that. Perhaps this is based on the way various tests were conducted and reported.

For general crop purposes, the minimum amount of manganese that should appear on our test results is 40 ppm. Depending on test methods, other lab minimum levels could be different. However, as other limiting factors are eliminated, manganese levels should at least be maintained above 80+ ppm, with an excellent level being 125+ ppm. In fact, when all other nutrients are properly supplied, the best wheat yields are attained at even higher levels of manganese.

In Germany, the highest wheat yielding soils on the farms that I work with have the highest manganese levels. Some will run as high as 250 ppm. A top yielding field set a record for that type of soil in Lower Saxony. When I started working there, it was a problem field, yielding 80 to 90 bushels of wheat per acre because it had been over-fertilized. In the fourth year after working with it, the wheat yield went to 131 bushels per acre. The manganese level in that wheat field was 240+ ppm.

The elements manganese and magnesium are often confused because they sound so similar. Magnesium is a secondary element generally supplied by dolomite limestone, magnesium sulfate, or other forms of fertilizers. Even manganese and magnesium deficiency symptoms are somewhat similar. In both cases the leaves of many plants turn yellow or white except for the veins, which remain dark green. But the difference between them is a manganese deficiency shows up first in new leaves at the top of the plant. Magnesium deficiency shows up first in the oldest leaves at the bottom of the plant.

Manganese plays a major role in photosynthesis as well as chlorophyll synthesis and enzyme system construction and operation. Some manganese sensitive crops are soybeans and dry beans, oats, sugar beets, table beets, lettuce and citrus fruit. I see the fastest response to manganese on beans. I have been in those heavy, black, soggy-type soils in northwestern Ohio where the manganese is deficient and farmers spray a foliar manganese. When it was time to quit and go to lunch, the grower could have driven the tractor to the house and not marked anything because, after lunch, those beans were already green to the row where he stopped spraying. The crop can assimilate the nutrient that fast.

Manganese deficient soybeans have a coloration best described as yellow. Once you drop below 40 ppm manganese, soybeans suffer, more so than most other crops. I am just as concerned about wheat. I do recommend use of manganese on some fields of soybeans and wheat in various areas. Manganese deficiency in corn really presents no signs until it drops below 30 ppm. Below 30 it actually stunts the growth of corn. It shortens internodes on the stalk.

In terms of the amount needed and how it affects all crops, manganese is the most important of all the micronutrients. However, on many fields where needed, it is not recognized as being necessary due to the latent deficiency (hidden hunger), that is low enough to affect yield, but not enough to show up in the leaves of the crop.

A soil analysis should always be conducted to determine present levels before any manganese is applied. This is especially true since manganese toxicity is possible in soils with a pH of 5.5 or less, depending on the levels available in any particular soil. Raising the pH from 5.5 to 6.5 decreases the amount of manganese available in the soil solution by 100 times.

Since manganese availability in many soils begins to reach critically low levels as pH rises above 6.5, the first rules to consider in order to provide adequate levels for a crop are, "Know how much is present and be careful not to over-lime your fields." Overuse of potassium or magnesium fertilizers can also reduce manganese availability because both of these nutrients increase soil pH too. Regardless of the pH level, unusually high potassium or sodium levels (in combination totaling 10% or more of a soil's base saturation) mean that manganese uptake will be blocked out of the plant, no matter what a test may show. In this case manganese is not tied up in the soil, it is still available, but the excessive saturation of potassium and/or sodium is so high that the manganese cannot be properly taken up by the crop. This problem occurs most often on lighter soils, and is especially troublesome for cotton, wheat, soybeans, peas, oats, tomatoes, citrus and grapes.

In addition, low sulfur levels can cause less manganese to be available to the crop. Also, very high organic matter (6% or above) and very low organic matter (less than 2 1/2%) can restrict manganese availability. Sufficient moisture, warm soil temperatures and adequate aeration are important factors which help provide an ample supply of manganese.

Sources of manganese include manganese sulfate for soil and foliar applications, manganese oxides, which, when taken up by the soil, can help on slightly acidic soils or as a water-soluble foliar application at low rates, chelated and complexed manganese, acidic manganese frits, and manganese sequestered in polyphosphates.

Despite many claims to the contrary, our best results for building manganese levels in the soil have been from the use of manganese sulfate at broadcast rates. When lime is applied the same year, a second application may be needed before levels show an increase, since liming tends to reduce availability of manganese. It is also effective as a foliar application, though chelates and other forms can also be used effectively at the recommended rates as a foliar.

The common source for manganese, and the one I rely on most, is manganese sulfate. In this form, it is the lowest priced and the easiest with which to build soil levels. It is generally styled 23 to 27% manganese sulfate.

The only time manganese oxide might be considered for building soil levels is when it is possible to absolutely pulverize the product into a powder and then build it back to a prell or a pellet. If it is pulverized first and then built back, it is possible to get a breakdown as good as with manganese sulfate. But if it isn't pulverized, it will simply rest there and fail to build up the desired nutrient levels.

Manganese chelate is something else. Many farmers in Ohio spray it on their soybeans. They have been told that manganese sulfate is no good for the purpose of building manganese levels. A more valid approach, perhaps, is to call around to see what kind of cost comparisons are available. If we have a 36 ppm manganese and put on 25 pounds of manganese sulfate, certain soils will be taken care of in regard to that manganese deficiency with one application at a cost of $7.50 for 25 pounds. As far as manganese chelate is concerned, it comes down to taking the amount of manganese usually fed into the leaf and supplying it as a foliar. That equivalent feeds the plant but will not influence soil levels. This means the procedure has to be done every year, year in and year out. In order to get enough manganese chelate on a soybean crop to be equivalent to the reaction from 25 pounds of manganese sulfate, it costs about the same. With the manganese chelate, this cost is repeated every year. Manganese sulfate, on the other hand, builds up soil levels. A caveat has to be added—*most times*. Certain soils can absorb manganese at 25 pounds per acre and improve the level a little bit. Applied a second time, the recorded level will go up a little bit more. And applied a third time, it will go up a little bit again. There are soils for which we really don't solve the manganese problem for very long. The level can be improved temporarily, and then it drops back down. So keep checking the levels in the soil. For most soils, however, the manganese problem is solved with the first application, and manganese sulfate is the most economical source to apply.

Why won't the chelates stay put? Actually, the manganese chelate contains a very minute amount of manganese, essentially the same payload the plant roots would forage from the soil. The chelate cannot increase the overall availability of manganese in the soil. With the chelate, you are using a small amount of manganese to get it into the leaf. Our objective in taking the soil route is to build levels to a point where the farmer doesn't have to keep spending money.

Another effective means of increasing manganese availability is the use of ammonium sulfate or ammonium nitrate, especially on alkaline soils. So if soil pH is above 6.5, these materials provide a special advantage in soils that are below the desired level in manganese.

Manganese availability is most affected after you get above a pH of 7. It is also affected when you have a pH even below 7 in heavy, soggy soils.

Now consider copper. When it comes right down to it, information on whether or not a farmer should be trying to increase the copper level in his soils can become very confusing. For example, one Midwestern university extension publication from the 1970s reads, "The amount of copper available for plant growth is not adequately known since a reliable soil test for copper does not exist." Then the author goes on to recommend how much copper to use on particular crops anyway. When it comes to micronutrient use, much the same thing still goes on today.

Copper is a micronutrient, needed in small amounts when compared to N, P and K, sulfur or limestone. And all of these nutrients are needed in adequate amounts before trying to increase production capabilities with trace elements such as copper.

Severe copper deficiencies are most common on boggy-type soils such as peat, muck or those unusually high in organic matter. Very sandy soils are also more likely to be copper deficient. But slight (latent) deficiencies—"hidden hunger"—are prevalent for some high yielding crops even on good mineralized soils. Such problems can occur due to heavy applications of nitrogen or high amounts of phosphate in the soil. Either of these can reduce copper availability. High soil pH levels (above 7.0 on our test) and drought conditions intensify any copper problems. Also, excessive zinc levels can lead to serious copper deficiencies in the crop. When neglected, copper can become the limiting factor in yield, especially in small grains, particularly wheat, corn, cotton, grasses, fruit trees and certain vegetables such as onions, spinach and members of the cabbage family, including rapeseed.

Copper is essential to chlorophyll formation in plants. It is also important in the reproductive stage of development, meaning better seed production. Copper helps increase the sugar content of fruits and vegetables. It contributes to both better color and flavor, and helps increase storage and shipping qualities. Copper will increase stalk strength in combination with adequate potassium and manganese, which enables crops to withstand higher rates of nitrogen without lodging problems. And in this regard, adequate copper seems to increase the uptake efficiency of plants receiving ammonium forms of nitrogen. This can be especially important to those crops receiving late applications of ammonia nitrogen such as wheat or medium to full-season corn. It is also important where manure or compost is used because ammonia can be directly used in the production of amino acids at late stages of growth and copper is involved in building and converting the amino acids to protein.

Regional Variations in the Mineral Composition of Vegetables

Samples of cabbage, lettuce, snapbeans, spinach and tomatoes were obtained from commercial fields of these crops in Georgia, South Carolina, Virginia, Maryland, New Jersey, New York (Long Island), Ohio, Indiana, Illinois, and Colorado. The total number of samples examined was 204.

The collecting had to be done during the mid-summer months, and this made it impossible to obtain samples of all five crops from all ten states. Fortunately, samples of snapbeans and tomatoes were secured from every state. This report, therefore, deals primarily with the findings on these two crops. Bountiful snapbeans and Rutgers tomatoes were chosen for collecting, and most of the samples belonged to these two varieties. Insofar as possible, the cabbage, lettuce, and spinach samples were confined to the Golden Acre, Grand Rapids, and Savoy varieties, respectively.

All samples were collected at the stage of growth when they were being harvested for market. Field collection was followed by as rapid transportation to the laboratory as possible. Only the edible portions were prepared for analysis, the outer leaves of cabbage and lettuce being discarded. All samples were rinsed in cold distilled water. The tomatoes were rubbed also with a clean cloth. The samples were dried in a hot-air convection oven at temperatures ranging between 70° and 80° C. Samples of the vegetables were wet-ashed with a mixture of nitric and perchloric acids and made up to volume. Aliquots were then analyzed for the major nutrient elements by standard procedures, including the use of the flame photometer for determining calcium, potassium and sodium. Another sample was dry-ashed at between 600° and 700° C, and analyzed for the minor mineral nutrient elements by the use of a spectrograph.

The soils involved in the eastern coastal plain states were of the Tifton, Bladen, Orangeburg, Portsmouth, Norfolk and Sassafras series. These belong to the podzolic group, including both the red-yellow and the gray-brown zones. They have all been developed from coastal plain materials and have been thoroughly leached, they have relatively low exchange capacities, and they contain only very limited supplies of mineral nutrients.

The soils involved in the east north central states were of the Wooster, Miami, Crosby, Brookston, Clarion and Webster series. The first four are members belonging to the gray-brown podzolic group, which have been developed on glacial drift, some of which was of a calcareous nature. Those of the last two series are prairie soils, which have been developed from calcareous glacial drift.

The Colorado vegetables were obtained from areas where the Laurel, Gilchrist and Berthan series predominate. These soils belong to the brown and planosol groups, and are under irrigation farming. They are high in calcium carbonate and in available mineral nutrients.

Fertilizing and liming practices influence the mineral composition of plants. Consequently it seemed desirable to make a survey of these practices as employed on the fields from which the samples were selected. The data from this survey are summarized in the table. It is important to note the relatively high rates at which fertilizer is applied in the coastal plain states as compared to the rates employed farther west. In the east north central states less dependence is placed on fertilizers and greater use is made of clover sods and manure. Only relatively small amounts of fertilizer are used in Colorado.

The rate of use of lime increases from Georgia northward to New Jersey. It varies considerably from farm to farm in the east north central states. No lime was used on the Colorado farms.

Data on the ash and mineral cation content of 46 samples of snapbeans and 67 samples of tomatoes are shown, state by state, in the table.

—*Firman E. Bear*
The Land News [Friends of the Land], 1949

Hands-On Agronomy

Average ash and nutrient-cation content of snapbeans and tomatoes and highest and lowest individual values* for these and 3 other vegetables

Ash in percentages and cations in milliequivalents per 100 grams dry matter

STATE	SNAPBEANS Ash	Ca	Mg	K	Na	TOTAL CATIONS	TOMATOES Ash	Ca	Mg	K	Na	TOTAL CATIONS
Georgia	6.50	14.5	38.3	51.7	1.3	105.8	7.78	6.0	32.9	85.7	3.0	127.6
S. Carolina	6.26	23.0	32.9	44.8	2.2	101.9	8.20	7.5	30.4	85.7	3.5	127.1
Virginia	5.98	17.0	25.5	50.9	1.7	95.1	8.44	7.0	33.7	97.2	2.2	140.1
Maryland	6.49	20.4	36.2	56.0	0.8	113.5	7.00	14.0	14.8	88.2	0.4	117.4
New Jersey	6.62	24.0	43.6	48.8	3.9	120.3	8.14	13.0	21.4	83.1	2.2	119.7
New York	6.34	25.5	39.5	64.5	3.0	132.5	8.95	14.5	17.3	107.4	1.3	140.5
Ohio	8.53	30.5	45.2	71.1	1.7	149.1	9.10	13.5	26.3	101.8	1.3	142.6
Indiana	6.59	30.5	46.0	67.5	1.3	145.3	9.18	15.0	28.0	101.8	2.2	147.0
Illinois	7.73	26.5	43.6	70.6	1.3	142.0	8.59	13.8	28.0	96.0	1.3	139.1
Colorado	7.68	29.0	48.5	56.5	0.4	134.4	11.54	15.0	33.7	111.0	0.8	160.5

	Ash	Ca	Mg	K	Na
SNAPBEANS					
Highest	10.45	40.5	60.0	99.7	8.6
Lowest	4.04	15.5	14.8	29.1	0.0
CABBAGE					
Highest	10.38	60.0	43.6	148.3	20.4
Lowest	6.12	17.5	15.6	53.7	0.8
LETTUCE					
Highest	24.28	71.0	49.3	176.5	12.2
Lowest	7.01	16.0	13.1	53.7	0.0
TOMATOES					
Highest	14.20	23.0	59.2	148.3	6.5
Lowest	6.07	4.5	4.5	58.8	0.0
SPINACH					
Highest	28.56	96.0	203.9	257.0	69.5
Lowest	12.38	47.5	46.9	84.6	0.8

*No two of these extreme values are for the same sample. Thus, for snapbeans the highest Ca, Mg, K and Na values were found in Colorado, Indiana, and New York, respectively.

Copper rarely ever occurs in significant enough quantities to be increased in the soil or plant by amounts contained in the usual mineral fertilizers. But sufficient applications of the proper materials can build up the levels in the soil for longer periods of time than is possible for most other micronutrients. Copper sulfate is the most effective form to use in building copper levels in the soil. It acts rapidly when applied to the soil, but such small amounts are required that it must be uniformly mixed or blended with other fertilizers in order to be spread properly.

Copper chelate, 2% to 7 1/2%, is an effective foliar source. However, applications as a foliar feed supply only the present crop and will have no significant effect on future copper levels or crops to be grown there.

The critical ranges for copper are these. Anything below 2 ppm copper means deficiency. Five ppm is excellent, and 10 ppm+ is excessive. Above 10 ppm, plenty of phosphates are mandated because copper can tie up phosphate exactly the way phosphate can tie up copper. It is better to stay between 5 and 10 ppm, but above 2 ppm, don't even start thinking about getting to 5 until everything else has been put into proper equilibrium, at which point it is time to re-evaluate how much money can be spent. Always test before adding copper to the soil. Continuing applications beyond the point needed for top production can lead to toxicity problems. Excessive levels can affect phosphate, zinc and iron uptake.

When it comes to copper, remember what happens when you put on extra nitrogen. Too much nitrogen stops the uptake of copper. Overuse of nitrogen can mean a copper deficiency.

Copper, per pound, is the most expensive of all the nutrient elements required for crop production. It is also the most stable element. Once the copper level gets built up, it does not have to be built up again for long periods of time.

If you put on 25 pounds of manganese sulfate, we generally expect that this is going to raise the manganese by about 3.5 ppm. When we apply copper as ten pounds of 23% copper sulfate, it will raise the copper level in a year's time by .6 ppm. Five pounds of copper sulfate will raise the level by .3 ppm. In other words, if you have 1.4 ppm and you want to get to 2 ppm, five pounds of copper sulfate will carry the soil system to only 1.7 ppm that first year, still short for wheat and other similar crops.

Except in the case of wheat and other small grains, if I tell you that you need ten pounds of copper sulfate and that amount represents a cost that is too high, you could consider putting on two pounds for the next five years instead of ten pounds at once without much affect on yields. You can build copper levels this way because that nutrient is so stable in the soil. Almost every soil I analyze is deficient in copper. The few exceptions are where there is a lot of copper in the soil and manure has been used, or along rivers where soil has been moved in by constant flooding, and where alluvial deposits keep the soil built up. The other place where we don't have copper deficiencies is where a lot of pesticides containing copper have been used in the past, and where turkey litter is commonly used.

When crops on soils with adequate fertility that test low in copper fail to respond to copper applications, a molybdenum test should be considered. Both need to be present in adequate amounts, since either one can influence the amount a crop can take up of the other one.

A farmer from Iowa I had worked with for eight years called me one day. He said he had a problem with some of his corn going down. He wanted me to look at the soil test. He had 80 acres split into four 20s, and one had a 1.5 copper, his lowest level. I told him that his copper was 1.5 ppm and he was going to have the weakest stalks there. It was true. He said, "Well, since that is true, what about the next field?" We went through all the data until he hit 2 ppm. In each case he lost corn from lodging, but the lower the copper level below 2 ppm, the worse the corn was lodged. Copper gives resilience to a plant. The other key to flavor after sulfur is copper. Copper doesn't move in the soil. If you see a copper deficiency at all, it is like sulfur. It shows the deficiency in the youngest growth first. Adequate nitrogen means you get better copper uptake. Too much nitrogen means you actually decrease the availability of copper to the plant. Wheat is a crop that responds well to copper. If the other needed nutrients are adequate, but you are below 2 ppm copper and you put enough copper on your wheat to get above 2 ppm, it will make an extra five bushels of wheat.

I went over to Germany in 1985. The client who asked me over there had me speaking to several groups of farmers. He told me to tell them just what I had done on his farms. In Germany, they use the taller varieties of wheat, but they also use growth retardants or growth regulators to keep plants short. When the subject turned to copper, I mentioned that if the soil had below 2 ppm and copper was put on, it would increase yields by five bushels per acre. I also told them that every soil I had checked in Germany was below that level. One man raised his hand, stood up and spoke for two or three minutes. The interpreter leaned over and said, "This is the man who is in charge of fertility for the university in this area. He is telling the farmers why they don't need to really worry about the copper that you said should be put on." When he had finished, a doctor of fertility research rose and reported a ten-year study (unknown to me) just completed which had shown exactly the same results I had mentioned on wheat production.

Copper sulfate, 22.5 or 23%, is water soluble and can be applied to soil or as a foliar. I won't bother with other copper sources if I can get copper sulfate because I know it works and I know how much can be applied safely. A ten-pound application of copper sulfate—in 12 months time—will raise the copper level by 0.6 ppm on the specific test we use. A copper level is the easiest to build, and zinc is the next in the pecking order. Both have staying power in the soil.

Zinc aids in the absorption of moisture. Along with potassium, think of zinc in critical moisture situations. It also helps transform carbohydrates. It regulates plant sugar use. Zinc plays a role in enzyme system functioning, as well as with the growth regulators normally present in the plant and protein synthesis. Consider zinc needs, especially in sensitive crops such as corn and grain sorghum, also soybeans and dry beans. As far as zinc levels are concerned, the minimum is 6 ppm. Below that, enough should be applied the first year to get up above the 6 ppm figure. There has never been a soil—in my experience at least—that required more than 30 pounds of zinc sulfate to completely take care of the worst zinc deficiency, provided limestone didn't have to be applied at the same time. If lime is applied, the lime won't drive out the zinc, but it will affect zinc availability. If you need zinc and lime and put on the lime but don't put on the zinc, expect your zinc level to get worse. Zinc probably gives a response more often than any other micronutrient when it is applied for crop production. I see many soils that need zinc. All can be taken care of, generally with excellent response. Only a few crops do not respond well to zinc when only slightly deficient, one of them being wheat. Again, 6 ppm is the minimum. Excellent means 10 ppm, and an excess is 20 ppm+.

A classic sign of zinc deficiency in corn is the whitish stripe in the leaf color, which looks much like a magnesium deficiency. In the field, often I can't tell whether it is a zinc deficiency or a magnesium deficiency. The difference between zinc and magnesium deficiencies should be that zinc will be white and magnesium will be white on top with a purplish color on the bottom.

Too much nitrogen also ties up zinc. High phosphorous, high calcium or high potassium levels can induce zinc defi-

A Nutritional Cure for Brucellosis

We fed manganese-iodide in approximately the same proportion as potassium-iodide with results that seemed almost incredible. In fact the herd to which this was fed was almost wholly infected with brucellosis and none of the cows had been able to deliver a calf—all of them aborted. To our surprise, after the feeding of manganese-iodide, many of the cows delivered living calves. To assure ourselves that this was not a coincidence, we tried the manganese-iodide in the feed of a second herd. All but three out of the 24 cows delivered a calf.

Whether or not manganese is an insufficient mineral we do not know, however, we proceeded to feed this to still another herd which was infected with brucellosis. We administered at least 10 grains of manganese sulfate, disregarding the iodine, and only one cow aborted.

Because of past experience in combining manganese-iodide with chloride of cobalt, we next added chloride of cobalt to the iron sulfate and manganese-iodide in the feed of certain cows which were obstinate cases and where an abortion seemed inevitable. To our great satisfaction the abortions were avoided and the animals delivered normal calves.

To get satisfactory results in the treatment of brucellosis, we tried an experiment. We took an infected cow and placed it beside a clean cow which was not infected and kept the two together in the same stall for a period of one year. At the end of the year, we found the infected cow still infected and the clean cow still clean. Our veterinarian concluded that the clean cow might be carrying some infection which would be a counteraction to the brucellosis germ, and "since he was not satisfied that the test was conclusive, he would not permit infected animals to be introduced into a herd of non-infected animals.

His precaution has proved wise for since the event of testing for brucellosis in cows, whole herds have been cleaned up by the isolation method, and now herds are being sold with a guarantee that they are a clean herd, and not infected with brucellosis.

Our conclusion is that iodine, manganese and cobalt are important elements in the feeding of cattle to eradicate brucellosis and should be given to high-producing cows in their feed rations.

—*Oscar Erf*
quoted in *The History of Randleigh Farm*, 1947

ciencies as does the overuse of nitrogen. Also, as the pH goes up from 6, zinc availability begins to decrease, and it can go as high as 7 before it stops decreasing that availability. Heavy cuts, such as when the field has been graded or the topsoil has been taken away, or when washed subsoils appear, strong zinc deficiencies become evident.

Zinc is not easy to leach away. It is held well on clay and humus. Once zinc levels are improved, it is relatively easy to keep them up. When zinc sulfate is applied, using our tests, an exact relationship between the amount of zinc and the soil can be expected. Zinc sulfate is 36% zinc. Application of ten pounds of zinc sulfate will exhibit a 3.6 pound increase of zinc on the test. The correlation is classic. Putting on ten pounds of 36% zinc sulfate means putting on 3.6 pounds of zinc per acre. A soil test—when the zinc is finished breaking down—will show an increase of 3.6 pounds of zinc. That translates into 1.8 ppm, meaning every 10 pounds of zinc sulfate applied will raise the zinc level by 1.8 ppm. There is one other thing to be remembered about pure zinc sulfate. Put on ten pounds of zinc sulfate today, then come back next year and pull a soil test on the same day. That zinc is only going to be halfway to its final level. You are only going to see a 0.9 ppm increase in the soil. When you put on sufficient zinc it will not reach the desired level for two years, but will supply enough zinc for the crops grown for both years.

Some firms say they have a 36% zinc product, it being a 36% oxysulfate. It is cheaper at the counter, but it will not build zinc levels. Apply ten pounds, the same as with 36% zinc sulfate, and next year the deficiency is still there. Pure zinc sulfate is the sure choice. There are some zinc oxide products that have been pulverized and then prilled which have also proved effective for increasing the levels in the soil.

With the exception of boron on most soils, the technology exists in order to build the levels of trace elements to a point that it is not an annual expense, but basically an initial expenditure and then afterwards it is a matter of testing and fertilizing as needed over the years to keep the levels up. Micronutrients, when applied in the right form, will build up the levels in the soil and help the crop yields accordingly.

Some farmers who have livestock have always felt they shouldn't have to be concerned with trace elements because their manure or compost would take care of it. I work with many farmers who use manures and compost, and this is rarely the case. Think about it. When a soil is deficient in copper and adequate copper is not being supplemented, how can enough be in the manure? Manure is generally low in sulfur, boron and copper—the nutrients most often lacking in our soils used for growing the crops. Keep in mind, when manure is applied, you can influence the soil nutrient level to only the extent of what is there in the first place. Nevertheless, manure is certainly helpful and in certain soils even sufficient to keep the trace elements that are present in a soil most available for plant use, while at the same time helping to recycle those that are picked up in the feed. And therefore, as the use of manures in an area declines, the need for trace elements will increase.

Most soils we analyze just do not have an adequate supply of trace elements to assure that the crop will do its best. So just because there is enough of the major elements for the crop, does not assure that trace element levels will be adequate also.

Under the present economic circumstances, every farmer needs to have the confidence that he is on a solid footing, and doing all he can to supply his crops the fertility needed from start to finish. The misconceptions and misunderstandings about soil fertility make this even harder to accomplish. The more farmers or those involved in a soil fertility program understand the reasons behind micronutrient recommendations, the more confidence there will be in those recommendations and the decisions made on how to use them. The lack of any nutrient, whether needed in major, secondary or trace amounts, hurts the soil and all that must live from it.

My-cor-rhi-za / ˌmī-ke-ʹrī-ze / *n* [NL, fr. *myc* + Gk *rhiza* root] **1** the symbiotic association of the mycelium of fungus with plant roots **2** an underground living complex that decomposes organic materials, making soils fertile by entering into symbiotic relationships with roots of higher plants to supply them with critically needed compounds

13

The Grower's Purpose

I ALWAYS STRIVE TO TEACH THE IDEA that a farmer needs a program. It is not merely a matter of needing a soil test. Rather, a good soil test that one can count on is mandatory, and there has to be a program to follow through on. I also strive to teach the idea that the products used must fit the plan. I never tout a specific product and then try to build a program around it. I do try to see where you are and then plug in products that are readily available. If that does not do the job, then additional education is in order. Both ends of the equation need to understand ways and means available to accomplish the grower's purpose. Let's say you have a farm and you would like to produce in the most economical way, but you can't handle manure. You don't have a manure spreader and you can't find anybody to spread the material. Or if you have manure and can spread it, then at least I need to know that and what type of manure it is. Once that information is available, we are ready to face reality. At that point I try to help the grower find the materials required. I don't sell fertilizer for a living, I sell my services as a soil fertility specialist, and the farmer works with the suppliers he chooses.

William A. Albrecht always stressed that if you want to do it right, look at nature and see how nature does, and try to get as close to nature as possible. So far, in this little book, we have looked at the structure of the soil, its composition—minerals, humus, air and water. We have looked at these in terms of chemistry and we have looked at them in terms of physics. But chemistry and physics can supply only two-thirds of the answer. For the full answer, we must now look at the biological side of the soil. In most instances, the biological side of the grower's equation gets slighted. For reasons that escape me, farmers are not quite as interested in biology. Yet they know they have to have 25% air and 25% water in the soil system. Microbes require plenty of air and water to live. Sandy soils generally have too much air and not enough moisture.

In a heavy clay soil, the mix goes the other way. We get more water saturation and not enough air space. There is less pore space because colloids stick closer together. So the biology of the soil needs the exact physical and chemical mix detailed here to do its business. Examine soils and you will conclude that every time the texture changes, so does the soil's ability to absorb moisture and deliver nutrients. Topsoil has to be completely saturated before water will penetrate into the next layer. When soils are worked, a chisel plow or offset disc is to be preferred. Unlike a moldboard plow, either implement will help keep nutrients on top where they belong. By way of contrast, a moldboard plow turns over the soil, creating a new and generally hostile environment for the microbes present.

Even a disc or a chisel plow keeps coarser particles on top, with the finer particles sifting downward.

We actually create a silt layer in the soil when we work at the same depth all the time. What difference does it make? You have to keep the soil open so that there are avenues for the water to travel through. Say that the first two-inch layer has more sand. It has to become saturated before water will penetrate the next layer. Then that layer has to be saturated before it allows water to move into the next layer. The soil system works best with coarse particles on top, with medium and fine particles below. When Mount St. Helens erupted in Washington state, I was in touch with a good friend who worked as a consultant in the area. A lot of farms had an inch of volcanic ash deposited on top of the soil. That ash was a finer textured material than the soil itself. He analyzed the ash for its nutrient content. He also wanted to see what the fines were, what the medium sizes were, and the character of the heavies. That volcanic ash matched out to a silty type soil.

The topsoil where he was working was a sandy type soil. The farmer who used a moldboard plow to turn under the ash created a new water barrier. If you have coarse sand on top, and then you put a silt layer down, all that sand has to get completely saturated with water before it will move into the silt layer. Then—if you have enough moisture—if you can keep it coming in, it will finally penetrate the silt layer and move down below it. When the plant wants to pull moisture back up, the task becomes nearly impossible if water didn't get past the silt layer. It has to complete the saturation process before water can wick back into the top. Farmers who knew enough to mix the volcanic dust into the top six inches of soil didn't have the problem created by those using a moldboard plow.

Any time you get a different consistency in terms of texture, you are impeding water movement. You can get some sediments near the surface if the soil is not kept open. The

The Grower's Purpose   295

first key to keeping pore space open is to keep a proper calcium saturation. The second key to keeping it open is to minimize compaction. And a third key is to offset compaction if indeed it occurs. A water penetration problem is also a root penetration problem. When you begin to see a brown color throughout the topsoil layer, you can know that something is working in the right direction. When the lower portion is gray or yellow in appearance, it indicates that soil will need extra help. A soil conditioner works well in this regard. As long as we keep the top 6.75 inches working and open, we have effectively canceled out the need to worry in terms of initial water penetration. But when the top is skinned to a subsoil level, then new problems arrive. Roots will not penetrate unless hardpans are eliminated.

Basically, the farm publications do not deal in soil biology. The reason is nobody is making enough money on microbes to be able to pay for the advertising or to pay the people to do the articles. The big money is made in herbicides and pesticides, which rate so much advertising space. I have heard many professionals say that farmers still aren't using enough phosphate and potash, so there is no need to worry about all these other things, like soil biology.

Most of the people in mainline companies imply that using natural systems is old fashioned. They feel it won't work in today's agriculture. They say you can't use natural systems because it would be tantamount to going back to the mule and the garden tractor, and neither enable megafarm management. Well, I am not talking about that kind of a natural system. I stress a natural system that works in a modern operation. You have to look at the natural cycles in nature to use the biology of the soil properly. There are cycles in nature and one of them is the nitrogen cycle. Rain will provide a certain amount of nitrogen from the air, about 4 to 5%. This blessing is available in a form the plant can use. Of course, manures go into the soil and confer nitrogen on the nutrient complex. Nitrogen can be fixed in the

Hands-On Agronomy

Versatility and Industry in the Soil

Every saltspoonful of soil on this planet contains at least two billion microbes. [A recent survey showed that there are more bacteria on and in every person's body than there are human beings on earth.] That is an incomparably larger population than those of the few microbial species we believe to be nuisances. Just as the astronomical hordes of bacteria covering our persons have no ill effects, and indeed are useful to us, so the microbial community in the soil is exquisitely well adjusted for coexistence with the plants, and animals, that it supports.

One of the key functions of soil microorganisms is to break down dead plant and animal tissues and return their nutrient chemicals to the soil. Yet in high summer a field of, say, turnips or potatoes can grow vigorously in intimate contact with billions of creatures specifically capable of destroying these vegetables. Only if and when the tissue has died can the scavenger organisms operate, and then they do so swiftly and efficiently. As with our skin inhabitants, there is a disturbing lesson here for those who believe in shattering the natural balance of the microbial world by chemical overkill.

—*Bernard Dixon*
Magnificent Microbes, 1976

soil biologically by *Rhizobium* bacteria. There are other forms of microbes and soil life that fix nitrogen, including the algae. We can harvest nitrogen from both plants and animals and recycle it as much as possible. In the soil, there are systems that bring nitrogen back out. Chemically, it goes from ammonia to nitrite to nitrate. It is used in forming proteins. It escapes the soil as nitrogen oxide in gas form. If bacteria fail to break it down again, it may re-enter the atmosphere. Nature's cycles—carbon and nitrogen—are more wondrous than anything man can account for. Academia can take 180 bushels of corn and show the amount of nutrients used by the crop according to the number of growth days. According to these data, 19 pounds of nitrogen are taken in by the corn during the first 25 days.

We also hear it stressed about having phosphate on the soil for seed production, or the need to have phosphate early for corn. In the first 25 days, a 180-bushel corn crop takes four pounds of P_2O_5 out of the soil. In the first 25 days, it also takes 22 pounds of potassium. But what do we hear stressed when we talk about raising a 180-bushel corn crop? The term is nitrogen, nitrogen, nitrogen. Yet it takes only 19 pounds of nitrogen for the first 25 days of that above-mentioned corn crop. But it takes 22 pounds of potassium in the same first 25 days for the same production record. The same corn crop takes more potassium than nitrogen during the first 25 days. At 50 days, the calculated intake is 103 pounds of nitrogen and 126 pounds of potassium. Yet we will come in and put on 200 pounds of nitrogen and, say, 90 pounds of potassium or less is enough. How can we do that? If you have good potassium levels in the soil, it works well. On the 75th day of 125 day corn, 198 pounds of potassium will have been taken up, as will 178 pounds of nitrogen. At 100 days, the numbers are 226 pounds of nitrogen and 234 pounds of potassium. At 125 days, nitrogen and potash basically balance out, 240 for nitrogen and 240 for potash.

On soybeans at 40 days, a 50-bushel crop takes 7.6 pounds of nitrogen and 6.1 pounds of potassium. It takes more nitrogen in this case, but remember, microbes are supplying 50 to 70% of the nitrogen requirement. If we look at what has to come from the soil, even if it is half, we are talking about 3.8 pounds of nitrogen versus 6.1 potash. Nitrogen gets well ahead of potash, but when you look at a 50-bushel bean crop, you need 257 pounds of nitrogen and 187 pounds of potash. But of that 257 pounds of nitrogen, at least 50% of it probably came from the soil.

Any time you overuse nitrogen, you cut off a portion of the potassium uptake. It is absolutely necessary to leave plenty of room for potassium because corn is going to take more potassium than nitrogen until the last 25 days in the growth cycle.

Now look at a 135-bushel per acre grain sorghum crop. The first 20 days take nine pounds of nitrogen, and 18 pounds of potassium. After 40 days, grain sorghum will have taken in 70 pounds of nitrogen and 121 pounds of potassium. After 60 days, the numbers say 130 pounds of nitrogen and 206 pounds of potassium. At 85 days, it is 157 versus 245—almost 100 pounds more potassium than nitrogen. At 95 days, the numbers are 185 pounds of nitrogen and 258 pounds of potassium. It becomes obvious that potassium really contributes to a grain sorghum yield in terms of pounds per acre.

I stress calcium and phosphorus requirements in alfalfa production. Potassium also has to be stressed, but in first cut alfalfa, yielding 2.35 tons, there will be 136 pounds of nitrogen, 50 to 70% of which came from the air. There will be 31 pounds of phosphates, 124 pounds of potassium and 50 pounds of calcium. A second cutting at 2.1 tons means 11 pounds of nitrogen, 24 pounds of phosphate and 107 pounds of potassium.

In the third cutting, 2.03 tons, and in a fourth cutting, 1.5 tons—now an eight ton total from four cuttings—the breakdown is 415 pounds of nitrogen, at least half of which came from the *Rhizobium* symbiont, 94 pounds of phosphorus, 401 pounds of potassium, 151 pounds of calcium, 36 pounds of magnesium and 26 pounds of sulfur. Convert sulfur to sulfate—26 times three—it turns out to be 78 pounds of sulfate sulfur versus 94 pounds of phosphate phosphorus. Sulfate is needed almost in as large an amount as is phosphate, even on alfalfa.

We put phosphorus on all the time, and it doesn't move. But do we really need to be concerned about the sulfur? Well, certainly we do. We need it. Corn is one of our highest yielding plants, yet it is only 2% efficient in utilizing sunlight at 150 bushels per acre. Theoretically, corn should be able to produce 400 bushels per acre. As far as using the microbial activity in the soil, clovers, soybeans and alfalfa require different types of bacteria, but they have to be *Rhizobium* species in order to do their best. Microbes in a healthy acre of soil will weigh as much as an average cow. I tell clients that the soil is alive and it has to be alive in order to get efficiency from fertilizer inputs. If that soil is not alive, there will be no efficiency from the fertilizer.

We hear nitrate nitrogen is what the plant uses. Well, if we didn't have the microbes there to convert it down, it would never achieve the right form. We add P_2O_5 phosphate to the soil. Microbes convert it and combine it with hydrogen before the plant can use it as a food source. If we put phosphate on and in the soil and have no microbial conversion, the plant will starve. William A. Albrecht fairly chafed at the statement that humus isn't necessary. He said, "People who say that don't know what they are talking about!" However, to say that you have to have a huge amount of humus is also mistaken. If you take all the humus out of a soil and try to grow a plant, nothing will happen. But put the smallest amount of humus back into that soil, and plants will start to grow again. I have never seen a soil that didn't have at least some humus in it. Admittedly,

300

some soils are very low in humus, but I haven't seen one for which we couldn't measure the humus.

From experience, I believe you can actually overdo the microbial activity in the soil just as much as you can overdo anything else. One of the most talked-about life forms in the world is called fungi. Fungi tolerate acid soils below pH 6. Bacteria, on the other hand, survive best above pH 7. But both do well on a soil that has balanced nutrients and the resulting pH of around 6.3 to 6.5.

Another life form that can be observed often, especially by farmers who have corn, is the actinomycetes. They are intermediate between bacteria and fungi. When you work the soil and detect that good fresh soil smell, actinomycetes are at work. In spring you can dig out a piece of cornstalk that lies buried and you see a kind of white mold. That, by scientific name, is actinomycetes.

Another microbial life form people do not talk about very much is algae. Some algae can fix nitrogen and some of them carry on a brand of photosynthesis. Microbial animal life in the soil includes protozoa and nematodes. Nematodes are eel-like in shape. They can be serious parasites, but it must be remembered that there are hundreds and hundreds of types of nematodes. Very few of them present problems. Most nematodes in the soil are beneficial. There is an analysis for nematodes. It involves a microscopic count of all the various types. If the soil chemistry is not balanced, a nematode that is actually beneficial to the soil can become parasitic. It can take from the plant what it actually should be getting from the soil. Nematodes are generally not the problem in heavy soils that they are in light, sandy soils.

At least 70% of the aerobic bacteria, the ones that need oxygen, work in the top two inches of a soil. And 70% of the humus in a soil is formed in the top two inches. That should tell us something. It takes aerobic bacteria to account for humus formulation. All humus is formed in the top five inches or so of a soil system. This is basically as deep as the fencepost rots. Below that, there is no oxygen. If there is no oxygen, anaerobic bacteria take over. They get their oxygen by breaking down residues. If you break down oxygen, you don't get the right carbon-nitrogen ratio, and you don't get humus build-up. So if you take your residues and crops that are grown on top and turn them down eight or nine inches, you have canceled out the ability of microorganisms to make humus.

It takes an average of one pound of nitrogen to break down 100 pounds of crop residue. If you can get that ratio with corn stover and soybeans, you can form humus. It really works out to be about 20 parts or less carbon to one part nitrogen. Manures are about 30 to 1.

As residues break down, the carbon to nitrogen ratio falls to somewhere between 1 to 10 and 1 to 20. In other words, if you have a lot of sawdust that you want to put on your field, you need to determine what the carbon content of the sawdust is. It is probably something like 400 to 1 in terms of the carbon to nitrogen that is in it. Let's bring it down to 300 to 1 because that is easier to calculate. That means you have one part nitrogen for every 300 parts carbon. You would have to use an extra 9 pounds of nitrogen to break down every 300 pounds of sawdust. An old Albrecht rule of thumb says the microbes eat at the first table. This means they take all the nutrients a plant normally might use, and they take it first until they no longer need it. If residue decomposition needs the nutrients, then there will be none for the plant. There always has to be enough for the microbes as well as for the crop. Microbes have to convert nitrogen and other nutrients into the right form before the plant gets its requirement.

Since we are talking about organisms, let's look at decomposition of organic residues with release of nutrient element constituents. To me, that is important and it is a natural cycle, but you can speed up that cycle by overusing nitrogen. When you overuse nitrogen and burn out humus, you release nutrient elements tied up in organic residues and eventually the elements that are constituent parts of humus.

Soil organisms are necessary to form humus in the soil, and to improve the physical properties of soils. Organisms help keep that soil friable. It is the same thing if you put mulch over a real hard soil. It loosens it up. Here, microbes do the work on the underside of the mulch.

There is a difference between mulch and working residues into the soil. If you put mulch on top, then you have the bottom of the mulch and the top of the soil where the microbes and the mulch come in contact to break down the mulch. As soon as you work mulch into the soil, you have permitted all kinds of microbial contact, allowing more nutrients to be digested by the microbes as a part of the increased decomposition process.

When you apply manures and composts, potassium and phosphate will increase in the soil by more than what is found in the manure. This is a consequence of plant nutrient release from insoluble, inorganic soil minerals—in other words, from the decomposed rock.

Soil mycorrhizae are fungi in the soil. They actually extend the root system of a plant. Mycorrhizae establish and enter the plant, and in turn the plant feeds the mycorrhizae in terms of the nutrients it needs. The mycorrhiza also conveys nutrients to the plant. One of the nutrients is phosphate. In short, mycorrhizae are feeders.

In 15 year studies with pines and oaks, researchers found that broadcast application of high amounts of commercial nitrogen to feed the trees will kill all the mycorrhizal fungi in the soil. Pine trees need mycorrhizae. Even if use of commercial nitrogen is ceased, mycorrhizae will not come back until boron has been increased to the toleration point. Once you get boron up where it is supposed to be, then you can bring back mycorrhiza fungi.

If you have a balanced soil, or a soil that is within the tolerances related in these chapters, what should be the ratios of one nutrient to another? A ratio will work in one soil and not in another because we haven't established the chemistry and the physics yet. For example, one statement that is made by the Sulphur Institute is that you need one pound of sulfur for every ten pounds of nitrogen. That isn't necessarily true. You don't always need a 1 to 10 ratio of sulfur to nitrogen. If you start looking at those ratios and try to match the soil—and you don't have the same chemistry in the soil that the so-called norm had in the adage creation experiment, that ratio is not going to work the same way. You need to look at the base saturation of your soil to determine the practical side of things.

I have a client in southeast Missouri with whom I worked for a couple of years. His son graduated from an ag college in another state. He had a major in plant science with a minor in agronomy. He was watching his dad's farm and he needed a job. He said, "You know, if it would work out, I would like to work with you." I hired him to pull samples and work with me. We worked together for two years. One day we were working the same farm together. We stopped to eat lunch, and he said, "You know, Neal, I have worked for you a couple of years. It took me 18 months or so to get my head straightened out. What you were telling me wasn't matching up with what I had been taught in school. I had to start seeing examples and watching and looking at the soils to learn how what you said applied. If someone had been saying, You need to know about cation exchange capacity and base saturation, I would have told him I knew about that. Our textbook had a section on exchange capacity, and it had a section on base saturation percentages, but it did not tell you how to use either on your farm. The problem was the professors didn't understand how to teach us to use it either. I never really learned how to use exchange capacity and base saturation until I started to work with you. I couldn't learn it sooner because of all the roadblocks that had been put in my head. When you go from

Revelations of Species

"Microscopic examination of the small feeding roots of any plant growing on a virgin soil," says S.C. Hood, "will show a network of fungus mycelia over the root surface. The thickness and density of this net will vary with the plant and the soil conditions. On most herbaceous plants it consists of two layers. The outer one is made up of mostly brown or gray septate (sectioned) hyphae spreading over the root surface and sending strands into the surrounding soil. This outer layer is made up of most Basidiomycetes. There are often tangles of mycelia in the surrounding soil, containing small rhizomorphs (root-like bodies) which present different forms and colors, according to the species represented.

"It has been fully demonstrated that this symbiosis is not involved in the process of photosynthesis, since the production of fiber and other carbohydrate materials goes on whether fungi are present or not. It is, therefore, a fair hypothesis that this fungus-plant root symbiosis of mycorrhiza promotes the production of amino acids for building of the protein molecules."

—*William A. Albrecht*
The Albrecht Papers, Volume III, 1989

farm to farm, it gets to where you can't deny it anymore, and even though you were taught one way you just have to realize it wasn't the right way."

It is ingrained into academia that all they need is pH, phosphate and potash. I put on a seminar about calcium-magnesium. It usually lasts a half day. I take what University of Wisconsin says about calcium-magnesium, what the University of Iowa says, what the University of Missouri says, and what various universities say, based on what they write up in their research publications. I read it to the farmers in the room because so much of it is exactly opposite of what I am telling them. The universities teach that if the pounds are found in the soil, you are okay, because by putting on N, P and K the pounds will release. They don't look at base saturation. Basically, with every university, what they write on calcium-magnesium will tell you that if you have a high magnesium soil, it makes no difference; and second, you can't do anything about it anyway. They will tell you that you can't change a high magnesium soil and get the magnesium out of it. I have clients who started with me in the late 1970s. They had 65% calcium and 25% magnesium. In five to six years they had 65% calcium and 15% magnesium. You can't get magnesium out of the soil if your calcium is below 60% base saturation. I have seen experimental farms at certain universities in the midwest that have less than 60% saturation of calcium. They have used nitrogen so long they have driven calcium out. When they put on lime, often they put on high magnesium lime. As a consequence, their calcium levels never reach the Albrecht minimum. In western U.S. soils, when they need lime, they rationalize that keeping the pH down is the key to success, for which reason they go to gypsum (calcium sulfate) instead of calcium carbonate. In reality calcium sulfate under such conditions will not properly adjust the calcium content in the soil. With base saturation below 58% calcium, gypsum will not successfully drive out sodium or magnesium

Symbiotic Relationship

It is probable that this symbiotic relation began when the first primitive plant forms left the primordial sea and took to the land. There were primitive forms of fungi and algae, both of which had developed in water. When cast on dry land, as separates, both were helpless. The fungi could not make carbohydrates. The algae could not secure mineral nutrients from the rocks. But united in a partnership, both could survive. The algae made carbohydrates for both, and the fungi extracted from the rocks the mineral elements needed by both of them.

[There is nothing to suggest that this relationship does not persist to the present, especially in the lichens, the first builders of soil. In their development of complicated structures, higher plants kept a part of this early relationship.]

—*S.C. Hood*
Hood Laboratory Report, private papers,
Acres U.S.A. collection

because calcium sulfate will not take calcium levels high enough above the 60% saturation required for this chemical miracle.

There is a phrase that isn't used very often these days. It is, *antagonistic action against plant pathogens.* This comes very close to saying, with Albrecht, that the anatomy of dealing with bacterial and insect attack is seated in fertility management, and not in buying toxic materials from Dow Chemical or Monsanto.

This makes exchange capacity and base saturation the most important discovery since van Helmont grew trees in a tub to nail down the role of earth minerals and air in plant production. In short, the chemistry has to be right so that the biology in the soil can function. Chemistry provides the physical structure of a soil so that it can provide the correct environment for biology. When soil organisms can do their job, the soil itself will in fact fight plant pathogens. Unfortunately, this objective does not mean single factor activity.

Still, it isn't unusual to hear a farmer say, once on the program, that he has less insect, disease and weed problems. One farmer told me, "The year you got me started using copper, I didn't have the problem with wheat rust that I used to have." Copper has a reputation for controlling rust.

The better the organisms in the soil work, the more strength they will confer on the plant. In any case, removal of toxicity from the soil—either the residue of pesticides or over-applications of minerals that rely on homeostatic control—falls within the purview of the microbial function.

The soil is alive and it has to be kept alive in order to deliver top yields and quality.

How can we know whether we have the right environment for the microbes? A good test is the earthworm population. With the right soil environment, not only are microorganisms going to do better, but also the earthworms and macroorganisms are going to do better as well. Elliott C. Roberts of the Lawn Institute once made an evaluation of live microbes in the soil. He said that there are approximately 900 billion microorganisms per pound of healthy soil. That is why we talk about a microorganism weight equal to an average size cow in every acre of soil. That is why failure to turn in residues is tantamount to starving the microbes. This, in turn, will starve the plant in terms of its ability to get what it needs. The microbes have to do the converting. The law of thermodynamics states that life can come only from life. If the soil is dead biologically, nothing is going to grow from it. The soil is the plant's stomach. If we do not have the microorganisms in our stomach to do the job, how are we going to live? Hans Peter Rausch of Germany put it this way. "Bacteria and other microflora in the area of the plant's root system, through which it receives nutrients from the soil, belong to the same group of bacteria and other microbes found in the intestines of humans and animals." The very microbes that are digesting nutrients in the area of plant roots are the same ones that digest the food we eat.

My wife was bitten by a spider, so they put her on some antibiotics. After she got over the spider bite, she had a terrible, terrible cold. We went to the doctor, albeit not to the same fellow who prescribed the penicillin. He said she should have taken Lactobacillus and gotten her system built back up. All she did in the earlier instance was kill off the beneficial microbes. Her body wasn't able to provide the materials she needed to fight off the cold germs.

I look for fields where earthworm castings are thick. Frankly, I don't see a lot of corn fields heavy with earthworm castings. However, I do find somewhat more soybean fields with earthworm castings. Often I can take a probe of soil and collect castings in abundance from the same area. I take a three by five card and rake the top of the casting pile onto it. I have purposely collected enough earthworm castings for a soil sample in a number of fields, and I have ordered out audits to see what the difference was between soil and castings. I have done this in several counties in southeast Missouri.

I have always heard that when the earthworm emerges from the soil, it actually balances out those castings with a better concentration of nutrients than contained in the soil itself. But instead, I have found that if the soil is high in calcium, the castings will be high in calcium. If the soil is low in calcium and high in magnesium, the castings will be low in calcium and high in magnesium. In terms of base saturation percentages, the percentages have been improved, but not enough to solve the excesses. What the worm had to digest is what you are going to find, except for one thing. The castings contain a higher concentration of micronutrients. The point I am trying to make is that when you get microbes and earthworms to work in the soil, a new level of micronutrient availability is foreordained.

We have all heard about the college that didn't recognize micronutrients, to which agronomist John Porter answered, "But the plants do, and they didn't go to college." Those castings not only concentrate micronutrients, the earthworms in fact write a meal ticket that enables microorganisms to do better. Eight to ten earthworms per square foot means up to one million earthworms per acre. One report states that a square foot of castings will contain 2.5 times more magnesium than the soil, three times more calcium, five times more nitrogen, seven times more phosphorous or 11 times more potash. Frankly, I have not found double rates of anything until testing the trace elements. I am not saying that earthworms are not valuable. I am saying that whenever you see results such as those mentioned above, you have to ask a few more questions.

Earthworms do help aerate the soil. They provide avenues for air and conduits for water, not just for entry down but also for capillary return.

Farm producers have various soils on their farms. They can't be so remotely located that a fertilizer salesman can't find them. This American original has a material to put on. He says if the farmer puts it on, he can quit using fertilizers. There are some products that are types of gypsum with compost in them. There are humates that work wonders. There are heavy clays with a high micronutrient content and an even higher exchange capacity. In terms of buying those things, I tell the client, "Until you get a calcium saturation between 60 and 70%, and magnesium between 10 and 20%, you are really never going to know whether these products measure up or not." When the physical structure is out of whack, or the nutrient balance is off, micronutrient products which generally help to stimulate microbes are not going to do the same job.

A man and his two sons had me sample their farm. When I returned to deliver the results, I sat down and told them what they should do. When we were finished, the father said, "Well, Neal, I hope this won't make you mad, but we are not going to do any of that." It didn't make me mad, but it sure made me curious. He told me about a company that had a certain product. He intended to start using the products at a rate of 300 pounds per acre for several years, and then he would cut back to 200 pounds per acre. He stopped using any commercial fertilizer except nitrogen. He had harvested some excellent crops. Now he wanted to see what the nutrient levels were in every one of his fields. "They tell me that when I put 300 pounds on," he said, "next year my phosphate and potash and other nutrients will be better than they are this year. All we are going to do is put that 300 pounds of material on and use some nitrogen." He asked if I thought he would get into trouble with this, and I said that he had been growing crops up to now, and with the levels he had, I didn't think he was going to achieve his top yields. If he had told me he was going to use this product in the first place, I could have told him in which fields he could expect to achieve better results, and which ones he wouldn't improve as we discussed each sample. As it was, this was important enough to go back over the samples again for just that purpose.

The next year father and sons had me come back and sample the whole farm again, The father said, "Neal, on every field where you said we would see a difference, we could see it. On every field where you said we wouldn't, we couldn't tell it was worth putting it on there." Where they could see the difference was where the calcium was between 60 and 70% base saturation, and where magnesium was between 10 and 20%.

I learned that due to a fellow up in Wisconsin who was selling a humate fertilizer. I went up there and helped put on a seminar. During an exchange, he said, "I can't understand it. I sell humates to farmers and I have some farmers who come out to meet me and pat me on the back and say that this is the greatest stuff he has ever seen. I go right down the road to another farm, and this guy is ready to run me off with a shotgun because, "all I did was take his money." Now maybe you could say that one farmer paid attention, and the other one didn't. But I'll have a farmer who will say that the humates worked just great *over here* but *over there* on that field it looks like he threw his money away." The key was the balance. He went back to the farms where there were fields that worked, and some that didn't. He told them that for the humate to work well, the calcium had to be up above 60%, and the magnesium had to be in the 10 to 20% range, and proved it by using a detailed soil analysis.

The humate is a material that delivers response via its micronutrients. These nutrients are seldom limiting factors until calcium and magnesium are available in proper supply. Inputs such as humates stimulate the microbial activity because they contain a lot of nutrients we do not know how to measure. We seldom have the soils the way we need them.

Hands-On Agronomy

What we really do is get them in the minimum basic shape, and then we start applying what I call a broad spectrum micronutrient rich material. At that point we enter the twilight zone of not knowing how to measure.

Those broad spectrum micronutrient mineral rich fertilizers support higher microbial populations in the soil. So far commercial agriculture makes little use of these materials because they are expensive. Most of the time only people who work with microbial inoculants and stimulants invoke the use of these materials, but the gap between knowledge and field application is closing.

Trade laboratories are now starting to measure the microbial content of soils. The cost can be high, but considered in terms of one sample of good soil and one bad soil, the bite out of a fertilizer budget is not astronomical.

Bi-o-log-ic / ˌbī-e-'läj-ik / *n* [G *biologie*, fr. *bi-* + *-logie* -logy] **1** a biological product used in medicine **2** a biological product used in agriculture and/or animal husbandry **3** special products that rely on life to lend an assist to crop production chiefly via nutrient release, nitrogen fixation and several leaf feeding and inoculation processes **4** products based on growth hormone principles, namely gibberellins, auxins and cytokinins **5** in general, life products that impact on the energy exchange of chromosomes and nucleotides

14

An Environment
for Microbes

I HAVE WORKED WITH FARMERS who use all types of materials. One product out of Utah is called Azomite. Another out of Mississippi has the trade name Flora-Stim. A humate out of New Mexico is called Clodbuster. Colorado furnishes material with the trade name Planters II. There are Leonardite products out of North Dakota, sea kelps out of Norway and the east and west coast, and algae out of Klamath Falls, Oregon. I have mentioned Nitro/Max, and I could mention a hundred other products—each with a purpose, each of value if used as directed under the right conditions. The pages of *Acres U.S.A.* advertise many products which have validity if used properly. But if used on a soil that is not properly balanced out, one may be hard pressed to see a response. Much the same is true of biologicals. If you don't have the right conditions for biologicals to work, they are not going to do a good job. A product will work great in one field and not at all in the next because the minimum condition has not been met. But if the soil is right, biologicals are easy to work with and the easiest to make the recommendations for. Jim McHale, a former Secretary of Agriculture in Pennsylvania, was among the first to prescribe biological products based on achieving maximum balance for major and secondary nutrients as a prelude.

I had a farmer client who grew sweet corn. He decided to use a seed treatment biological on his crop. The directions read, mix ten parts water with one part biological and mist on the seed. He didn't have time to mist it on the seed so he just took the seed and soaked it in that stuff and planted it. To the row where he did that, the sweet corn didn't come up to a stand at all. He just overdid it in terms of that inoculant. The company will tell you if you soak it, you will get a worse response, not a better response. If you don't know for sure, just follow the instructions. Just because a little is good does not mean more will be better.

I planted green peas in my garden, using the same biological. One row was a control. I soaked the seeds with the 10 to 1 mixture for the second row. And I planted the peas in the third row after spraying the material over the row of peas. Peas were planted in cold soil. A biological inoculant should cause those to emerge faster if the material is used properly. One morning the row that I sprayed over the top was up from one end to the other. The other two rows were barely popping through. The next day it was still uneven as to how they came up. By the third day, they were all up. The treated ones were a day and a half to two days ahead in terms of growth.

There are other advantages to biologicals besides getting the plants up fast. I feel there are some health advantages just because we stimulate the microbes and there are some advantages to getting the root down deeper and faster. After all, the plant is going to send its roots down before it pushes growth out the top. If you stimulate faster root growth, you can get the plant to come up faster.

A lot of the companies that sell biologicals want to do all the work with the farmer themselves. As a result, there are a number of these materials that I have never worked with and probably a lot more of them that I have never heard of. The ones I am most familiar with are AgraLife, Nitro/Max, Agrispon and Vitazyme. These are hydrogen oxide chelated trace minerals and specific plant extracts. In other words, the fabricators take minerals, plant extracts and hydrogen oxide and put them together in certain combinations. All have their own formulas. Vitazyme makes use of four different seaweed extracts, two fish extracts and one extract from corn. All the extracts supply basically a kinin response. Growers can view it much as they would a cytokinin effect. Cytokinin is a growth regulator that governs the germination of a seed.

I have viewed biologicals from almost every point of view. Several companies have hired me to help solve their field problems.

If you have a soil that has the right amount of minerals specific to available calcium and phosphorus, and you have four to five inches of crumbly soil with few residues that have to be broken down, you can use a biological inoculant both in fall and spring and not have to use a heavy amount of commercial nitrogen. In some cases, I have had a nitrate test run and found that there is enough nitrate nitrogen, and that no extra nitrogen is required in order for the nitrogen replacement product to work.

I have clients who have farmed with biologicals since 1975 and raised corn every year, and never have used a commercial nitrogen at all. When they started they were not organic or natural farmers in any sense of the word. They were simply commercial farmers. I don't have thousands and thousands of them, I don't even have hundreds and hundreds of them. There are just a few of them out there. Needless to say, it is hard to find university documentation on these materials. In 1978, I met a microbiologist named Dr. Dwayne Vance at North Texas State University. One of the companies hired me to join him on a trip to Europe. We were to make presentations to the various organizations and administrations that had say-so over sales in Europe.

I went because of my field experience, and he as the laboratory expert. He had taken AgraLife and run a sealed vacuum test. A sealed vacuum test involves putting soil in a growth chamber. The only thing that gets in is whatever is pumped in. They start with the soil and they pump argon into the chamber. When you pump argon in, it drives all the nitrogen out. Then they inoculate the soil with a biological. No nitrogen increase shows up in that soil at all. Then they pump the argon out and put nitrogen back in via regular air with nitrogen in it. At that point they start to see a nitrogen increase in the soil. No commercial nitrogen is added. Only the activity between AgraLife, the soil and the air is involved.

They can also start by having air in the chamber. The microbial stimulant is added. It starts to work immediately, and nitrogen levels start to increase. What that means, and what Vance was saying, is that there is some mechanism that enables the plant to get the nitrogen it needs from the soil, with the nitrogen coming directly from the air and not from a commercial source.

Vance visited the Sloan-Kettering Institute about a month before we went to Europe. He said that Sloan-Kettering had already developed a material for soil application that would take nitrogen directly from the air, into the soil and into the plant. They reported that the only problem was the energy source. It was so expensive that commercial nitrogen was lower priced.

Growth Hormones

There are three groups of growth hormones, each of which can interact to affect plant changes and growth patterns. There are the *gibberellins*. Unfortunately, these degrade rapidly and lack functional stability. They can easily be produced by plants if nutrition is ample and proper. There are the *auxins*. These are very complex compounds related directly to environment and character of nutrition. They decompose or can be degenerated rapidly in each type of environment. . . . Most herbicide compounds are auxin-like, albeit without nature's finely tuned governing capacity or application apparatus.

Last, there are *cytokinins*. These are produced in culture systems under laboratory control. They are stable, natural, and exchangeable to the biological energy field of soil and plant systems. They are basically cell dividers. That is to say, they stimulate cell division and enlargement. They cause differentiation of plant tissues and bud formation. They regenerate shoots from root segments, increase rate of germination, and induce flowering. They reverse the effect of plant inhibitors such as excess cold or heat, or improper light conditions. They offset coumarins that prevent germination and eliminate the need for infrared stimulus or magnetic effects on seed germination.

Cytokinins used in all areas of life systems can increase the capacity of those systems to utilize fertilizers 20 to 30% better. Cytokinins stabilize and enhance chlorophyll efficiency, and tend to improve protein synthesis and function in leaves of plants. Thus they increase photosynthesis capacity. In relying on this fact the farmer must make certain that the soil's nutritional capacity is equal to the task of filling the increased demand for leaf production. Cytokinins mobilize plant nutrients and tend to draw elemental nutrients to the areas of application, either on seeds, transplants, or leaves. Finally, the cytokinin input from any good eco-farming product has the effect of delaying senescence or early die-back of plants because now the plant can overcome and correct nutritional deficiencies.

—*Charles Walters & C.J. Fenzau*
An Acres U.S.A. Primer, 1975

I have worked with Dr. Robert Fischer at Virginia Commonwealth University. He is a microbiologist, perhaps one of the best in the United States on the workings of these products in the soil. DuPont has hired him to consult on microbial development. He became interested in biological products because he found that if used at the proper rate he could calibrate in hours how much faster radish seeds would sprout, the cytokinin response. His cotyledon studies, published in *Acres U.S.A.*, are classics. His work on lettuce seed sprouting is also a matter of record. When he tried to take his findings into the field, he really got discouraged. We sat up all one night until 5:00 a.m. talking about what had happened with biologicals.

At the beginning, in 1975, I thought by 1985 every farmer in the whole United States would be using biologicals. Unfortunately, many roadblocks surfaced to sour the situation. In one meeting, Vance told of the many legal and commercial barriers invoked to keep biologicals out of the mainstream. He saw the educational system as the main drawback. By the mid-1980s, it had become a case of the school of sciences versus the school of agriculture.

"There is a real rift between us," one professor told me. "When you enter course study in preparation for microbiology, chemistry comes first. But the students who are going to major in agronomy are treated differently. They get to take an easier chemistry course for their second unit. Those in the school of science have to take a harder course. Everybody ought to take the hard course because they would come out and understand the same things we do. As it is, they really didn't get the basics down in terms of all the required chemistry. So what really happens is that there is a gulf between the microbiology department and the agronomy department. That is why you are never going to find very many agronomists who understand how biologicals work."

One major state university had three different experimental farms. They were going to test two of the products I am talking about. They had to provide all the information about how they ran the tests and when I came there to see it, the control was better than where they had used either of the biological inoculants. I had never seen that before. They had a control, a gallon per ten acres of AgraLife, a gallon per ten acres of another biological, quarter-rate fertilizer, half-rate fertilizer and full-rate fertilizer. They ran soil tests before they started and it was pH, phosphate and potash all the way. It was in the contract that the company could also run soil tests. Fischer went down and took the samples. They told him they already had soil tests and they didn't want him to take any more. He said that it was in the contract and he was going to take soil samples out of each and every plot, which he did. The fellow in charge got angry and upset. The reason he got angry was because you could see exactly what those fellows could do. The control had a better exchange capacity and a better humus content than any one of the plots on which the biological had been used. The plot that received the biologicals had the lowest organic matter and the lowest exchange capacity on all three farms, and this replicated over several different plots.

They had a field day at another major eastern ag school. One part of an area that was not on the tour was used for biological tests which looked as good as those with commercial fertilizers. There was another part where all the tours came together. Everything was clearly marked. The plots where they had used biologicals were worse than the controls, much as in the prior example. They kept insisting that they could not show what had been used on those plots in the past until a court case forced the issue. In the court case they produced research material that revealed what they had done in the past. On the very plots that they selected for application of biologicals, they had used a program some three years earlier that left toxic cadmium levels.

The biologicals were used on these exact plots. For these several reasons, what I have to say about biologicals is not based on university research.

In the area of Gibson City, Sibley and Melvin, Illinois, the dealer who sold AgraLife had a good reputation. He farmed about 500 acres and he also sold seed corn. He wanted to try a biological "on ten or 20 acres." He had other growers "trying it on ten or 20 acres" of corn and beans. Applications were made by helicopter. They sprayed 1,400 acres and then they had to move over to spray another 600 acres. Where they sprayed the 1,400 acres they could see a difference in the corn within a week. Then they got to the last 600 acres, and when they sprayed they didn't see any difference in the corn. It was the same product, the same guy spraying it, too. They forgot about the water source. When they moved, they changed from one town's water to another town's water. The water they changed to had fluorine and chlorine in it. When they found that out, they switched and redid the whole 600 acres, and got the results.

There are enough case reports to paper the farm country from one end to the next. Let me relate the experience of a farmer who used commercial nitrogen on one side of a field. The other side got no commercial nitrogen, though all of the land got hog manure. On the one side, he had 154 pounds of actual nitrogen plus hog manure. On the other side, he had hog manure and one gallon AgraLife per ten acres, one time. This non-irrigated land had yields all the way from 170 down to 100 bushels per acre. That particular year it was somewhat dry, and the yield was 128.63 bushels per acre with 28% nitrogen. The biologically treated soil made 137.03 bushel per acre (and he didn't spend money on commercial nitrogen).

Another farmer had 1,000 acres and the dealer came to see him about using it on 20 acres, and he made a mistake. He talked to me and I advised him not to do it. I told him to try it on a little bit, but he used it on every acre of corn

Hands-On Agronomy

and he didn't leave a check. It is always a mistake not to leave a check. The corn looked great when I was in the area in July.

But that fall I saw the farmer and asked him how his corn checked out. He said it actually didn't do very good. He made about 40 bushels less corn per acre than neighboring farmers. He grew corn on corn. He used the biological without any other nitrogen source whatsoever. He had a half inch of crumbly soil.

It comes right back to what I have been saying all along. When you use biologicals, remember that first of all they utilize the microbes in the soil. There might not be any microbes in the product, but they utilize microbes in the soil to do the job. The next thing to be considered is that if you don't have enough aeration, the microbes are not going to be able to work the way they must to get nitrogen out of the air. The air must be inhaled into the soil. It has to be in contact with the work site. With such products, if you don't have four or five inches of crumbly soil, or do something to achieve it, you are going to have to rely on commercial nitrogen or lose a part of your corn crop. The farmer in question told me that his leaves started turning yellow in August. I asked him how many leaves turned and he said about four. He called the dealer and the area supervisor, but a lot of the guys selling biologicals then knew too little about nitrogen in agriculture. The supervisor said not to worry about it. Unfortunately, a non-worry disclaimer won't compensate for the loss of 40 bushels of corn per acre.

Still, there are things you can do even late in the season to avoid this situation. Even after you find four yellow leaves, if the corn is in the silking stage or before, put on 40 pounds of actual nitrogen in the form of ammonia nitrate (120 pounds of the product as sold) and you won't lose a bushel of corn. Once you get past that four-leaf stage there will be some loss. If three leaves show nitrogen deficiency, put on 30 pounds of nitrogen. If four leaves show nitrogen deficiency, put on 40 pounds of nitrogen, and if five leaves show nitrogen deficiency, the maximum amount to use is still 40 pounds of nitrogen. If you are going to fly it on, use ammonium nitrate. If you have a high-boy with drops on it, and you can get across the corn, you can use 32% liquid. The 32% can burn the corn leaves unless you get it down. The best thing to do when using a biological is to get a nitrate and ammonia analysis before the corn tassels.

Be sure that you have one pound of nitrogen per 100 pounds of residues in addition to a biological. If you have 40 pounds of nitrate nitrogen in a soil and you are going to use a biological, you do not have to worry about using additional nitrogen except to decompose any corn stalks you have left. If you don't know what the nitrate nitrogen level is and you are going to use a biological, then put on 40+ pounds of actual nitrogen if you are going to raise any high nitrogen requirement crop.

In terms of legumes, soybeans, alfalfa, dry beans, you don't have to worry about four inches of crumbly soil if the biological approach is to be used. First, you don't get the big response as is the case with a high nitrogen crop. Take soybeans. Farmers who have used the biological approach can go out and put it on at planting time, one application. With adequate lime and phosphate, they will harvest about five or six bushels more beans per acre. Expect to get a better protein content in soybeans and alfalfa with these microbial stimulants. In alfalfa, if you want to know how your potassium is being taken up, take a knife and cut the alfalfa plant off at the ground. Take the top of it and bend it down to the tip and see if you have leaves setting on the bottom half. The better your leaves set, the better utilization of potash you are getting. If you get up to the middle and you don't have any leaves you are not getting enough potassium into that alfalfa. Cotton is a woody type plant and it is a high nitrogen requiring plant, but it doesn't require the amount of nitrogen that corn does, and it works very well with the biologicals, with or without additional nitrogen.

A working equation for crop production runs as follows: where 200 pounds of nitrogen on corn is indicated, a maximum of 100 pounds of nitrogen on cotton is the norm. You can often find poor aeration and the magnesium levels at 20% or higher in a cotton field. Just pull up the stalk and look at the root. You should have one tap root that goes straight down. But when that magnesium level gets up to 18 or 19%, that tap root will split in two and fork. Where farmers have applied a gallon per ten acres of Nitro/Max at planting time, the tap roots will go straight down. Something happens that enables that plant to push the root straight on through. Take a knife and cut through a corn stalk with a biological and another with only nitrogen. The thinnest rind will be the one with commercial nitrogen. Now if you have 2.5 inches of crumbly soil, commercial nitrogen will beat the biological if you use it by itself. But if you use the biological and apply nitrogen by tassel time on such a soil, you won't lose out to the commercial nitrogen. If you have four or five inches of crumbly soil and you start out with 40 parts per million nitrate and enough added nitrogen to break down residues, you are not going to have a problem. If you probe between the rows and find that you have four or five inches of crumbly soil, don't worry. If you don't have it, and the corn is short enough, and you can come through with an anhydrous applicator, points deep, but without any anhydrous in the tank, and get some air into the soil, you won't have to come with 30 or 40 pounds of additional nitrogen.

When I first started working with Agrispon, I told Joe Walters, M.D., in California that I was going to send him a pint of this material to use in his garden. He got excited and said, "You mean you have a material that will do that! Don't send me a pint, send me a gallon." I sent it and then the telephone rang a few days later. It was one of his patients, the TV and movie personality, Eddie Albert. He got interested because his doctor was interested, and because he was a proponent of natural agriculture. That was in 1976. In 1978, a big company in Hawaii decided it would use the biological on corn. This was decided via contact with Eddie Albert. I tripped to Hawaii and met both Art Lowe and Eddie Albert. We went out and looked at their fields.

Up to that point, this was the hardest soil that I had ever seen. It tested 45% calcium and 40% magnesium. It needed 12 tons of lime to the acre, and they didn't have any lime. They raised 180 bushel corn in the summer, 165 bushel corn in the winter and they took three crops of silage corn per acre off this land every year. They left check plots. They sold silage down the road to Meadow Gold Dairy and received a premium because it was fresh.

How did they get corn to grow on that soil? They used 160 pounds of nitrogen and they also used four tons of chicken litter for each of the three crops of silage. This soil was so tough they would get a big John Deere ripper, and go in and rip it out. It would come out in chunks like paving stone. Then they would water the chunks and run over them with a big disc to break them up. When the clods were reduced in size suitably, they would plant again. That is where I came in—to run a test before using a biological. Here was the scene. They had a half-inch of crumbly soil. It was tight and heavy with an exchange capacity between 40 and 50. There was a calcium deficiency and a magnesium excess. They put four tons of chicken litter on all of the field. They used 160 pounds of nitrogen on the so-called commercial side. They used no nitrogen, and, just a gallon per ten acres of the biological on the other side. They made seven bushels more corn per acre where they used the biological over where they used the commercial nitrogen.

How could they come in there and do that on such a tight soil when I am telling you all these other things? Number one is that they ripped the soil deep three times a year.

Number two, the manure was put on at four tons per acre which got the microbial population working and kept that top loose enough to allow air to enter. They also aerated the soil.

You can have all these adverse conditions and still make a biological work if you keep in mind the things related up to now. They didn't use 40 pounds of nitrogen, but they didn't need to because they had four tons of poultry litter.

If I were to summarize these few lessons in a whiplash line or two, I would say leave a check plot, walk your fields, and see what you look at. If you farm with a certain viewpoint for 50 years, you are going to be making a mistake if you don't leave a check plot. One of my clients in Illinois farmed about 500 acres. He decided a biological worked, so he used it on every acre. One year he told me he got to wondering whether or not he would be doing better if he had kept on using commercial nitrogen. He said he didn't have any place to compare it so he just went to his neighbor and got some liquid nitrogen and put it on a field near his house. He made two rounds on a relatively even field. He harvested 12 bushels more corn where he didn't use that nitrogen. But if he had kept a test plot, all doubts could be handled year to year.

Directions for use are important. It always amazes and amuses me when a farmer decides to substitute his judgment for years of experiments most suppliers have invested in their products. I have in mind a product used in cotton production. The companies that work with Agrispon will tell you it lasts about six months. They will say for best results, put it on in spring and fall. In one case, a farmer didn't discover until he got to the end that he had failed to turn the sprayer on. You could see right where an application had been made all the way around the field. Growers who take slide photographs can point to stops and starts, results are often that dramatic. It might not show up as much in soybeans, but it will in high nitrogen requiring crops such as wheat, cotton and corn.

I was up in Illinois one day with Eddie Albert and a group of farmers looking at soybeans. The grower had taken a field and split it into three parts. He was intending to grow soybeans on it the following year. He treated ten acres in fall, and in spring he treated the same ten acres again. Another ten acres adjoining this plot were also treated that spring. The last ten acres received no treatment. In that part of Illinois it is standard practice to omit fertilization on soybeans. I dug up some soybeans. On the basis of nodulation alone I could tell where two applications had been made compared to none. There was triple the nodulation. It was double the nodulation where an application had been made in the spring. Yet looking out over the field, I couldn't see a difference in the size or appearance of the beans at about 12 inches in height. Many a farmer has said, "No difference," even in the hopper, until he weighed the areas separately at harvest.

The results do not seem to respect geography. I have assembled records from corn plots in Virginia, to Campbell's tomatoes in Ohio. Each entry has its related story. Campbell's ran a test with biologicals the first year, and it was "all systems go." They ran a test the second year and spent a large sum of money to have the experimental acreage hand weeded so as not to possibly flaw the test. The people who set it up didn't go back to counsel with them. After they got word they had a problem, the company asked me to go up there. They had water standing in the fields. The plot with the gallon per ten acres was not better than the control. When I put the probe into the soil, I could see they had no aeration at all. If they had just come earlier and run something down the middles, they could have taken care of that problem.

Wheat was the first crop to receive this venturesome type of fertility assist in Illinois. Wheat harvest in the area is gen-

The Physiological Approach
to Livestock Nutrition Problems

While broken bones, depraved appetite and other gross physical symptoms first called our attention to the needs of animals for minerals, bones and blood studies and balance techniques have been the tools by which quantitative needs for all-round nutrition have been established. There is ample evidence of the urgent need for many more of these physiological studies to fill in the gaps of our knowledge of the mineral nutrition of livestock. We were all amazed by the identification of a lack of *cobalt* as the cause of the losses among grazing animals in Australia, New Zealand and elsewhere, and of the minute amount of the element required to prevent the troubles. Recently, areas of cobalt deficiency have been located in the United States, (Baltzer et. al., 1941). Recently, also, large areas where *copper* deficiency is a practical problem have been discovered, apparently involving other physiological functions besides blood regeneration. Additional instances of *iron* deficiency are being uncovered, and *manganese* and even *magnesium* can no longer be neglected in certain feeding situations.

These recent discoveries regarding mineral elements teach us several things. In the first place, we cannot rest on the assumption that, aside from salt, calcium, phosphorus, and iodine in special situations, commonly fed rations will always meet mineral needs. We know of too many cases were this is not true, and we have learned that the same feed may vary widely in mineral content. More important, these recently discovered cases of mineral deficiency in practice were uncovered where the shortage was bad enough to develop acute physical symptoms which demanded attention. Are there much more widespread cases of deficiencies too mild to be detected by gross observations? Here we should learn a lesson from vitamin research—that the subacute troubles recognizable only by physiological tests, may be the more numerous and the more important.

—*L.A. Maynard*
paper delivered before the American Society
of Animal Production, 1941

erally in June. A portion of a field had a fall and a spring application at a gallon per ten acres. The treatment made about ten bushels more wheat per acre than where the traditional 100 pounds of actual nitrogen had been used. If a good biological is used on wheat and a low spot presents a tell-tale yellow before the crop has headed out, think *airplane*. Fly on 40 pounds of nitrogen. It will result in an extra ten bushels of wheat per acre.

In any country, the farmer seems to expect miracles. No wonder he is often a victim of foo-foo dust salesmen and so partial to snake oil. And yet the way many farmers use perfectly valid products would make anything like a secret formula whispered by a dying monk to a titled traveler pure hokum. But as Paul Harvey says, there is the rest of the story.

I recall a German baron who decided that he would use a material then called AgroVita, and the company guaranteed him that whatever loss he experienced, they would make up the difference. He turned in a bill and they sent me over there to check it out. The bill was based on a loss because the rye crop was not making heads. When I got there I had to sludge through water. I had on boots and sludged through water halfway up the boots while in the fields. It was April and they had an unusual amount of rain. Obviously, a biological is not going to work in such a situation because there is no air. I doubt that you are going to get anything else to work under such conditions either. Huge piles of stubble from the last crop were also in evidence. With residue that hadn't broken down, and with a nitrogen shortfall, there wasn't enough nitrogen to feed the crop and break down the residue at the same time, thus the lack of grain heads.

The reports are endless. One farmer collected soybeans from the side on which he had used a biological, and kept some in a box. When he harvested the other side of the field, he also kept some in a box. He marked the boxes. He said, "You can blindfold me and I can figure out which one is which." He would put some of each in a cup and take a ruler and level them off, put the beans on a postage scale and weigh them. He concluded that the beans that got the biological would weigh heavier, and indeed they did.

I recall a Texas ryegrass pasture. The grower used ammonium sulfate on most of the pasture, holding back about ten acres in each pasture where he used an inoculant. The root system with ammonium sulfate and the root system with the biological made a significant contrast. There was no other nitrogen source. I didn't try to get him to use ammonium sulfate, but he had not used commercial nitrogen in the past. Basically, the idea was to see if a biological inoculant versus ammonium sulfate would deliver a difference. And there was a difference.

Biologicals and related products have their place, just don't count them as miracle products that will solve all the fertility problems of agriculture. But for farmers interested in natural systems, count these products as valuable and worthwhile tools to learn about—and use!

Hands-on / ˈhan(d)-ˈzän / *adj, oft attrib* [ME, fr. OE; akin to OHG *hant* hand; akin to OHG *ana* on] **1** the act of learning by doing, as in agronomy—the primacy of practical knowledge over subjective textbook fare [*subjective*, in turn, must be defined as a product of the mind without reference to outside reality **2** a colloquial term used in agriculture for agronomists who take scientific knowledge into the field **3** manual skills in trades and farming based on physical ability mixed with practical intellectual skills

AFTERWORD

AT THE END OF A RATHER LONG BOOK, it might seem super-fluous to append an Afterword. After all, we touched the bases, and farmers, soon enough, grow weary of more itera-tion and reiteration. Still, any pragmatic hands-on manual must deal with suggestions closer to home than glittering generalizations or far-out abstractions. A truly effective pro-gram for soil building and crop production must consider the following test.

Take a good uniform area of land. Follow whatever pro-gram you think would make the best comparison on half of it. On the second half, using the same dollars per acre if needed, use my program of soil fertility. Give the program three years, comparing costs, production and overall results each year. From each side take two sets of soil samples be-fore the project begins as per instructions from the particular programs used. (I offer a brochure on how you should pull soil samples to send for analysis which is printed as the Appendix of this book. If you would like a brochure, just enclose a stamped, self-addressed envelope, addressed to Kinsey's Agricultural Services, P.O. Box 7, Bertrand, Missouri, 63823.) Send tests from both sides to be analyzed by each of the soil labs used in the fertility program. Take samples again at the same time of year for the next three cropping seasons. Note any changes in soil fertility as shown by tests over the years, as well as costs and benefits from each program. Let the results tell the story, but carry on through for the entire three years.

When soil tests indicate a need for more than the budget will permit, don't give up. Just call back to ask for a 1-2-3 order of importance for needed materials. This can be provided only when adequate details of the last crop and yield on the field and the proposed crop to be grown are provided.

Farmers need to know that there are soil analyses they really can trust. This book strives to help establish that fact, and gives the steps to take for those who want further proof. The tests advocated are detailed enough to use in evaluating the land's productivity and future potential. These tests are not some vague generalization that only points the farmer in the right direction. Instead, they provide the necessary foundation for long-lasting, concrete, productive fertilization procedures necessary for each individual area.

There is a tremendous need for increased attention to building soil fertility. This factor is neglected even though it could make more difference than any other decision for field or farm. Agriculture presently is not considering soil fertility nearly enough. Seed variety, row width and plant population get more attention than the proper program of fertilizer and lime these days. Not that such considerations are not important, but in agriculture fertilization needs that are not being met are costing the farmer and landowner more production than any other factor.

Many farmers are missing out because they are content with yields of "good" soil instead of building soil for its top potential.

Another point easily overlooked is how chemistry, physics and biology work in harmony on the most productive soils. By starting with N, P and K fertilizers, you have skipped over an integral part of soil fertility. Fertilization is the chemistry. But soil chemistry can function properly only when the soil's physical structure is in line. For that, we must concentrate on calcium and magnesium, the two ingredients that most influence the soil's physical structure, namely the proper amount of water and air space interspersed with the humus and mineral content of the soil. Then and only then are we actually set to provide the environment needed for the biological portion of the soil to function. Consequently, all of these work together to unlock the tremendous potential of a soil. There are many farmers who get the chemistry and physics right, but fail to consider the biological aspects of the soil's function. For example, when the humus content is below 2.5%, soil microbes survive only on a starvation diet. Without proper attention, such soils will never have a chance to respond correctly.

I have compared samples on literally thousands of areas from all over the United States as well as other countries. Top yielding soils show the same fertility levels time after time. There are exceptions when the weather is just perfect for this or that crop in a given year on a tolerable soil. But soils that yield exceptionally well year after year for a variety of crops fit a pattern. These soils can be picked out from the analysis sheet.

One client wrote recently his comments on my work with his soil fertility and resultant production. He stated that from the beginning he could make 120% of the average in seed corn production using my fertilizer recommendations.

Still, it took time to get his soils in shape. Now, after six or more years on the program, his seed corn produced 140% of the average previous year. Another client receives awards for his exceptional corn yields. Yet no one accepts the low amount he tells them he uses in terms of the nitrogen program recommended for him. Another client put one farm in my program. A second farm was used as a control. After several years, that changed. When I began, the farm not on the program was the good farm with the best yields of the two. But as time went by, the problem farm continued to improve until it became the best of the two. That's when the decision was made to include the second farm in the program. The results tell the story.

I stress to my clients, you may be able to grow an excellent crop without fertilizer when conditions are right, but you can never grow even a good crop without adequate fertility. There really are no short-cuts to a successful fertility program. Without a specific nutrient, any number of programs may postpone the inevitable, but in the end the decline in the fertility level will be evident, and, if allowed to persist, productivity will suffer. Testing can detect this.

To build a program of top fertility will require enough desire to study your soil tests and work at it. But the requirements have more to do with being interested and consistent than they do with being hard to understand or difficult to achieve. Farmers don't have to have a college education to put this program into practice. Just using good common sense and a detailed soil analysis with the figures interpreted correctly can accomplish great strides.

I have one of the best jobs in the world, thanks to my clients. They make all the effort and time expended worthwhile year after year. Nothing about my work is more rewarding than a phone call or a letter from a client who has been helped in some way that is special enough to report back.

Hands-On Agronomy

APPENDIX

The Soil Sample

THE RECOMMENDATIONS YOU RECEIVE FROM SOIL TESTS will only be as good as the samples you send for analysis.

Soil samples may be collected any time. Late spring and early summer sampling avoids the rush, shows the soil's fertility at its best and gives time to plan a fertility program which can begin directly following harvest, if necessary. However, if no samples have been taken within the last two years, the best time to sample is as soon as possible. Sampling should be done every year if fertility is high and/or trace elements are being used to achieve top yields.

These are the basic steps for soil sampling. A soil probe is recommended for easiest and best sampling results. Stainless steel probes are generally available for $30 from the

Neal Kinsey Consulting Service. This includes shipping anywhere in the U.S.

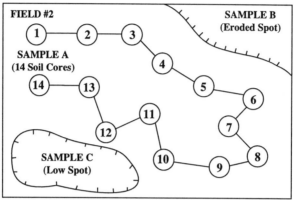

Prepare a map of the areas tested as detailed in Chapter 2.

A good map makes your sampling repeatable from year to year and is useful at the time of fertilization.

Designate a number for each field. Use permanent lines such as roads, ditches and fences for boundary lines.

Divide the field into areas that have the same color, slope, texture, drainage and past history of erosion. Each area should have the same cropping history, fertilizer and manure treatments and the same intended crop for all the soil within that area. Assign each of the areas sampled a letter. For example, Field #2 (see map) could have three areas: A-the high ground, B-the sloping ground, and C-the low level ground. The numbers written on the sample bags would then be 2A, 2B, and 2C.

One area should not generally represent more than 20 acres, (8 to 10 hectares), the first year our testing program is used, even though soils are uniform in texture and relief. The next time samples are taken, combine areas which by analysis have been shown to be alike. As a general rule, any area that is different in slope, texture, color, weed growth, etc., and large enough to be fertilized separately should also be sampled separately. Otherwise, stay out of such areas

Hands-On Agronomy

when taking the soil sample. You may wish to combine small areas that have all the same characteristics. Sample at least 300 feet away from crushed limestone roads and stay at least 20 feet away from fence rows or the edge of a field.

Avoid, or sample separately the following:

- Eroded hillsides or low spots.
- Terraces, ditch banks, old fence rows, and roads.
- Animal droppings, urine spots, old manure, straw or hay stacks.
- Areas around sheds, barns and/or where buildings have formerly stood.
- Lime, fertilizer, chemical spill areas and fertilizer bands.
- Dead and back furrows.

Collect the sample according to the following rules.

Using a soil probe or shovel, sample down to plow depth or 6 to 7 inches (4 inches for no-till pastures and lawns). Remove any obvious debris (roots, leaves, etc.), being careful that none of the soil is removed with it. Put the soil into a sample bag or plastic container. Zip-lock bags are fine as long as they have never been used, but put tape over the writing or attach masking tape to write on because all types of ink can rub off the bag during shipment. Do not use paper sacks from the grocery store, bread wrappers, etc., due to possible contamination. Avoid using a plastic bucket used for other purposes to collect samples. Repeated washings of a bucket used to mix salt and minerals for feed can still result in contamination. Probe the soil every 50 to 100 paces, always taking a minimum of 5 probes per composite sample for small areas, and one probe for every one to two acres from larger areas. Only a small amount of soil is necessary for analysis. Just be sure your sample represents the entire soil profile, if mixed, in order to send only a small portion. Remember, this will be a very detailed analysis, which will only be as accurate as the sample you send.

Pack the samples tightly. For larger packages (more than 2 or 3 samples), we recommend UPS. Soils may be sent wet or dry. Use a zip-lock or plastic lined bag for wet samples. Samples can be dried at home by spreading them on waxed paper and air drying. *Do not dry in an oven.* It is okay to leave samples to dry in the sun.

Label the bags as follows. Include your name, the farm name if any, field number and sample area letters on the sample bag. Make sure the labeling on the bag matches the number of the field and area on the map it has to represent. Labeling the bags to match the areas before taking the sample helps.

Fill out a worksheet. Please fill in your name, address, phone number, any special tests required, last year's crop and yield, the crop to be grown, fertilizers available as well as any special goals, to help us in making recommendations. We have a soil worksheet available for your convenience, but samples may be sent without it. In the U.S., send the information along with your samples and payment to our address shown below. Due to USDA regulations, special arrangements for exemption stickers and address labels must be provided for soils which are shipped from other countries. A soil test includes boron, iron, manganese, copper and zinc plus recommendations. Call our office for current charges. Rush samples are not accepted without prior approval.

The contact point for Kinsey's Agricultural Services is P.O. Box 7, Bertrand, Missouri 63823. Telephone 314-683-3880. Use any service you like, but keep the above directions in mind.

I'll end this book with a note of thanks. Special thanks go to all who have become and those who have remained clients throughout the years. These folks have put a smile on my face and a song in my heart. I know that our combined efforts will leave the land and all it produces better than would otherwise be the case.

Hands-On Agronomy

ACKNOWLEDGMENTS

In addition to those named in my dedication, I wish to acknowledge my debt to the following: to Bill Shriver, Bill Swirbul and Brookside Farms Laboratories, and to those who tolerated my leanings toward natural systems. I want to particularly thank Bob Boehle, Lou Flohr, Jan Zweip and Andy Skapura for their help and inspiration during my Brookside years. And finally, a special thanks to Dr. J.F.L. Childs, who has continued to give support over the years, and was the first to begin a persistent encouragement concerning getting the material I use down in book form. Without these people and many others, what is printed here would not be possible.

Readers will note the use of boxed materials to support—much like a condiment—the digestibility of the general text. Thanks are due the following for permission to use copyrighted materials in those boxed presentations. The other boxes are amply credited in the presentation itself.

Page 5. "Remember That You are Dust," from *Soil, Grass & Cancer*, 1959, pp. 1, 4.

Page 13. "Weeds—Guardians of the Soil," from *Weeds, Guardians of the Soil*, Devin-Adair, 1950, pp. 11-12.

Page 25. "The Land," from *Earth Foods*, Follett Publishing Co., 1972, pp. 53-54.

Page 41. "The Inportance of Calcium for Large Yields," from *More Food From Soil Science*, Growers Chemical Corp., 1965, p. 72.

Page 67. "Silica," from *Silica: The Forgotten Nutrient*, Alive Books, 1990, pp 27-28, 74.

Page 109. "Application of Fertilizer," from *Natural Food & Farming*, Natural Food Associates, 1961.

Page 121. "Quality Produce Demands Proper Composting," from Natural Food Associates Convention speech, 1961.

Page 173. "Calcium and Phosphorus," from *Health From the Sea and Soil*, Exposition Banner Book, 1962, p. 152.

Page 213. "Comparisons of Manures," from *Humus & The Farmer*, Rodale Press, 1949, p. 120.

Page 245. "Only Small Quantities of Minerals are Needed," from *Food Power From the Sea*, Earth Foods Association, 1977, pp. 185-186.

Page 297. "Versatility and Industry in the Soil," from *Magnificent Microbes*, Atheneum Press, 1976, pp. 11-12.

INDEX

INDEX

AAA program, 35
acid soils, 75, 84
acidity, 144
acids, mineral, 50
Acres U.S.A., xi, xii, 2, 315, 320
Acres U.S.A. Primer, An, xii, 7, 47, 133, 134, 143, 153, 247, 319
ADP, 154, 158
adsorption, 34
aerobes, 64
AgraLife, 317, 318, 322
Agri-SC, 102
Agricultural Testament, An, 201
AgriSpon, 113, 116, 317, 325, 327
AgroVita, 330
Ahlson, Charles B., 173
Albert, Eddie, 325, 326, 327
Albrecht, William A., 2, 3, 4, 9, 14, 15, 16, 18-19, 43, 133, 137, 149, 165, 171, 179, 202, 208, 217, 223, 249, 294, 305
Albrecht Papers, The, xii, 247
Albrecht Papers, The, Volume I, 137, 149
Albrecht Papers, The, Volume III, 18, 19, 305
Albrecht System, The, 44
alfalfa, 9, 68, 77, 88, 108, 110, 116, 143, 212, 218, 324
algae, 301
American Society of Animal Production, 329
amino acids, 107, 108
ammonia, 138, 141; analysis, 128
ammonium nitrate, 136, 138, 139

ammonium sulfate, 133, 134, 140, 148, 227
anhydrous ammonia, 131, 141, 142, 144, 148, 150
anion, 29; defined, 28
antibiotics, xiv
apatite, 153
Application of Fertilizer, 109
Arizona, Scottsdale, 23, 24
Arkansas, northeast, 20
ash and nutrient cation content of vegetables, 283
atomic absorption, 32
Atomic Energy Commission, 8
ATP, 154, 158
auxins, 319
azalea, 68
Azomite, 315

bacteria, xiv, 68
bacterial conversion, 72
barley, 9, 254
base saturation, 53
bases, 34
beans, dry, 324
Bear, Firman E., 282
Beltsville, Maryland, USDA station, 59
Bertrand, Gabriel, 5
bindweed, 12, 14
biologic, defined, 314
biological, xii
biologically ripe food, xv
biologicals, 113, 122, 261

bionomics, 39
biuret, 121, 198
blueberries, 50, 65, 66, 77
borate, 268
Borate 44G, 268, 270
Borate 48, 268
Borax, 268
boron, 60, 68, 145, 240, 242, 251, 264, 265, 266, 267, 271; defined, 258
Bray, Roger, 59
British Columbia, 21
brittle bones disease, 248
broccoli, 254
Brookside Farms, 2
buffer capacity, 62
Bulldog Soda, 254

cabbage, 254
calcareous soils, 84
calcitic limestone, 74, 75
calcium, xiv, 3, 12-14, 16, 18, 23, 30, 32, 33, 34, 36, 41, 43, 45, 50, 52, 53, 54, 64, 65, 68, 73, 74, 78, 79, 80, 81, 83, 84, 86, 87, 89, 90, 91, 92, 93, 95, 96, 106, 108, 119, 128, 129, 146, 147, 149, 172, 212, 217, 253, 256, 257, 263, 299; carbonate, 76, 77; deficiency, 76, 79; defined, 56; /magnesium, blood levels, 205
Calcium and Magnesium, 87
Calcium and Phosphorus, 173
California, 24
carbohydrates, xiv
carbon, 106
carbon dioxide, xiv, xv
CAST, see Council for Agricultural Science and Technology

cation, 29, 32, 64, 65, 68, 89; defined, 28; exchange capacity, 32, 33, 34, 78, 85
Cation Exchange Capacity, 33
Cato, 13
cauliflower, 254
CEC, see cation exchange capacity
cellulose, xiv
Chelation, A Unique Union of Metals and Organic Molecules, 222
chemical myth, xi-xix
chloride, 101, 150, 251
chlorine, 246; defined, 238
chlorophyll, 83, 107, 108
chlorosis, 272
clay, 20, 26, 31, 49, 60, 63, 66, 96; gumbo soil, 2; yellow, 30, 35
Clodbuster, 315
clover, 9, 172; red, 88
cobalt, 269
Cocannouer, Joseph A., 13, 109
Colburn, Zoell, 154
colloid, soil, 30, 31
compaction, 58, 96
Comparisons of Manures, 213
compost, 197, 203, 204, 208, 254, 72
copper, 54, 79, 142, 232, 233, 240, 243, 248, 251, 256, 265, 279, 280, 284, 285, 286, 291, 308; defined, 260
corn, 9, 11, 107, 127, 134, 135, 144, 145, 147, 157, 174, 175, 212, 228, 244, 265, 271, 298, 323, 324, 324, 326; sweet, 316
Corrective Treatment, The, 160
cotton, 2, 20, 53, 135, 265, 271, 324
cotyledon studies, 320

Hood, S.C., 305, 307
hormone-enzyme systems, xiv
horse manure, 210
horsetail, 67
Howard, Sir Albert, 1, 109, 201
human wastes, 215
humates, 312
humus, xiv, xv, 16, 17, 20, 30, 31,
    49, 58, 60, 63, 64, 145, 146,
    225; defined, xx
Humus and the Farmer, 213
hydrogen, 30, 33, 34, 53, 106,
    212; defined, 238; exchange-
    able, 256
hydroponics, xiv, xv

I conceit, xviii
imbalances, 72
Imperial Valley, 24
*Importance of Calcium for Large
    Yields, The*, 41
indole, 121, 198
*Influence of Calcium on Magne-
    sium*, 91
Insoluble Yet Available, 133, 137
integrated pest management, 230
iron, 79, 251, 256, 265, 272, 273;
    defined, 258

Journal of Applied Nutrition, 222

K-Mag, 93
Kaufman, Klaus, 67
killer agriculture, 1
Kinsey, Dad, 1, 2
Kinsey, Neal, xii, xviii
Kritchkovich, Paul, 214

Land News, The, 59, 282
Land, The, 25

law of the little bit, 8
Law of the Maximum, 6, 54
Law of the Minimum, xiii, 54
Lawn Institute, 309
leaf analysis, 78, 230-234
leather leaf fern, 34
legumes, 11, 107, 120, 165, 267,
    324; inoculants for, 10
lemons, 44
Leonardite, 315
Leow, Oscar, 10, 91
life, in the soil, xvi
light, xiv, xvi
lignin, xiv
lime, see calcium
Lime Your Soils for Better Crops, 18
limestone, 78, 80; calcitic, 74, 75
liming, 73, 75, 76
Little Dixie (northern Missouri),
    29

magnesium, xiv, 20, 32, 33, 34,
    41, 50, 52, 53, 54, 64, 65, 68,
    80, 82, 84, 85, 86, 87, 88, 89,
    90, 91, 92, 93, 95, 106, 110, 116,
    119, 128, 129, 134, 143, 146,
    148, 151, 217, 256, 275, 277,
    324, 329; carbonate, 76; defi-
    ciency, 72, 76, 84, 220; defined,
    82; limestone, 43; sulfate, 93
Magnificent Microbes, 297
manganese, 77, 79, 234, 243, 251,
    256, 265, 274, 275, 276, 278,
    279, 287, 329; defined, 259
manure, 13, 34, 62, 72, 117, 119,
    197-216, 254, 274, 291, 302,
    326; dairy, 209; defined, 196;
    feedlot, 199; fresh, 214; hog,
    209; horse, 210; odors, 197;
    poultry, 118, 203, 210; sheep,

210; value of, 199
Marco Polo, 39
marl, 74
Marshall, C.E., 143
Maryland, Beltsville, USDA station, 59
Maynard, L.A., 329
McCalla, T.M., 115
McHale, Jim, 316
ME, see milliequivalents
microbes, 58, 63, 124, 145, 262
microbial activity, 202
microbial materials, 63
micronutrient application, 264
micronutrients, 55
microorganisms, 293-313
Microorganisms and Soil Structure, 114
Miller, John J., 222
milliequivalents, 33
minerals, balance of 58; chemistry of, 57
Minerals in Nutrition, Present, Past and Future, 222
mining, 1
Mississippi, 35
Mississippi River, 2
Missouri Agricultural Experiment Station's *Research Bulletin 765*, 39, 115
Missouri, southeastern, 136
molybdenum, 77, 243, 244, 246, 264, 265; defined, 236
monoammonium phosphate, 166, 167
Monsanto, 3
More Food from Soil Science, 41
Mount St. Helens, 295
mycorrhiza, 293-313; defined, 292
myth, chemical, xi-xix; organic,

xi-xix

N, P and K, xiv, xvi, 7
National Cotton Council, 140
natural systems, 113
Natural Food and Farming, 109
Natural Foods Associates, 121
negative charge, 30
nematodes, 301
night soil, 121, 198
Ninety Mile Desert, 248
nitrate, 138, 141, 150; analysis, 128; nitrogen, 107, 212
Nitro/Max, 111, 262, 315, 317, 325
nitrogen, xiv, xv, 23, 54, 60, 72, 74, 79, 86, 88, 105, 106, 108, 110, 111, 112, 116, 117, 120, 123, 124, 126, 127, 130, 131, 133, 134, 135, 139, 142, 144, 145, 146, 150, 212, 225, 284, 287, 297, 298, 299, 302, 304, 324; defined, 104; inhibitor, 131; starvation, 106
nodulation, 107
North Africa, 39
North Texas State University, 318
nucleic acids, 107
nutrients present, 202
nutrition, xiv
Nutritional Cure for Brucellosis, A, 288

Oklahoma, 36
Only Small Quantities of Minerals are Needed, 245
organic camp, xi-xix
organic matter, 49, 61, 62, 128, 142, 146
organic myth, xi
organic nitrogen, 108